THE HANDBOOK OF

EAST ASIA

Michael G. Kort

Twenty-First Century Books
Minneapolis

Flags and captions courtesy of Whitney Smith, the Flag Research Center, Winchester, MA

Acknowledgement: *The Handbook of East Asia* is my fourth volume in a series that includes works on the former Soviet Union, the Middle East, and Eastern Europe. Amy Shields was my editor for all four books, and her creativity, energy, and dedication immeasurably improved each of them. I hope a simple thank you here will convey the deep gratitude I feel for her many contributions to these books.

Twenty-First Century Books
A division of Lerner Publishing Group
241 First Avenue North
Minneapolis, Minnesota 55401 U.S.A.

Website address: www.lernerbooks.com

Library of Congress Cataloging-in-Publication Data

Kort, Michael, 1944–
    The handbook of East Asia / Michael G. Kort.
       v.   cm.
    Audience: "Age: 12-up."
    Includes bibliographical references and index.
    Contents: What is East Asia—The People's Republic of China—The Republic of China—Japan—North Korea and South Korea—Mongolia.
      ISBN-13: 978-0-7613-2672-4 (lib. bdg.)
      ISBN-10: 0-7613-2672-3 (lib. bdg.)
      1. East Asia—Juvenile literature. [1. East Asia.] I. Title.
    DS504.5.K686 2006
    950—dc21   2003008205

Manufactured in the United States of America
1 2 3 4 5 6 – BP – 11 10 09 08 07 06

In Memory of

SIEGFRIED SIMON KORT,

my father's cousin.

*Interned for four years in a concentration camp in Italy,
he escaped on April 18, 1944. Soon thereafter he led
six British soldiers across German lines to safety, for
which he was officially recognized by the British
government, the same government that had
denied him asylum from the Nazis in 1939.
His parents and sister were murdered at Auschwitz.*

CONTENTS

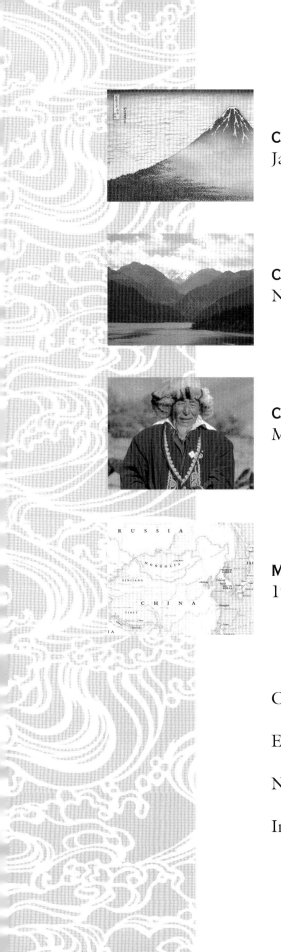

PREFACE

East Asia is home to one of the world's great civilizations, whose history stretches back in time for at least four thousand years. The origin and center of that civilization was China, although over time, Korea and Japan learned and borrowed from China and developed unique and creative cultures of their own. East Asia's achievements in art, literature, science, philosophy, and other fields are all the more remarkable because they took place in relative isolation. For about three thousand years, great distances, towering mountain ranges, and virtually impassable deserts separated East Asia from other ancient centers of civilization. It was largely cut off from Egypt and Mesopotamia in the Middle East, the Mediterranean world of the Greeks and Romans, and the Hindu civilization of the Indian subcontinent, which was a neighbor to East Asia in terms of distance but on the opposite side of one of the world's most formidable natural barriers, the mighty Himalaya mountains.

Today modern technology has made the world a much smaller place, and East Asia is looming ever larger in that shrinking world. It contains the world's most populous country, the People's Republic of China (PRC or China), and the world's

6

third- and sixth-largest economies, those of Japan and China. China, with its huge population and modernizing economy, is probably the only country in the world with the potential to join the United States as an international superpower. Japan, although only one-tenth the size of China in terms of population, is an economic giant nonetheless and the only country that rivals the United States in technological prowess. South Korea is another emerging economic powerhouse, as is the Republic of China (ROC), a small country that occupies the island of Taiwan in the shadow of its enormous and hostile mainland neighbor, the PRC. Even North Korea, plagued by a tyrannical Communist regime and a collapsing economy that has left its people starving, is able to make waves internationally, at least in a negative sense, because of its manufacture and export of guided missiles to aggressive countries in other parts of the world and its ongoing program to develop nuclear weapons.

Despite its historical importance, there is no precise definition for what constitutes East Asia. Defining this enormous region involves both geography—that is, what has been shaped over millions of years by natural forces—and history—that is, what has been created over thousands of years by human effort. In geographic terms, East Asia is that part of the Eurasian landmass east of the arid expanse of Central Asia, south of the forests and tundra of Siberia, and north of the warm and humid Indian subcontinent, or South Asia. In historical terms, East Asia includes most of the area whose cultural development has been heavily influenced by the civilization that first arose in ancient China more than four millennia ago.

This book will define East Asia as including six countries: the People's Republic of China, the Republic of China, Japan, South Korea, North Korea, and Mongolia. A quick look at the map and a good history book will reveal that this definition does not strictly follow either geographic or historical/cultural criteria. In terms of geography, Siberia, which is part of northern Asia, stretches northeastward beyond East Asia to the Bering Strait, the narrow strip of frigid water separating Asia from North America. This means that *northern* Asia extends more than 1,000 miles (1,600 kilometers) farther east than does *East* Asia. In this case, cultural history has trumped geography, mainly because northern Asia has never been within the zone of Chinese cultural influence. At the same time, East Asia does not necessarily include the entire sphere influenced by Chinese civilization, which long extended beyond the countries mentioned above, especially into Vietnam and other parts of Southeast Asia. In *this* case, natural geography, and to a lesser extent recent history, have trumped millennia of cultural history. In any event, these exclusions still leave this book with a vast and important region to cover, one with an ancient history full of remarkable achievements that increasingly is playing a major role in the modern world.

ONE

WHAT IS EAST ASIA?

Six countries share the vast expanse of East Asia: the People's Republic of China, the Republic of China, North Korea, South Korea, Japan, and Mongolia. This short list includes two pairs of countries, each of which for centuries once formed a single political unit. Both pairs—the People's Republic of China and the Republic of China, and North and South Korea—arose out of events that shook the region during the 1940s.

The People's Republic of China and the Republic of China emerged from China's civil war of 1946–1949. The victorious Communists ended up controlling mainland China, virtually all of the country, which they called the People's Republic of China. The defeated Nationalists retreated across 100 miles (160 kilometers) of water and occupied the island of Taiwan. There they survived under the protection of the United States, calling the small area they controlled the Republic of China. Since

1949 the Communist Party that governs mainland China has been trying to complete its victory by bringing Taiwan under its rule, regardless of the wishes of the people who live there.

The division of the Korean Peninsula into two states took place between 1945 and 1948 as World War II was ending and the Cold War beginning. Unlike the Chinese, who fought against each other for control of their country and thereby decided their own fate, the Korean people and their leaders lacked control over their country when it was divided. Nor did any armies, Korean or otherwise, clash as the country was cut in half. Between 1910 and 1945, Korea had endured brutal treatment as a Japanese colony. After 1945 its fate became the object of Cold War sparring between the Soviet Union and the United States, the respective leaders of the Communist and capitalist worlds. Their confrontation on the Korean Peninsula in the early days of the Cold War gave birth to Communist-ruled North Korea and capitalist South Korea.

The division of Korea resulted in two countries that became bitter enemies, and that hostility led to war. The Korean War (1950–1953) began when North Korea invaded the South. It was one of the two hot, or shooting, wars the United States fought during the Cold War (the other was the Vietnam War). In support of South Korea, American soldiers fought both North Koreans and Communist Chinese troops in a bloody seesaw struggle that moved up and down the Korean Peninsula. The war ended with Korea physically devastated and still divided. Not even the dramatic events of the late 1980s and early 1990s that swept away the Communist regimes of Eastern Europe and the Soviet Union, and the end of the Cold War in 1990, ended the division of Korea. In fact, the end of the Cold War did not even officially end the Korean War. An armistice had stopped the fighting in 1953, but to this day there has not been a peace treaty to formally end the war. Nor did the end of the Cold War end the division of China. The two Communist regimes that respectively rule most of China and the northern half of Korea have the distinction of being among a mere handful of Communist states in the world that survived beyond the early 1990s.

The two other countries of East Asia—Mongolia and Japan—have in common the good fortune that they are not divided like their neighbors. Aside from that similarity, these two countries are profoundly different from each other. Mongolia, a huge territory of prairie and desert with a tiny population, was a Communist dictatorship for seven decades. That regime collapsed between 1990 and 1992, leaving behind a poor and economically backward country. Japan, a densely populated island nation, became a fascist dictatorship in the 1930s, fought unsuccessfully to become the dominant power in Asia during World War II, and in the half century that followed emerged as East Asia's dominant economic power and one of the most technologically advanced and richest countries in the world. While Mongolia was isolated from the rest of the world during the twentieth century, Japan was deeply engaged in international affairs, as a combatant in several major wars before 1945, and then after 1945 as a leading manufacturing and trading nation and an ally of the Western democracies in the Cold War.

THE GEOGRAPHIC SETTING

East Asia begins where towering mountain ranges and vast deserts cut across the continent of Asia, the world's largest landmass. It extends eastward to the coastal seas that are fringes of the Pacific Ocean, where it includes several large islands just offshore: the four main islands of Japan in the north, the island of Taiwan in the center, and Hainan Island in the south. Four seas—the Sea of Japan, the Yellow Sea, the East China Sea, and the South China Sea—and three straits—the Korea Strait, the Taiwan Strait, and the Qiongzhou Strait—wash the eastern coast of the Asian mainland and the coastlines of its offshore islands. Beyond them lies the seemingly endless Pacific. East Asia's southern limits are the Himalayas, the world's highest mountains, which cut off South Asia from the rest of the continent, and, farther east, the network of mountains and dense jungles that mark the northern fringe of Southeast Asia. The subarctic forests of Siberia are evergreen sentinels standing astride East Asia's northern limits. East Asia covers an area of more than 4.5 million square miles (12 million square kilometers), slightly more than a quarter of Asia.

The huge expanse of East Asia is divided into four main geographic zones. In the southwest is a mountain and plateau region aptly known as the Roof of the World. From south to north it consists of the Himalayas, the Plateau of Tibet, and the Kunlun Mountains. The Plateau of Tibet, ranging in altitude from between 13,000 and 15,000 feet (4,000 and 4,500 meters) above sea level, is by far the highest landform of its kind in the world. It is the source of several of Asia's major rivers, including the Indus and Brahmaputra, which flow into South Asia; the Mekong, the main waterway of Southeast Asia; and the Yellow and Yangtze, the two most important rivers of China.

Directly to the north of Asia's roof, and running eastward for about 2,000 miles (3,200 kilometers) across Mongolia and most of northern China, is an arid region of basins, mountains, and plateau land, most of which is between 2,000 and 5,000 feet (600 to 1,500 meters) above sea level. It begins in the west with the Tarim Basin, a bleak desert region that is ringed in the north by the Tian Shan Mountains. Farther north still are the Altai Mountains. East of the Altai Mountains is the Mongolian Plateau, whose northern section is a prairie and whose south is the forbidding gravel-strewn Gobi Desert. The Gobi, the world's northernmost desert, straddles about half of the Chinese-Mongolian border and covers an area of 500,000 square miles (1.3 million square kilometers), almost twice the size of Texas. Its name comes from a Mongolian word meaning "waterless place," and it usually receives less than 3 inches (8 centimeters) of rainfall per year.

Some geographers have referred to the entire territory running approximately from the Himalayas to the Kunlun Mountains to the eastern edge of the Mongolian Plateau as High Asia, a name that aptly summarizes the topography of this gigantic upland.

East of the Plateau of Tibet and south of the Mongolian Plateau are East Asia's lowlands: the Manchurian Plain, the North China Plain, and—farther west and at a slightly higher altitude—the Sichuan Plain (or Basin). These lowlands give way to hills and relatively low mountains in northern China and on the Korean Peninsula. They merge into a similar landscape, although with higher mountains, in southern China. Both the Yellow and Yangtze rivers flow through this region, which is as densely populated as any on Earth.

Finally, along East Asia's Pacific coast is a great arc of mountains that actually extends well beyond East Asia, running southward into Southeast Asia, northward through the Kamchatka Peninsula in Russia, and eastward deep into the Pacific Ocean. Many of these mountains are volcanic. Over millions of years, two colliding plates of the Earth's crust and eruptions of molten lava from deep below the Earth's surface pushed these peaks above the level of the sea to form several groups of islands. In East Asia they include Taiwan and the islands of Japan, an archipelago comprising four main islands and thousands of smaller ones.

CLIMATE

East Asia's climate is governed by the interaction of airflows from the interior of the great Asian landmass to the west and from the even greater expanse of ocean to the south and east. In winter, cold, dry air from the interior, the so-called dry monsoon, flows outward to the sea. Winters in the southern and eastern parts of East Asia therefore are cool and dry. In spring and summer, the flow is reversed. Air in the interior heats up and rises, drawing in moist ocean air. This is the wet summer monsoon, which brings heavy rains to this same region. This humid subtropical climate pattern, which affects eastern and southern China, southern Korea, and southern and central Japan—combined with the right soils—has permitted the growing of rice, and often two crops per year. This in turn allowed the region to support a large population. It therefore is no accident that since ancient times East Asia has been the home to more people than anywhere else on Earth aside from South Asia, where conditions are similar. This section of East Asia also lies in the path of severe tropical storms called typhoons, which in the Western Hemisphere are known as hurricanes. Typhoons often cause flooding and great destruction when they sweep over the land during the late summer and fall. In parts of northern China, as well as in northern Korea and Japan, there is plenty of moisture but milder summers and colder winters, giving this region a humid continental climate. Unlike the mainland, the islands of Japan receive rainfall all year long.

Conditions are very different farther inland, where the moist ocean breezes do not reach because of the distance from the sea or mountain barriers. From northern China westward across the Mongolian Plateau the climate is cold, often bitterly so, and dry in winter and hot and dry in summer. Most of the region is either a dry prairie or desert. The Plateau of Tibet and its surrounding mountains is a region of extremes, with very cold winters, cool summers, and decreasing amounts of rain as one moves south to north.

THE VEGETABLE CIVILIZATION

The diet of East Asia has been based on grains and vegetables for thousands of years. Because the climate and soils of large parts of East Asia were suited for rice, and rice produced a great deal of food per unit of land, the region was densely populated from early times. A dense population in turn meant that all available farmland had to be used to produce food, whether grains or vegetables, suitable for humans. There was no room for grazing land or land to grow fodder crops like hay for animals. This made it impossible to raise large animals that produced milk or could be killed for meat. The few large animals that could be kept were draft animals used to work the fields. A few barnyard animals such as chickens, ducks, and pigs could survive because they lived on scraps, adding eggs (in the case of the poultry) and small amounts of meat to their owners' diets. People living on the islands of Japan had easy access to seafood. But, with the exception of the nomads of the interior, East Asians rarely ate meat and never ate dairy products. They depended largely on the crops they grew in the ground. That is why East Asia has sometimes been called "the vegetable civilization."

THE PEOPLES OF EAST ASIA

Since ancient times most of the people living in East Asia belong to what anthropologists refer to as the Mongoloid racial group. People of this group generally are relatively short and have fleshy narrow eyelids. These characteristics may have developed as protection against the cold in northeast Asia, the probable original home of all Mongoloid peoples. Archaeological evidence indicates that this group of people spread from the northern and central parts of East Asia southward and toward the coast, until they finally reached the islands offshore, a migration that still was taking place in some areas during the past thousand years. For example, the ancestors of most Japanese probably did not settle the islands of Japan until about 2,300 years ago. Chinese settlers did not come to Taiwan in large numbers until the seventeenth century, about the same time as the Pilgrims settled in Massachusetts.

The main difference among most of the peoples of East Asia is linguistic, that is, the languages they speak. The great majority of East Asians speak languages belonging to the Sinitic family, of which Chinese is by far the most important. Chinese has been spoken in what today is northern China for as long as records exist, and today more people speak Chinese as their mother tongue than any other language in the world. However, that does not mean that all people who speak Chinese can in fact speak to each other. That is because Chinese has been spoken over such a large area for such a long time that it has evolved into many distinct sublanguages, or dialects. These dialects are as different from each other as Spanish is from Italian or Swedish is from German; a speaker of one dialect cannot understand the speaker of another. Aside from Chinese, other Sinitic languages spoken in East Asia include the Miao-Yao languages of southwestern China and several dialects of the Tibetan language spoken on that lofty plateau.

Altaic languages, named for the Altai Mountains in Mongolia, are spoken by the Mongols, the Uighur people of northwestern China, and the Tungus peoples of Manchuria in northeastern China. Most experts agree that Korean and Japanese are Altaic languages, which makes the Altaic family the second most widely spoken language group in East Asia.

There are small groups of peoples scattered across East Asia who speak languages that are neither Sinitic nor Altaic. The indigenous people of Taiwan speak languages similar to those spoken in parts of Southeast Asia such as Malaysia and Indonesia. These languages belong to what is called the Austronesian family. In northwestern China, some people speak a language that belongs to the Indo-European family, which includes English and the other major languages that evolved in Europe. The Ainu people, the indigenous people of Japan, who today survive in the far north in tiny numbers, speak a language that does not fit easily into any major language group.

EAST ASIA'S HISTORICAL PHASES

East Asia's first historical phase is by far its longest: the period of more than three thousand years when its peoples developed their cultures in relative isolation from major civilizations elsewhere in the world. In particular, this is the period of East Asia's history before its large-scale encounter with the modern West after 1800. Of course, East Asia's isolation was far from complete. More than two thousand years ago, China was trading with the Roman Empire along an overland route that came to

Aberdeen Harbor, in Hong Kong, is a striking blend of the old and new China.

be called the Silk Road. The Chinese also had contacts with the Indian civilization of South Asia, from which they learned about the Buddhist religion as early as the first century A.D. There also were contacts with the Middle East dating from ancient times, and the Chinese had their first encounters with Arabs, both in battle and in trade, during the eighth century. The Mongols, when they built their great empire in the thirteenth century, increased Chinese contact with lands to the west via the Silk Road. The first Europeans to arrive in East Asia by sea were the Portuguese, who reached China and Japan in the sixteenth century.

However, none of these contacts were extensive or powerful enough to pose a threat to East Asia's cultures. This changed after 1800, when Western European merchants and military forces arrived in the region in growing numbers and strength. For the first time, the dominant cultures of East Asia faced a rival civilization that far exceeded them in technological capability, and therefore in military power. China and Japan, the region's two leading powers, responded differently to the Western challenge, which required mastering Western technology. The Japanese met this demand far more successfully than the Chinese. This second period—when traditional East Asia first had to confront the modern West—may be said to have lasted until the mid-twentieth century.

The third major period of East Asian history covers the past half century, when Japan and China both became major powers capable of competing with the modernized West. Once again these two proud countries with long and distinguished histories have responded to the West in very different ways, and with different degrees of success. Korea, still divided at its geographic midpoint, has had more difficulty emerging from the shadow of foreign power, but that too seems to be happening, at least in terms of South Korea. How the process of modernization will shape East Asia in the twenty-first century, and how successfully the nations of the region will control their own destinies, remains to be seen.

TWO

THE PEOPLE'S REPUBLIC OF CHINA

The Chinese have never doubted their place in the world. In ancient times they proudly called their county the "Middle Kingdom," a name that had much less to do with its geographical location than what they considered its historical importance. As the Chinese saw it, their country was the center of the civilized world. The farther one traveled from China and its benevolent influence, the less civilized and more barbarian that world became. Chinese legends recorded how the Middle Kingdom's earliest emperors taught the human race about everything from fire, hunting, and agriculture to writing, the knowledge of medicine, and how to make musical instruments. The emperor himself was the "Son of Heaven," and he ruled "everything under heaven." In short, the ancient Chinese claimed that they had created human civilization and that their culture was superior to any other.

These claims, of course, are myths and do not reflect historical reality. Yet in reality the Chinese have no need for these or any other myths to establish their place in history. Theirs is a culture that can trace its history back more than four thousand years. China may not have created the world's first civilization: Those developed by the ancient inhabitants of Mesopotamia, Egypt, and the Indus River valley began at least one thousand years earlier. But those cultures, and the people who built them, have long since disappeared. The Chinese and their distinct culture are very much still here. Or, to be more precise, they are still there, that is, in China. Among all the peoples of the world, only the Chinese can claim a four-thousand-year-long unbroken line of one continuous civilization in the same place, dating from the Bronze Age to the Space Age. The unified state they forged more than 2,200 years ago survives, despite long periods of disunity and eras of foreign conquest.

China's ancient system of writing, while not as efficient as the phonetic system developed later in the Middle East by the Phoenicians, from which we derive our alphabet, nonetheless spread across East Asia and remains in use today. It became the vehicle for a literary tradition of prose, poetry, drama, history, and philosophy so rich and prolific that half of all books written before 1750 were written in Chinese. The Chinese called their four basic writing inventions—paper, brush, ink, and inkstone—their "four treasures." Their deep respect for knowledge went well beyond an appreciation of its value as an end in itself. It also reflected a profound commonsense understanding that knowledge and learning are essential keys to a better life. As Confucius, the most influential thinker in China's long history, put it:

> Love of humanity without love of learning soon becomes silliness. Love of wisdom without love of learning soon becomes lack of principle. Love of rectitude without love of learning soon becomes harshness. Love of courage without love of learning soon becomes chaos.[1]

Chinese civilization appreciated the world of beauty as well as the world of ideas. Its calligraphy and landscape painting were part of a remarkable artistic heritage, as were the magnificent bronzes of the ancient Shang dynasty. The Chinese also were unusually skilled at combining form and function. An excellent example is their porcelain, a seventh-century invention. Porcelain became a standard for high-quality ceramics for so long that it simply became known as "china." An even older product is silk, the soft, beautiful thread produced by the humble silkworm as it feeds on mulberry trees. The Chinese carefully guarded the secret of silk production for hundreds of years—smuggling silkworm eggs out of the country was punishable by death—and it is easy to understand why. Chinese silk was prized throughout the ancient world; in Rome it was considered as valuable as gold. It was so important in international trade in ancient times that the main trade route through Central Asia linking China to the Mediterranean world was called the Silk Road. Eventually, the secret of silk manufacturing did escape China, passing to Korea and Japan by about 200 B.C. It did not reach the West until it became known to the Byzantine Empire almost eight hundred years later.

China's technological achievements also are impressive. The Chinese are justifiably proud of what they call the "four inventions": paper, printing, the magnetic compass, and gunpowder. But these four are only the start of a long and impressive list. The modern horse collar (vital for transportation and agriculture), the watertight ship compartment, canal locks, suspension bridges, and the crossbow are all Chinese inventions. The Chinese were casting iron and making steel centuries before these processes reached Europe. The 1,500-mile (2,400-kilometer)-long Great Wall and the 1,100-mile (1,700-kilometer)-long Grand Canal are monuments to engineering skills that matched any in the ancient or medieval worlds. The Great Wall was begun in the second century B.C. and expanded and rebuilt over many generations to keep out the warlike nomad horsemen to the north. And until the nineteenth century, traditional Chinese medicine—a complex combination of thousands of herbs, ancient religious beliefs, and rational thought, analysis, and observation—matched anything available elsewhere in the world.

Science was another area of Chinese excellence. Chinese astronomy dates from 1300 B.C. Chinese astronomers spent centuries studying sunspots and mapping stars, and in A.D. 1054 they recorded the explosion of the Crab Nebula supernova. Chinese mathematicians made the ancient world's most accurate computation of pi and developed coordinate geometry. They discovered the algebraic triangular pattern for coefficients about five hundred years before it became known in Europe (where it was called Pascal's Triangle in honor of its French discoverer). After the seventeenth century, when European thinkers developed the scientific method, scientific leadership passed to the West. But for a remarkably long period of about seven hundred years, from approximately A.D. 700 to 1400, China was the most technologically advanced civilization in the world.

CHINA'S CONFUCIAN TRADITION

Throughout its long history, China has been one of the most regulated societies in the world. Ancient Chinese society developed in this way because it depended on its ability to control water. In the north, in the Yellow River valley, inadequate rainfall meant that survival depended on a complex system of irrigation, while farther south, in the Yangtze River valley, growing rice required flooding and then draining the fields for each crop. This in turn meant people had to work together and cooperate on a daily basis and that large numbers of workers had to be regularly mobilized for large water-control projects. These demands produced a way of life sharply different from what we know in the modern West, where maximizing individual freedom and opportunity is the main goal of society. In traditional China, the individual was unimportant and strictly subordinated to the group. Each individual had to learn his or her place in society and fulfill the corresponding obligations without question. Chinese society was a rigid social pyramid in which the small minority at the top controlled the great majority at the bottom and whose most important goals were order and stability.

The family played a primary role in preparing people for their places in society and in keeping them there. The father was the supreme authority. He had almost total control over family members, from his wife, whom he could divorce at will, to his children, whose very lives often were in his hands. Age dominated over youth. Children owed their parents what was called "filial piety," a concept of strict obedience that extended into adulthood. Thus *The Twenty-Four Examples of Filial Piety*, a book compiled in the fourteenth century, told of a seventy-year-old man who acted like a child, dancing and doing somersaults, in order to please his parents. Women were subordinate to men. During times of famine, baby girls were denied food to save the boys. When a young woman married, she went to live with her husband's family, where she often was treated by her mother-in-law as a servant. While a husband could divorce his wife at will, a woman's only escape from an unhappy marriage usually was suicide. Women had no property rights other than their marriage dowry, and they had to share their husbands with other wives and concubines. A poem from China's *Book of Songs*, which contains works composed between 1000 and 600 B.C., shows how unequally the Middle Kingdom valued men and women:

> Sons shall be born him.
> They will be put to sleep on couches;
> They will be clothed in robes . . .
>
> Daughters shall be born to him.
> They will be put to sleep on the ground;
> They will be clothed in wrappers . . .
>
> A clever man builds a city;
> A clever woman lays one low . . .
> For disorder does not come from heaven
> But is brought about by women.[2]

Matters became even worse during the tenth century A.D., when the new custom of foot binding added injury to insult. This crippling practice started at the royal court and eventually spread to most levels of Chinese society. It consisted of binding the toes of young girls—often as young as five years old—under their arches. The feet were bound with cloth strips day and night. As they grew, the arches broke. The results of this painful process were the so-called "three-inch golden lily" feet that were about half the size of normal feet. They were considered a sign of female beauty in China and a great help in arranging a marriage. By the nineteenth century more than half of all Chinese women had bound feet, their supposed beauty having been bought at the price of constant pain and great difficulty in walking. Running was an impossibility.

The philosophic underpinning of the traditional Chinese way of life was called Confucianism. Confucius (551–479 B.C.) was a scholar and teacher who developed and expanded ideas already deeply rooted in Chinese culture well before his time. The main goal of the doctrine that bears his name is what the Chinese called a harmonious society, which meant a well-governed society in which there was order and stability. Order and stability in turn required inequality. The key to a harmonious society, given that it was based on inequality, was that each person accept his or her place in it, whether high or low on the social ladder. This idea was enforced by the concept of *li*: conduct according to status. Unlike in the modern West, where people expect that rules of conduct and the law will be applied equally to all individuals, the concept of *li* stressed that people behave according to rules appropriate to their place in the social pyramid. It was proper for a husband to strike a wife or a son, but a wife who struck her husband, or a son who struck his father, would be severely punished. Thus the classic texts record that Confucius himself "spoke out boldly" when addressing a social inferior but "spoke respectfully" when addressing a superior.

These and other Confucian rules applied primarily to the upper classes. Strict laws and punishments were used to control millions of ordinary Chinese peasants. At the same time, those in power were expected to deliver good and moral government. This could only be done, Confucianism taught, if they lived and ruled according to Confucian rules and moral teachings. Their virtuous conduct would serve as an example to others and enable them to govern effectively and assure social order.

The Chinese Confucian ideal, then, was an ordered society based on inequality run by a government that was a benevolent despotism. But it was still a despotism. In China the law served the state, not the people. The people also served the state, not the other way around. More than six hundred crimes were punishable by death, and torture was used to get confessions.

Confucianism did not become the official ideology of the Chinese state until late in the first century B.C., more than three hundred years after the great sage's death. By then it was accepted that the key to knowing how to behave, and hence how to govern properly, lay in the classic Confucian texts. Eventually China developed a unique system for selecting officials who would serve the emperor and govern his realm. All officials had to pass extremely difficult examinations, a task that required years of study. Most dynasties funded schools to prepare young men for these examinations, ranging from village schools up to universities. Aside from the sons of slaves and men from several small low-ranking groups, all males were eligible to take these exams. However, with the rare exception when a poor youth might find a sponsor, only the sons of wealthy landowners could afford the tutors and time required to prepare for the examinations. Only a select few passed and thereby qualified as scholars eligible to become government officials, who were considered the elite of the realm and given important privileges. Though the examination system varied from dynasty to dynasty and certainly had its flaws, it gave China a loyal bureaucracy steeped in Confucian values, and probably made ancient and medieval China the best-governed country in the world.

At the top of Chinese society stood the emperor. Unlike his officials, he inherited his position. His whim could destroy the career of even the highest officeholder. One emperor, for example, forced 107 high officials to kneel outside his palace for five successive days, and they were far better off than some of their colleagues who were whipped to death with bamboo poles. But even in their insecurity, officials were far better off than ordinary peasants, who spent their entire lives at the mercy of the officials ruling over them. For ordinary Chinese, the state, with its strict laws and harsh punishments, was something to be feared and avoided. In a society where the collective was far more important than the individual, an entire family could be punished, and even executed, for an illegal act committed by one of its members.

Confucianism lost its official status as the guiding ideology for the state when the Chinese monarchy was abolished in 1911. Along with most traditional Chinese values, Confucianism came under direct attack after the Communist takeover in 1949. Furthermore, a great deal changed as China modernized during the twentieth century and new ways of doing things became part of the country's daily life. But Confucianism and other traditional Chinese values did not disappear. They survived both the republic that was established in 1911 and the attacks of the Communist regime that has ruled China for more than fifty years. At a time of rapid and often painful change, they still provide a measure of guidance for millions of people.

CHINA'S PLACE IN EAST ASIA AND THE WORLD

Even before it was unified for the first time in 221 B.C., China was the cultural center of East Asia. Once unified, China's power and influence expanded, at times as far as parts of Southeast and Central Asia. All of its immediate neighbors, in particular Korea and Japan, were within the Middle Kingdom's cultural orbit, even if it did not control them directly. This situation did not fundamentally change when China suffered periods of disunity, or even when it was conquered by nomads from the north, as happened in the thirteenth century A.D. The most significant influence from outside East Asia was the arrival of the Buddhist religion, which came to China from India along trade routes during the first century. However, no state could challenge China's preeminent position in its part of the world. China correspondingly had at best only a marginal influence on the civilizations beyond the geographic barriers to its south and west.

China's power in East Asia was reflected in the way the Middle Kingdom treated its neighbors. The Middle Kingdom dealt with foreign states according to the tribute system, which was based on the Confucian view of the world ordered by inequality. China set the rules. In order to establish and maintain relations with China, representatives of foreign states were expected to bring tribute, or gifts, to the emperor. They then had to perform the *kowtow*, an exercise in which one kneeled and bowed, gently tapping one's head on the floor several times. The kowtow left no doubt which country was superior and which was inferior. Since China, except during periods of disunity, was by far the most powerful state in East Asia, it was able to enforce the tribute system on its neighbors for centuries.

This favorable situation changed dramatically for the worse after 1800, when, weakened by internal decline and domestic problems, China was simultaneously confronted in its own backyard by powerful intruders from the West. Unable to defend itself militarily against the Western powers, and eventually unable to match even the Japanese in military strength, China was gradually reduced to the status of a semicolony of several foreign powers. The Middle Kingdom endured more than a century of humiliation at the hands of these powers that lasted from the early 1840s until the end of World War II. In the Revolution of 1911 the two-thousand-year-old Chinese monarchy and dynastic system collapsed, to be replaced by a weak and ineffectual republic, which in fact was little more than a military dictatorship. That regime survived only until 1949, when a civil war gave birth to a Communist dictatorship led by a charismatic revolutionary named Mao Zedong.

Under Mao, China went through a series of internal upheavals, as Mao and his dedicated colleagues led an effort, often fired by fanaticism, to build a perfect communist society. China under Mao also reasserted itself as a powerful nation able to play a pivotal role in East Asian affairs, and even a significant role in world affairs, especially after it developed nuclear weapons in the 1960s. After Mao's death in 1976, China's Communist Party maintained its control over the country, but certain policies became far more pragmatic. While maintaining its political dictatorship, often by brutally repressing dissent, the regime's economic reforms allowed private enterprise to flourish. This produced dramatic economic growth. At the same time, economic equality, the main promise of the Communist revolution, was sacrificed. Today China has reestablished itself as the leading power in East Asia, not in a cultural sense as in ancient times, but in a political, economic, and military sense. It is a major world power as well. But it has serious internal problems that are getting worse, which means it faces some difficult choices in the near future.

GEOGRAPHY

With an area of 3,695,500 square miles (9,571,300 square kilometers), about a fifth of the landmass of Asia, China is the third-largest country in the world behind Russia and Canada and slightly larger than the United States. China is really the size of a small continent, about 90 percent the size of Europe and 15 percent larger than Australia. It borders on fourteen countries: Russia and Mongolia to the north (and Russia again to the northeast); Kazakhstan, Kyrgyzstan, Tajikistan, Afghanistan (for barely 50 miles, or 80 kilometers), and Pakistan to the west; India, Nepal, Bhutan, Myanmar, Laos, and Vietnam to the south; and North Korea to the east. Only Russia borders on as many countries. China's 8,700-mile (14,500-kilometer) -long coastline is washed, north to south, by the Yellow, East

China, and South China seas. Beyond the first two seas lies the Pacific Ocean, while the South China Sea separates the Asian mainland from island archipelagoes that house the Philippines, Indonesia, and Malaysia. Directly offshore are five thousand islands, including tropical Hainan Island in the far south, the largest island under PRC control. Most of China is hilly or mountainous. More than 60 percent of the country lies at least 1 mile (1.6 kilometers) above sea level, and only about 10 percent of China's territory is suitable for farming.

The PRC is divided into twenty-two provinces, four metropolitan regions (Beijing, Shanghai, Tianjin, and Chongqing) with provincial status, and five autonomous regions with non-Chinese majorities. It also has two cities, Hong Kong and Macau, that were under foreign control until the late 1990s and now are called special administrative regions (SARs). The PRC also claims it has a twenty-third province, the island of Taiwan, which remains outside its control as a separate country, the Republic of China.

China's huge territory includes a great variety of landscapes. They break down into four major regions, each of which occupies about a quarter of the country: the northeast, which contains the temperate and, in the extreme northeast, cold regions; the semitropical and tropical center and south; the arid and semiarid north and northwest; and, in the west, the Tibetan Plateau. The first two regions, minus the extreme northeast, constitute what is called China proper: the territory where ethnic Chinese (or Han Chinese) have long formed the majority of the population. China proper, with an area of about 1.5 million square miles (4 million square kilometers), is home to the great majority of the country's population and is one of the most densely populated regions on Earth.

Two great rivers, both of which begin on the high Tibetan Plateau, cut through China proper: the Yellow River (Huang He) in the north and the Yangtze River in the center of the country. The Yellow River valley is the ancestral home to the Chinese people and where Chinese civilization first took shape.

It is the fifth-longest river in the world, about 3,395 miles (5,464 kilometers) in length. The river cuts across what is known as the North China Plain, a region covered to a depth of 150 feet (46 meters) by a yellow, powdery, and fertile soil called loess, which was carried out of inner Asia by enormous storms during the last ice age. Beijing ("Northern Capital"), the capital of the PRC, is located on the eastern part of the North China Plain about 100 miles (160 kilometers) from the seacoast. Despite receiving only 20 to 25 inches (51 to 64 centimeters) of rain per year, the Yellow River valley with its fertile soil was an ideal spot for Stone Age hunter-gatherers to make the transition to agriculture.

From the start, however, the Yellow River has been a taker as well as a giver of life. Its name comes from the color of the easily eroded loess soil floating in its waters, soil that has had little to hold it in place since the region's forests were cut down to create farmland thousands of years ago. The Yellow River carries so much soil, or silt—about a billion tons a year into its lower sections—that it has been called the world's muddiest river. Over time, as the silt settled to the bottom, it raised the river floor, often causing the river to overflow its banks or burst through the dikes built to contain it. Dikes built by the back-breaking labor of uncounted generations of peasants actually increased the danger of a disastrous flood. As the river bottom rose, peasants built the dikes higher, until in some places the river flows more than 70 feet (21 meters) above the surrounding plain, held in check only by man-made walls needing constant maintenance to do their task. The terrible floods that resulted when the dikes failed gave the Yellow River its second name: China's Sorrow. The importance of the Yellow River is reflected in the meticulous records the Chinese have kept of their struggle to control its waters. They show the river has breached its dikes and flooded the surrounding countryside about 1,600 times in the past 2,500 years. The worst disasters occurred when the river changed its course, a dreaded event that has occurred ten times since 602 B.C.

Nor did modern times bring relief to the Chinese. China's last dynasty, the Qing (1644–1911), created a special position to deal with the Yellow River floods, the Governor of Yellow River Affairs. The man who held it was the second most powerful official in the country, but it was not enough. In 1852 dikes along the river, weakened by years of neglect, collapsed, and the river cut a new route that brought it to the sea 250 miles (400 kilometers) farther north than before. In 1931, some 34,000 square miles (88,500 square kilometers) were flooded, resulting in the death of almost 1 million people and making millions more homeless. In 1938, the government deliberately destroyed the dikes to slow the advance of the invading Japanese army, and the river was returned to its old course. Between 1896 and 1946, the Yellow River burst its dikes more than two hundred times. Today, silt in the river continues to raise the downstream riverbed by 4 inches (10 centimeters) per year, greatly increasing the threat of flooding.

The town of Lanzhou is in northwest China, along the Yellow River. The town was a stop along the ancient path followed by traders known as the Silk Road.

Although Chinese civilization began in the north along the Yellow River, it is the Yangtze that has been China's most important river for the past 1,500 years. The Yangtze follows a course of 3,900 miles (6,300 kilometers) from the Tibetan Plateau to the East China Sea, making it China's longest river and the third longest in the world, trailing only the Nile and the Amazon rivers. Its official Chinese name—Chang Jiang— means "Long River." Only three rivers in the world carry more water. After tumbling down from its source more than 16,000 feet (5,000 meters) high on the Tibetan Plateau, the Yangtze flows through the Red Basin in Sichuan province, home to more than 80 million people. It then enters the spectacular Three Gorges, much of which will be disappear under a huge reservoir when the world's largest dam, currently under construction, is completed.

Once the Chinese settled the Yangtze River valley, its suitability for growing rice made it the country's agricultural heartland. Generations of Chinese peasants literally have moved mountains of earth to create the rice paddies that produce two rice crops a year to feed China's enormous population. The Yangtze has more than seven hundred tributaries, including eight major rivers, and drains about 20 percent (more than 750,000 square miles, or 2 million square kilometers) of China's landmass. More than 400 million people live on or near its banks, and the region produces about half of China's agricultural output. The Yangtze is less likely to flood than the Yellow River, but when floods occur they are especially disruptive because of the large number of people in harm's way. In 1931 the river's worst flood of the century in terms of lives lost caused destruction that affected 28 million people and left 145,000 dead. A flood four years later killed almost as many people and affected 10 million. Another flood in 1954 killed 31,000 people and affected almost 19 million. Floods in 1998, with more people than ever packed into the Yangtze River valley, affected more than 180 million people, but the death toll was held to about 4,100.

Unlike the Yellow River, the Yangtze is a deep river for long stretches along its lower sections, allowing large ships to travel about 700 miles (1,100 kilometers) inland from the sea. The river carries so much cargo and passenger traffic that it has been called China's Main Street. Shanghai, China's largest city and most important industrial center and port, stands on a small tributary to the Yangtze where the great river reaches the sea (Shanghai means "near the sea"). China's third-largest river is the Pearl (or West) River, which drains a large part of extreme southern China before reaching the sea near the cities of Guangzhou and Hong Kong. However, the country's third most important waterway, at least in terms of the historical role it has played, is man-made: the Grand Canal. Stretching from the Yangtze to Beijing and the longest canal ever built, the Grand Canal today suffers from many years of neglect. Most of it has been filled with silt and is no longer navigable.

The part of northeastern China once known as Manchuria is not considered part of China proper. It is the home of a non-Chinese ethnic group, the Manchus. They conquered China in the mid-seventeenth century and established a dynasty that lasted 267 years, the last dynasty to rule China. Today Manchuria's territory is part of three different provinces; the PRC does not use the name Manchuria. The region, larger than Alaska, is a huge expanse of lowlands and wooded mountains blessed with fertile soil and abundant mineral resources. The Japanese seized it from China in 1931 and ruled it as the puppet state Manchukuo until the end of World War II, when it reverted to Chinese control. It contains the 800-square-mile (2,000-square-kilometer) Changbai Shan nature reserve, the largest in the PRC. Baitou Shan (White Head Mountain) on the border with Korea—where it is called Mount Paektu—is considered sacred by both the Manchus and Koreans.

China's north and northwest territories have varied topographies but are united by their dry climate, which ranges from semiarid to desert. The northwest is an area about four times the size of California consisting of mountains, a deep natural basin, and desert. Formerly it was known as East Turkestan, a name that reflects its predominantly Turkic and Muslim population. Today it is called Xinjiang province. Probably the most striking feature of Xinjiang is the Tarim Basin, which covers 207,000 square miles (540,000 square kilometers), and is the largest of its kind in the world. The Tarim Basin is rimmed by the Kunlun Mountains in the south and the Tian Shan (Heavenly Mountains) range in the north, where some peaks are more than 20,000 feet (6,000 meters) above sea level. In its center is the Taklimakan Desert, an area the size of Germany. A large salt lake, Lop Nor, at the eastern edge of the basin has been China's nuclear test site since the PRC exploded its first atomic bomb in October 1964. Not all of the Tarim Basin is desert or wasteland. There are some areas suitable for farming, and the growing season, thanks to the mountains to the north that shelter the basin from polar air, is seven months long. Xinjiang province also has thousands of square miles of natural pastures that are known for their scenic beauty. The Turpan Oasis at the northern edge of the Taklimakan, 505 feet (154 meters) below sea level, is the lowest point in China.

East of Xinjiang is the Gobi Desert, whose heart is the rocky Alashan Plateau. The Alashan Plateau is virtually uninhabited and is used by the PRC military to test guided missiles. The forbidding Gobi, the world's northernmost desert, straddles the Chinese/Mongolian border as it stretches northeastward across China's Inner Mongolian Autonomous Region.

Directly south of Xinjiang is the Tibetan Plateau, which has an average elevation of 13,000 to 15,000 feet (4,000 to 4,500 meters) above sea level. The bulk of Tibet's 471,000 square miles (1.2 square kilometers) is uninhabited. The local climate is harsh, dry, and extremely cold. The landscape is largely a barren expanse of snow, ice, rock, and gravel. A few pasture areas support woolly yaks, oxlike animals that provide Tibetans with food and clothing. Most of the 2.4 million people who live on the plateau are concentrated in the valleys of the Brahmaputra River and its tributaries. The heart and soul of Tibet is Lhasa, the holy city of the Tibetan version of Buddhism, which has been the central feature of Tibetan culture since the seventh century.

NATURAL RESOURCES AND THE ENVIRONMENT

China is rich in natural resources. It has large iron deposits and is the world's largest iron ore producer. China also has the world's largest deposits of tungsten, titanium, and molybdenum, as well as large deposits of tin, antimony, copper, uranium, gold, mercury, aluminum, salt, and other minerals. There are also large deposits of oil—China is one of the world's top ten producers of oil—and small amounts of natural gas. However, China's oil deposits are not large relative to its huge population and rising energy demands. Oil production does not meet the country's needs, and it is expected to become one of the world's major oil importers in the future. This is because as China continues to grow economically its need for oil will increase very quickly. Hopes of major oil discoveries in the South China Sea and the Tarim Basin have not materialized. On a more positive note, the country's swift rivers, including the Yangtze, give it the world's largest potential for producing hydroelectric power.

China's most abundant natural resource is coal, but in recent decades that has become as much of a curse as a blessing. China has the world's third-largest deposits of coal behind the United States and Russia and is the world's largest producer and consumer of that energy source. There are seventy major production centers in China scattered across every province. About three quarters of China's energy is produced from coal. As a result, since burning coal produces so many pollutants, much more than either oil or natural gas, China has one of the worst pollution problems in the world. Nine of the world's ten most polluted cities are in China, and the growing number of cars and trucks clogging the city streets adds to the pollution from coal-fired power stations. Burning coal also has created a serious acid rain problem that affects about 40 percent of the country as well as both Korea and Japan. Since China's use of energy is soaring, its pollution problems, and their effect on global warming, are certain to get much worse during the twenty-first century.

Some of the coal burning in China produces no useful energy at all. All across the world, thousands of underground coal fires are burning out of control. These fires have spread in recent years as increased mining has exposed coal seams to fires (some natural and others set by humans) and to the oxygen that feeds them. They last for decades, or even longer, and defy human efforts to put them out. One coal fire in Australia is estimated to be more than two thousand years old. Recently a report by the Clean Coal Center of the International Energy Agency warned that these fires, which produce huge amounts of carbon dioxide, are contributing significantly to the process of global warming.

The worst underground coal fires in the world are in China and India. Hundreds of them are in a belt stretching completely across northern China. The fires are consuming about 200 million tons of coal a year, an amount equal to 20 percent of China's annual coal production. They produce nearly as much carbon dioxide each year as all the cars and small trucks in the United States.

China has fertile soil, but less than it needs. Most of China's best soil is in its southern and eastern sections. Intensive farming techniques developed over many centuries have made China the world's largest producer of rice; about a third of the world's rice is grown in China. Wheat, sweet potatoes, tea, peanuts, corn, sugarcane, and cotton are other important crops. However, China's long-standing overuse of its soil, an ancient problem, and other environmentally destructive practices have exacted a high price on the land. The country has lost an estimated 20 percent of its farmland since 1949 because of erosion and economic development that has converted farmland to other uses. Deserts are spreading in the north at the rate of about 925 square miles (2,400 square kilometers) per year. Too much water has caused damage farther south. The massive floods of 1998 in the Yangtze Valley, the worst in many years, left millions of acres under water. A major cause of these floods was deforestation, which left no trees to absorb and hold back heavy rainfall. The Chinese government has long been aware of the problem—deforestation began in ancient times and has cost China most of its forests— and has been planting trees for decades. This campaign has doubled the size of China's forests since 1949.

China also has a serious problem with its water supply. The north in particular faces a long-term water shortage. Meanwhile, the water that is available is increasingly contaminated by untreated waste products from industries, sewers, and agriculture. Each year China's rivers carry about 3 billion tons of untreated, polluted water to the sea.

THE PEOPLE OF THE PRC

With more than 1.26 billion people, China is the world's most populous country, and was the first to pass the 1 billion mark. About 20 percent of the entire human race lives in China. Although China's cities have grown rapidly in recent decades, 64 percent of the population still lives in rural areas.

China's people are divided into fifty-six officially recognized nationality groups, but about 92 percent of the population is ethnic Chinese, or Han Chinese. The minority nationalities have an importance far beyond their numbers. They occupy about half of China's territory, which also mostly happens to include sensitive border areas. Two groups, the Muslim Uighurs of Xinjiang autonomous region in the northwest, and the Tibetans on their high plateau in the west, have a long history of tension with the Han Chinese. Although both groups live in autonomous regions, these territories are in reality under strict government control. Both groups resent increased Han immigration into their homelands and government pressures on their cultures, and separatist sentiments are strong in both regions. In fact, the influx of Han Chinese into Xinjiang, mainly into urban areas, has reduced the Uighur share of the total population from about 80 percent forty years ago to 45 percent today. Although the Uighurs remain the single largest group in their autonomous region, Han Chinese dominate the cities, including the provincial capital, where they are 80 percent of the population. Like other minority groups in the north, the Uighurs speak a Turkic language related to Mongolian. While agriculture is the main source of their income, they also are known for carpet weaving.

The largest minority nationality in China is the Zhuang people, who number more than 15 million and live in southwest China. They speak a language related to that spoken in Thailand but are more assimilated into mainstream Chinese society than most other minority peoples.

Although today the Chinese are a majority in most of southern China, the Zhuang and other groups who live there today as minorities were in fact there first. The Chinese began expanding southward from their original base in the north perhaps three thousand years ago. After occupying the Yangtze River valley, they continued to push toward the subtropical lands to the south in the third century B.C. An ancient Chinese historian described the lure of the warm and humid south:

> Since the land is so rich in edible products, there is no fear of famine, and therefore the people are content to live from day to day. . . . In the regions south of the Yangtze and Huai rivers no one ever freezes or starves to death.[3]

But the south was inhabited by a variety of non-Chinese groups, including the ancestors of today's Thai people. As has happened on every continent and in every age when technologically advanced settlers confront weaker peoples, the original inhabitants of southern China were overwhelmed. Some were driven into inaccessible mountains; others were gradually assimilated by the more numerous Chinese; and still others simply were wiped out. The cultures that were destroyed or displaced ranged from tribal societies to substantial and advanced kingdoms, but to the advancing Chinese they all were "treacherous" and "barbarous," unworthy of a better fate.

RELIGION

The People's Republic of China claims to be governed by Marxist ideology, which considers religion as nothing more than superstition that prevents human beings from dealing with their problems in the real world. The PRC officially is an atheist country, and, in fact, a majority of Chinese consider themselves as having no religious beliefs. Nonetheless, hundreds of millions of Chinese do practice religions of various sorts. The government does what it can to discourage religion, a policy that at times turns into outright persecution, but does recognize five religions: Buddhism, Daoism, Islam, Protestantism, and Roman Catholicism. Muslims account for perhaps 2.4 percent of the population, and all Christians combined for no more than 1 percent. Buddhism and Daoism have much larger followings. Buddhism took root in China almost two millennia ago, and Daoism is even older, dating from the sixth century B.C. Today most Tibetans follow their local version of Buddhism, or Lamaism, despite government pressures and often persecution. Daoism is based on the concept of *dao*, the way of the universe and order behind all life. It preaches that people should strive to live in harmony with the natural order of the universe. Since Confucianism, which dates from about the same time as Daoism, is really a philosophic outlook on life rather than a religion, Daoism is considered by many to be China's native religion, the only major religion that originated in the Middle Kingdom. The Falun Gong, a new spiritual sect that recently has developed a large following in China, has met with severe government persecution that has included thousands of arrests.

In A.D. 2, China conducted its first census, recording a population of about 59.9 million people, most of whom lived in the Yellow River region. The population probably remained at about that level for almost a thousand years. It then seems to have started to rise, reaching perhaps 100 million between the tenth and thirteen centuries and close to 150 million by 1600. While no exact figures exist, China's population probably was about 200 million in 1750. Then it jumped, rising from that figure to 400 million by 1850. There probably were two main reasons for this increase: a long era of peace and an increased food supply resulting from new land being brought under cultivation, and new crops, especially faster-growing varieties of rice. Whatever the causes, and experts have different opinions on the matter, historians have called this rapid increase China's "demographic disaster" because in the long run it undermined the Chinese government's ability to control society and the country's capacity as a whole to maintain its standard of living.[4] Yet the population continued to grow, passing 600 million in the 1950s, 800 million by the 1970s, and a billion by the 1990s. By 2002 more than 1.2 billion people lived in the People's Republic of China.

The first serious attempts to limit population growth began in the late 1970s, when the government began its one-child-per-family program; it was proclaimed a "basic national policy" in 1980. The government had some success with the program in urban areas, where living space was extremely tight and education levels, especially among women, were relatively high. The problem was in the countryside, where most Chinese still lived and where children were needed to help work on the farm, especially as parents became older. Another reason to ignore the rules was the desire for a male heir to carry on the family line in accord with ancient tradition. Young couples resorted to all sorts of measures to get a male heir. When ultrasound scanners (which reveal the sex of the fetus) became available in some regions after

This is Shanghai's Bund district, known as "The Paris of the Far East." China now has many modern cities, complete with heavy traffic and vibrant nightlife—a radical change from the austere days of Communism.

1979, some pregnant women who found out they were expecting a girl had abortions. New parents often hid the birth of a girl by not registering her with the authorities or, far worse, either abandoned female infants or killed them so they could try again to have a boy. By 1999, 117 boys were being born in China for every 100 girls. (Normally, more boys than girls are born, but the statistical average is about 105 boys per 100 girls.)

The government used education, propaganda, and economic incentives, including monthly payments and upgraded medical care, to convince young couples to adhere to the program. Couples who tried to have more than one child faced severe punishment. Women were forced to have abortions, even in their ninth month of pregnancy, or sterilized. Families that violated official directives had their homes destroyed. At the same time, the government tried to prevent parents from choosing the sex of their child. Doctors who performed ultra-sounds were forbidden to disclose the sex of the fetus to parents, but many ways were found around that prohibition.

According to one estimate, China's birth control policies prevented 200 million births by the mid-1990s. Meanwhile, the policy had evolved by the year 2000. In rural areas, Chinese couples who had a girl on their first try were permitted to have a second child. Women who had the permitted number of children were required to wear IUDs (intrauterine devices) to prevent further pregnancies. Non-Chinese ethnic minorities also were allowed to have more than one child, in some cases (in rural areas) as many as four. Those who violated the rules faced fines, the loss of social services, demotion in their jobs, and other punishments. Local officials who failed to prevent excess births also faced penalties.

Yet very serious problems remain. China's population is very young, and life expectancy has increased dramatically since 1949. This means the population will continue to grow until about 2030. Despite the widespread use of contraception, about 30 percent of all births are unplanned. Meanwhile, many female babies still are aborted or killed at birth. As a result, the male/female imbalance has grown along with the overall population, especially in rural areas. In rural areas as a whole there are 120 boys for every 100 girls; in some areas the ratio has even reached 140 boys for every 100 girls. This in turn means that millions of young men are unable to find wives. The government has predicted that by the end of the century, China will have 90 million bachelors. This abnormal situation is unacceptable to a large percentage of the population, especially in rural areas, where both traditional values and economic necessity require that men marry and produce heirs. The grim consequence is a profitable trade in human beings. Each year in China hundreds of thousands of poor women in rural areas are kidnapped and sold on a thriving black market. A 1999 government report said that 10,000 women were being rescued per year, but that clearly is only a fraction of those kidnapped in the first place. Nor are young boys safe: They risk being abducted and sold to families without sons, and therefore without prospects of producing an heir. As of 1999, the number of abductions of women was rising by 30 percent per year, while that of boys was increasing by 15 percent per year.

China has yet another population problem. Uncounted millions of children, girls *and* boys, not registered by parents who want to have more children, exist in China as nonpersons. Because they do not legally exist, they are not entitled to education or any other government benefits and face bleak lives eking out a living in the dark shadows of society or on its margins.

CHINESE HISTORY: CONFUCIANISM TO COMMUNISM AND BEYOND

China's history prior to the twentieth century is divided into ruling dynasties. Myths tell about the Xia dynasty that supposedly existed from about 2200 to 1700 B.C. But while recent excavations have unearthed urban sites and bronze implements from that era just north of the Yellow River, there is no solid evidence of a functioning dynasty in the region. The existence of the Shang dynasty (1523 to about 1027 B.C.) ruling a state in the Yellow River valley is supported by archaeological finds, especially thousands of bones and shells on which writing is carved that is recognizable as Chinese. The Shang culture is known for its magnificent bronze vessels and ornaments. The Shang kings actually controlled only part of northern China and were frequently at war with their neighbors. Eventually they were conquered by one of their former vassals, the Zhou, who originally lived west of the Yellow River. Although the Zhou dynasty claimed to rule much of the North China Plain from about 1027 to 256 B.C., in reality it stood at the head of a feudal rather than a united state. During the so-called Spring and Autumn period (722–481 B.C.) aristocratic families and alliances fought each other until only seven major states were left. Despite the disorder, this was an era of major technological advances and intellectual and cultural achievements. It was when both Laozi (570?–490? B.C.), the founder of Daoism, and Confucius lived, and the period itself takes its history from the *Annals of Spring and Autumn*, a history some experts say Confucius wrote. The so-called Warring States period (403–221 B.C.) finally brought China to the verge of unification. The most notable thinker of that era was Mencius (370–300 B.C.), who is considered the outstanding interpreter of Confucianism after the master himself.

IMPERIAL CHINA, 221 B.C.—1911

In 221 B.C., the state of Qin completed its conquest of six rival kingdoms and united China for the first time. It is from the name Qin—pronounced "Chin"—that we get the name China. The man who accomplished this remarkable feat called himself Qin Shihuangdi, or "First August Emperor." China's first emperor standardized weights and measures, the country's currency, and much more. Most important, he standardized the Chinese writing system. Qin Shihuangdi was utterly ruthless and determined to let nothing stand in the way of building a strong centralized state. Hundreds of scholars who opposed his rule were executed. His notorious "Burning of the Books" destroyed thousands of priceless volumes that expressed ideas the new emperor considered dangerous or outmoded, in the process robbing China of an important part of its cultural heritage. China's "First August Emperor" drafted hundreds of thousands of laborers to connect walls in northern China that various states had built to keep out northern nomads. These efforts produced the Great Wall—later it would fall into disrepair and be rebuilt several times—that stretched across northern China. The construction was done at breakneck speed and cost uncounted thousands of lives. Qin Shihuangdi paid for this and other building projects with extremely high taxes and enforced his harsh laws with severe punishments. He expanded China's borders in every direction, especially southward to the coast of the South China Sea. The burdens he imposed on the Chinese people drove them to despair, and a rebellion overthrew his dynasty almost immediately after his death.

The Han dynasty that followed the short-lived Qin lasted for four hundred years (206 B.C.–A.D. 220) and completed the job of fusing China into a single nation. During the Han dynasty Confucianism became China's official ideology, and the first examination system for selecting officials was established. It was a system of government that worked, and later dynasties built on it. The Han thus established a monarchy based on Confucian values that would last in China for more than two thousand years. The Han era also saw important technological progress. Along with porcelain and paper, perhaps the two most important inventions of that era, the Chinese invented the horse collar, new techniques for producing textiles, the water-powered mill, and techniques for making high-quality iron. They even developed the world's first seismograph for measuring earthquakes, and a wheelbarrow so well designed that it could carry 300 pounds (about 140 kilograms). During the Han dynasty the Silk Road, a caravan route leading from China across Central Asia to the Middle East and the shores of the Mediterranean Sea, first became a major highway for trade. The Silk Road brought China and Rome, the two greatest empires of the age, into contact, albeit tenuously and through several intermediaries. By the time the Han dynasty collapsed in the second century, it had done its job. China's cultural heritage had cured into a bond strong enough to survive the periods of political disunity and chaos that followed.

China's political fragmentation lasted for more than 350 years. The Sui dynasty (589–618) that fused the country together again, like the Qin, lasted only a short time. However, again like the Qin, the Sui dynasty was succeeded by another long-lived and successful dynasty, the Tang (618–907). The Tang dynasty has been called the golden age of Chinese history.

Literature, painting, sculpture, and especially poetry flourished. Woodblock printing set the stage for the mass production of books. A dazzling array of technological breakthroughs during the Tang and Song (960–1279) dynasties transformed agriculture. Advanced water management techniques (including improved dams and the invention of the sluice gate), better and faster ripening seeds (that permitted the double cropping of rice), and new and better fertilizers combined to dramatically increase crop yields. Progress was across the board. New drainage systems improved urban health, and expanded knowledge of anatomy improved medical care. Personal hygiene took a significant step forward with the invention of the toothbrush. The Chinese added gunpowder, firearms, and even bombs to the technology of warfare. (Gunpowder actually was invented by Daoist monks who had been mixing sulfur, charcoal, and saltpeter in an effort to create an elixir that would bring eternal life.) The Tang dynasty also improved China's system of government by revamping the examination system and reorganizing the state bureaucracy. During the Tang and Song dynasties, China was the most technologically advanced and urbanized society in the word; it also was probably the world's best governed country.

The Tang dynasty collapsed from a combination of foreign pressure and internal discontent. During the Song dynasty the outside threat grew stronger, and in 1126 nomads from beyond the Great Wall conquered northern China. The Song dynasty continued to rule China from the Yangtze Valley southward, where it held on until 1279. At that point all of China fell to the Mongols, whose conquests already stretched into the Middle East and Eastern Europe and constituted the largest empire ever built. With their victory over the Song in 1279, the Mongols became the first foreign group to conquer all of China. It was while the Mongols ruled China as the Yuan dynasty that the Italian traveler Marco Polo visited and lived in the Middle Kingdom. His writings gave Europeans the most detailed description of China up to that time, dazzling them with information about the Middle Kingdom's culture, technology, and wealth.

The Mongols ruled the Middle Kingdom with an iron hand. They treated the Chinese as third-class subjects: the Mongols at the top, their allies from Central Asia next, and the Chinese at the bottom. The Mongols forbade intermarriage among the three groups. Ultimately this system of rule back-fired; not even the Mongols' extraordinary military skills enabled them to hold power for long. In 1368 a rebellion drove them from China, and a new native dynasty, the Ming (or "brilliant" dynasty) took their place.

The Ming would rule China for almost three hundred years. Perhaps the most remarkable event of the Ming era was a series of naval expeditions between 1405 and 1433 that took Chinese sailors to Southeast Asia and then westward across the Indian Ocean to the Arabian Peninsula and Africa. The Ming ships were the most advanced of their time, but the dynasty did not build on what it accomplished during those expeditions. Instead, China turned inward. Technological progress in many areas slowed to a crawl. China began to lag in military technology, especially compared with what was being developed in Western Europe. Meanwhile, in 1514, Portuguese sailors, the first Europeans ever to round Africa and reach China by sea, landed in the southern city of Guangzhou. The Ming emperors paid relatively little attention to the new visitors. They were more concerned with old threats from north of the Great Wall, and with good reason. The Ming were growing weaker, and by 1618 they were under attack from the Manchus, who had been growing stronger since the mid-1500s. The Manchus took the Ming capital of Beijing in 1644, becoming the second non-Chinese conquerors of the entire Middle Kingdom. They established a new dynasty, the Qing (pronounced "Ching"), which means "pure." It would rule China until 1911—the last dynasty, it turned out, in Chinese history.

The Manchus were effective rulers for about 150 years. Although they, like the Mongols, were foreigners, the Manchus, while also forbidding intermarriage between Manchus and the far more numerous Chinese, at least made some effort to make their dynasty acceptable to the people they had conquered. The Manchus expanded China's borders to its greatest extent ever, conquering Tibet, Mongolia, and large parts of Central Asia (the present-day Xinjiang Autonomous Region), regions all populated by non-Chinese people.

By the late eighteenth century, however, decline had set in. The Manchu armies, once seemingly invincible, had been weakened by easy living and corruption, and the Manchu emperors themselves no longer equaled the vigorous men who had founded the dynasty and led it in its early days. Corruption, ineffective government, high taxes, and other abuses led to a massive rebellion that began in 1796 and was not put down until 1804. It turned out to be the first of many internal upheavals, a grim sign that the Manchus were losing their grip. In 1850 the Taiping Rebellion began in southern China. The Taiping Rebellion was not simply an attempt to overthrow the Manchus. Its leaders rejected the inequities of Confucianism and promised to rebuild Chinese society based on equality and communal ownership of land. The rebellion rallied millions of poor peasants to its banner, quickly spread to the Yangtze valley, and turned into a titanic civil war that lasted for fourteen years and claimed more than 30 million lives before it was suppressed. A series of other rebellions swept other parts of China, from the far south to the far north. The nineteenth century had become a complete disaster for the Manchus and for China.

CHINESE CIVILIZATION IN CRISIS

The decline of a dynasty was nothing new for China. What was new in the nineteenth century ran far deeper. Since at least the fifteenth century, technological progress in China had stagnated. This was true in almost every area, from agriculture to military techniques. Confucianism, which had done so much for so long to maintain order in China, was in part to blame for this. The Confucian tradition stressed memorization, not critical thinking. It also stressed the past, and therefore was in many ways closed to new ideas. At the same time, China's population had grown too large for its limited resources to bear. With less food and other necessities per person to go around each year, China gradually but unstoppably was being transformed from a rich society into a poor one. Meanwhile, far to the west the Scientific Revolution and then the Industrial Revolution, both based on new ideas and ways of thinking, were transforming the countries of Western Europe. Soon they were knocking at China's door, bringing with them a challenge to Chinese civilization far more powerful and fundamental than anything yet seen in the Middle Kingdom.

THE COMING OF THE WEST

The Chinese were not impressed with the first visitors to arrive by ship from Europe, neither the Portuguese, who arrived in 1514, nor the British, whose first ship docked in China in 1637. One Chinese scholar described some early European visitors this way:

> They all look alike, though differing in height; some being very tall. My present idea of them is ugliness and stiff angular demeanor. . . . Their cheeks are white and hollow, though occasionally purple; their noses are like sharp beaks, which we consider unfavorable. Some of them have thick tufts of hair, red and yellow, making them look like monkeys. Though sleepy looking, I think they have intelligence.[5]

At first the Chinese were able to dictate rules to the European traders, as they were accustomed to doing through the tribute system with their East Asian neighbors. The Europeans, whose conduct the Chinese considered unruly, would not be allowed into the country but restricted to small areas on the coast. In 1557 the Portuguese were allowed to establish a trading base and colony at the tip of a peninsula about 40 miles (60 kilometers) west of the city of Guangzhou (Canton), their reward for clearing pirates from the area. Beginning in 1699, the British were allowed to establish a trading base near the city of Guangzhou. Over the next sixty years what was called the Guangzhou system evolved. The British and other Western traders had to do business and live outside the city. They also had to conduct all their business with a special group of Chinese merchants that had a monopoly on foreign trade. Making matters worse, while the British, the most active European traders in China, were very interested in Chinese goods, especially tea, the Chinese had little interest in British products. That meant the British had to pay for their tea with scarce gold and silver.

The Guangzhou system survived only as long as the Chinese had the power to enforce it, and that era ended in the early nineteenth century. By then the Manchu dynasty's weakness and declining living conditions had increased the hardships on the Chinese people. To escape their misery, many of them turned to smoking opium. In defiance of Chinese law, British and other Western traders began smuggling the drug into China. When China tried to stop this illegal trade by seizing the opium before the traders could sell it, the British government declared war on China. The First Opium War (1839–1842) showed how weak China had become. The British easily defeated the Chinese. In the Treaty of Nanjing (1842), the British forced the Chinese to open up more ports to British trade. The British also took control of the island of Hong Kong, where a city soon grew up. The Treaty of Nanjing was the first of a series of "unequal treaties" that China was forced to sign with several Western powers, and later also with Japan. Two of those treaties were with the expanding Russian Empire, which between 1858 and 1860 annexed tens of thousands of square miles of Chinese territory in the northeast.

Most humiliating of all for the Middle Kingdom, in 1894–1895 it was defeated by Japan, a former tribute state and therefore supposedly an inferior, in a war over Korea. The victorious Japanese became the most influential power in Korea and, even worse, annexed the island of Taiwan. That disaster quickly was followed by what the Chinese called the "carving of the melon," when Britain, France, Germany, and Russia took control of small but valuable pieces of Chinese territory. The foreign powers did not turn these "concessions" into official colonies, but they controlled them nonetheless and could do what they wanted without being subject to Chinese law. The decaying Manchu dynasty was too weak to stop any of this.

China attempted to strengthen itself through reform during the second half of the nineteenth century. The reformers, who included prominent Confucian scholars, hoped to save the Confucian system by borrowing Western technology but keeping Western ideas such as democracy out of China. Their attempts failed completely, and China continued to weaken. Eventually ordinary Chinese took matters into their own hands. In 1900, tens of thousands of laborers and peasants staged an uprising against foreigners in China known as the Boxer Rebellion. The people who took part in this uprising were called "boxers" because their system of martial arts looked to Western observers like boxing. The Boxers attacked and killed both foreigners and Chinese associated with them. The Chinese government supported the uprising, which was put down by soldiers from Britain, Russia, Germany, Japan, France, Austria, Italy, and the United States. Once again, China had been defeated and humiliated by foreigners. Attempts at reform both just before and after the Boxer Rebellion changed nothing.

In 1911 an uprising in several Chinese provinces easily brought down the decayed Manchu dynasty. The revolutionaries were not part of a unified movement, but the Manchus were so weak that it did not matter. Following the Revolution of 1911, the decision was made to abolish the monarchy and establish a republic. The old Confucian system, which had governed China for more than two thousand years, had collapsed. The great challenge was to build a new system able to take its place.

Replacing Confucianism did not prove to be an easy task. In the decades before the collapse of the Manchus and the dynastic system, Chinese intellectuals were learning about Western ideas and becoming increasingly critical of Confucianism. By the beginning of the twentieth century, many of these intellectuals were convinced China could never become a prosperous modern society until it rejected Confucianism and adopted Western ideas and methods. These thinkers included Sun Yat-sen (1866–1925), a doctor who had been educated in Hawaii. By the 1890s, Sun had abandoned medicine for politics and committed himself to overthrowing the Manchu dynasty and turning China into a republic similar to what he saw in the West. He later played a central role in founding a political party called the Guomindang (Nationalist Party, or GMD) and the Chinese Republic. (The Guomindang was also known as the Kuomintang, or KMT.) To this day, Sun is considered the father of modern China. Other important figures of that era were Lu Xun (1881–1936), a poet, essayist, and novelist who is considered China's greatest modern writer; Hu Shi (1891– 1962), a writer who look the lead in urging fellow intellectuals to write in Chinese as it was actually spoken, not in formal Mandarin Chinese that only scholars could read; and Chen Duxiu (1879–1942), who founded the influential magazine *New Youth* to publicize new ideas and later became a founder of the Chinese Communist Party.

Hu Shi, Lu Xun, and Chen Duxiu were among the founders and leading lights of a cultural and literary phenomenon known as the New Culture Movement. They were joined by people like the youthful poet and painter Wen Yiduo (1899–1946), the first poet to take the structure of traditional Chinese verse and integrate it with the rhythm of spoken Chinese. His poem "Prayer" is one of the most popular examples of that effort:

> Please tell me, who are the Chinese?
> Show me how to cherish memory.

Please tell me of this people's greatness.
Softly tell me; don't shout it out.[6]

The ideas of the New Culture Movement spread gradually. They received a major boost from a wave of street protests against Western and Japanese imperialism in China that erupted on May 4, 1919. The New Culture Movement (after 1919 usually called the May Fourth Movement: the two are for practical purposes inseparable) was a literary and cultural phenomenon that drew heavily from ideas of the European Enlightenment. It involved thousands of students and intellectuals and, in fact, has been called China's Enlightenment. Young people, the core of the movement, openly rejected traditional arranged marriages for relationships based on "love and romance." Young women ignored Confucian limits on their activity and began to seek education and socialize with men like Western women did. There were hundreds of new journals and magazines with names like *New China* and *New Man*. Some intellectuals, like Chen Duxiu, were attracted to the theories of Karl Marx, an influential German socialist thinker. Marx's ideas had provided inspiration for a number of European revolutionaries, including a group led by Vladimir Lenin that had seized power in Russia in 1917 (and a few years later changed the country's name to the Union of Soviet Socialist Republics, or Soviet Union). In 1921 about twenty Chinese Marxists met in Beijing and founded the Chinese Communist Party (CCP). One of the men at that meeting was a young assistant librarian at Beijing University named Mao Zedong (1893–1976). In 1921, Mao was very much a junior member of the party; twenty-eight years later he would be its undisputed leader when it came to power in China. The CCP was set up with the help of the Soviet Union. Like other Communist parties, it was not an independent group, but looked to the Soviet Union as its model and took its orders from the Soviet regime.

Meanwhile, the Chinese Republic got off to a bad start. Sun Yat-sen became its first president, but he lacked an army and therefore power, and resigned as president after a month. From March of 1912 to 1916 the president of the Chinese Republic was a former general who ruled as a dictator, even briefly attempting to make himself emperor. After 1916, China's central government virtually collapsed. Most of the country was run by regional strongmen known as warlords whose only concern was building their own power. The Chinese people suffered from constant warfare, ruinous taxes, and a virtual lack of government services. Matters began to improve slightly in 1923, when Sun Yat-sen, once again president of China, worked out an alliance between his Guomindang and the CCP. The agreement was brokered by the Soviet Union. It called for the two parties to combine efforts, with the Guomindang, a much larger group, in the role of senior partner. The Soviets promised to aid the GMD, including military assistance. The GMD would then be able to expand from its base in the southern city of Guangzhou and start unifying the country. The Soviets were prepared to help the Guomindang because they reasoned that if it were able to unify China, it would expel the European powers from the country and thereby weaken them. This in turn might speed up Communist revolutions in Europe, a major Soviet goal.

The linchpin holding the alliance together was Sun Yat-sen. The CCP was not interested in a permanent partnership with the GMD. That was a short-range strategy designed to help the party gain strength. Like all Communist parties, in the long run the CCP intended to take power and establish a dictatorship similar to the Communist Party dictatorship in the Soviet Union. Many Guomindang members knew this and therefore did not trust the CCP. One of them was the Guomindang's top military man, Chiang Kai-shek (1887–1975). When Sun died of cancer in 1925, Chiang became the new Guomindang leader. In 1926, with Soviet and CCP help, he began a military campaign to unify China called the Northern Expedition. Neither the CCP leaders nor their Soviet advisers expected Chiang to betray them. They were mistaken. In 1927, barely a year into the campaign, Chiang turned on the unsuspecting CCP and almost wiped it out. A few of its members succeeding in avoiding Chiang's murderous assault by escaping to the countryside. One of them was Mao Zedong, who took refuge in the mountains of southern China.

In the decade that followed, Chiang Kai-shek tried and failed to complete the unification of China under his control. One obstacle in his way was Mao Zedong, the most effective of the CCP's leaders. Between 1927 and 1934, Mao was able to build up a Communist base in southern China beyond GMD control. He built an effective guerrilla army, and fended off several Guomindang military campaigns during the early 1930s. In 1934, however, Chiang's army, aided by advisers and weapons from Nazi Germany, mounted a new military campaign that overwhelmed Mao's Communists and forced them to flee. Their escape, against all odds, is known as the Long March. It lasted for a year and covered a twisted route more than 6,000 miles (9,700 kilometers) long. The Long March brought the CCP to a remote area in northern China, where, under Mao's leadership, it once again started to rebuild. The Communists' future looked grim—until 1937, when Japan launched an all-out attack on China. In 1931 the Japanese had occupied Manchuria, setting up a puppet state under their control they called Manchukuo. Chiang at first had been able to ignore that aggression and focus his attention on the CCP. But by 1937 that was impossible. He had to give up fighting the Chinese Communists and focus on the Japanese invaders. The CCP and GMD therefore formed a new alliance, this one to fight the Japanese. Neither side trusted the other at all, but the ferocity of the Japanese attack on their country forced the two parties into an uneasy truce until the Japanese could be defeated.

WORLD WAR II IN CHINA AND THE CHINESE CIVIL WAR

Japan's attack on China became part of World War II, which began in 1939. The Japanese treated the Chinese with great brutality, murdering enormous numbers of people. Probably the worst single act of murder, though far from the only one, took place when Japanese soldiers took Nanjing, the GMD capital. What followed was a rampage of killing, rape, and pillage that probably took 150,000, and possibly as many as 300,000, lives. In December 1941, after the Japanese bombed Pearl Harbor, the United States entered the war. It provided Chiang and the GMD aid to fight the Japanese, although Chiang's government never did so very effectively. Chiang considered the Communists a greater long-term enemy than Japan: He referred to the Japanese as "a disease of the skin," contrasting this to the Communists, who were "a disease of the heart." The Communists actually did a better job in the struggle against Japan, an effort that won them increasing public support. Chiang's government meanwhile was plagued with corruption. During World War II it lost much of its public support. When World War II ended with Japan's defeat in September 1945, between 15 and 20 million Chinese were dead. The Communists, who had been on the ropes in 1936 despite having escaped from Chiang during the Long March, were far stronger than ever before. They controlled a large part of China and had a capable, well-equipped army. They were ready for a showdown, which was not long in coming.

The United States tried and failed to get the CCP and GMD to agree to share power. Neither side was interested, as each was confident it could defeat the other. Civil war between the two sides broke out in 1946. Despite winning some early victories and receiving large amounts of American aid, the GMD could not overcome its own internal corruption. By 1949 the CCP had swept the GMD from the mainland. Chiang Kai-shek and the Nationalists fled to the island of Taiwan, 100 miles (160 kilometers) off the Chinese coast. There they continued to use the name Republic of China for the small patch of the country still under their control. On the mainland, Mao Zedong and the Communists, having survived disasters in the 1920s and 1930s, fought the Japanese during World War II, and defeated Chiang Kai-shek and the GMD in the civil

war, now stood ready to face what would prove to be a far
more difficult challenge: turning China into a prosperous
Communist country.

COMMUNIST CHINA, 1949–1976

The Chinese Communist Party embodied two ideals. One was
straightforward nationalism supported by millions of Chinese
with a variety of political views. Mao expressed this ideal when
in the fall of 1949, a few weeks before officially proclaiming the
founding of the PRC, he told the Chinese people and the world
a new era had dawned in East Asia:

> Our work will go down in the history of mankind, demon-
> strating that the Chinese people, comprising one quarter of
> humanity, have now stood up. . . . Ours will no longer be a
> nation subject to insult and humiliation. We have stood up.[7]

To some extent, even in 1949, Mao and the leaders of the
CCP could take satisfaction that they had at least made a start
in achieving their first goal. The other, and primary, ideal was
socialism. In 1949 the goal of turning China into a socialist
society loomed before the CCP as far from realization as ever.
And no wonder. Mao and his colleagues were determined to do
nothing less than completely change how the Chinese people
lived. As followers of the Marxist version of socialism, their goal
was to end all economic inequality. This would be done by
abolishing all forms of private property—by which Marxists
mean private ownership of land, factories, mines, and anything
else that produces wealth—and placing all of the nation's
wealth under the control of the state. There would no longer
be rich and poor: Whatever was produced would be distributed
fairly and equally, guaranteeing a decent standard of living for
all people. As in the Soviet Union, the state would plan and
control all economic activity. It would invest all available
resources to make the economy grow, and thereby raise every-

one's standard of living. Of course, the Communist Party would control the state, and it would operate without opposition. Mao and his fellow Communists had no intention of allowing any other political party to exist.

BUILDING SOCIALISM

In fact, the CCP would not turn to building socialism for several years. Its first years in power were devoted to consolidating power and repairing the damage done by years of war. In additio, a land reform program was begun to break the power of China's landlord class once and for all. Its land was taken away and redistributed to millions of peasants who previously had little or no land. A new marriage law broke with Confucian tradition by giving women legal equality with men. Meanwhile, the PRC became involved in a war in Korea. The war had started in 1950, when Communist North Korea attacked South Korea. When the United States intervened to protect South Korea and decisively defeated the North Korean army, the PRC sent hundreds of thousands of troops to save the North Korean regime from collapse. That brought the PRC into direct conflict with the United States. The war itself became a bloody stalemate before ending with a cease-fire—not a peace treaty—about where it began, at the 38th parallel that had divided North and South Korea back in 1945.

Mao and the CCP turned to building socialism in 1953 with a Five-Year Plan that included collectivization of agriculture and an intensive campaign to build industry. Collectivization meant abolishing all private farms. Individual peasant families would have to give up their land and join collective farms that would be under party control. These new, larger farms in theory would be more productive, since they would be able to make use of modern machinery, make better use of advanced farming methods, and use the labor more efficiently than was the case on small farms. The CCP used both persuasion and, when necessary, force to carry out collectivization and finished the job by 1957. At the same time, having taken control of all of China's industries, the government focused on expanding industries such as steel, coal, and electricity, which were considered the basis of a modern industrial economy. Industries that made products people used in their everyday lives received less attention and grew much more slowly.

Although collectivization was completed and Chinese industry grew rapidly under the First Five-Year Plan, problems emerged quickly and had major consequences. Collective farming was not a success. Peasants often resisted it, and many farms were mismanaged because the party leaders in charge lacked experience and managerial skills. Food production in China, in fact, had increased far more quickly *before* collectivization than after it. There also were disagreements about how China should manage industrial development. The CCP leadership fell generally into two camps. One, led by a distinguished veteran named Liu Shaoqi, argued that when problems arose it might be necessary to slow the pace of change and rely on practical expertise and careful planning to solve those problems. This camp also argued for policies that would allow peasants on collective farms to keep small plots of land for their own use. They could grow what they wanted in these gardens, raise animals such as pigs and chickens, and sell anything they did not eat themselves in order to make a little extra money.

The other camp opposed these ideas. It had the advantage of being led by Mao, who as party chairman had been the undisputed CCP leader since the 1940s, towering above anyone else in terms of authority. Mao believed that any concession to what he considered personal greed, such as allowing peasants to have private gardens, was a dangerous concession to capitalism. It would undermine the effort to build socialism. He and his supporters further argued that the key to overcoming whatever problems arose in the effort to build socialism was the will to confront obstacles and overcome them. Human will, Mao insisted, not the careful planning of people like Liu, was what had brought the CCP to power in the first place and would now enable it to turn China into a socialist society. To Mao, Liu and his supporters were "tottering like women with bound feet, constantly complaining that others are going too fast."[8]

During the First Five-Year Plan, these disputes usually were settled by compromise or by splitting the difference. For example, collectivization was completed according to Mao's schedule, but peasants were allowed to keep private gardens as Liu suggested. The problem was that Mao Zedong was not a man to accept compromise for long. Soon he had a new program to break the impasse between his supporters and Liu's, a program that Mao promised would allow China to take a giant leap forward that would turn it into a modern socialist society almost overnight. Or, as Mao put it, if China followed his advice, it would have "hard work for three years, happiness for a thousand."

THE GREAT LEAP FORWARD

Mao called his program the Great Leap Forward (GLF). The leap from China's current backward state to communism would be accomplished by tapping the unused revolutionary energy of the Chinese people. Mao used a physics analogy to illustrate his point:

> Our nation is like an atom. . . . When this atom's nucleus is smashed the thermal energy released will have really tremendous power. We will be able to do things we could not do before.[9]

Mao determined to release that untapped energy by setting up what were called people's communes. During 1958, within a period of a few months, more than 500,000,000 Chinese peasants became members of about 26,000 people's communes. The communes were essentially gigantic farms—an average commune contained about 25,000 people and farmed 100,000 acres (40,500 hectares). Aside from farming, commune members were also expected to build factories and produce industrial goods. The most important point about the communes was not their size, but how they were organized. The people's communes would run according to what Mao believed to be communist principles; no compromises would be made to individual incentives, which to Mao amounted to capitalism. Thus, to ensure equality, all people, regardless of the work they did, or how much, or how good, were paid the same. Private plots were abolished. Families ate in huge mess halls in order to free millions of women from housework for other supposedly more productive tasks. Millions of peasants were drafted into huge work gangs and sent far from their homes to labor on major projects such as dams and irrigation canals. People all over the country worked at the so-called "backyard furnaces" to produce steel, but only after putting in a full day's labor elsewhere. All of this was backed by endless propaganda that filled the press and blared from loudspeakers.

Work went on at a frantic pace that exhausted the people while wasting their labor in schemes that more often than not failed completely. For example, the steel produced in the primitive backyard furnaces was useless, while planting rice seeds closer together left no room for growth and reduced the crop. Dams built in haste collapsed during heavy rains. Deep plowing, which was done to make use of fertile soil that supposedly lay beneath the surface, instead caused soil erosion. A campaign to kill sparrows to prevent them from eating crop seeds did kill millions of birds; it also allowed the insect population to explode, which led to greater crop losses than before. Overused and poorly maintained machinery broke down. Manufactured goods left out in the open because there was no place to store them were ruined. Overworked and overregimented peasants and factory workers became demoralized and worked poorly. The list goes on and on.

By 1960 the Great Leap Forward had collapsed. But it did not simply fail; it caused a catastrophe. One of the CCP leaders who opposed the GLF wrote a poem in 1959 describing what he saw in the countryside as a result of Mao's fanaticism:

Millet is scattered all over the ground.
The leaves of the sweet potatoes
   are withered.
The young and the strong have gone
   to smelt iron.
To harvest the grain there are children
   and old women.
How shall we get through the next year?[10]

The situation was so bad that Mao, whose position had seemed beyond challenge before the Great Leap Forward, suffered a political setback. Although he retained his most important post, chairman of the CCP, in early 1959, Mao was replaced as president of the PRC by Liu Shaoqi. This removed Mao from the day-to-day running of China. Liu was ably assisted by a number of party veterans. They included the tough and experienced Deng Xiaoping, whose tasks included removing party officials who had supported the GLF and replacing them with more practical-minded people. With Liu, Deng, and their team in charge, China gradually recovered, although not quickly enough. China went through what those who lived through it called the "three bitter years." The drop in food production that resulted from a combination of Mao's policies and bad weather caused the worst famine in history: By 1962 at least 25 million people had died. Liu did not mince words when it came to assigning the blame. In 1962 he commented that 30 percent of China's difficulties during the GLF was due to natural causes and 70 percent due to human error. He did not have to say which party leader was primarily responsible for that 70 percent.

Liu and his colleagues reversed the GLF policies. The people's communes, while not officially disbanded, in practice were broken down into much smaller units. Peasants again were paid according to work done and allowed to farm small gardens and sell what they raised in rural markets. Factory managers again could pay workers according to what they produced. It seemed that common sense had returned to the leadership of the CCP. That conclusion, however, turned out to be premature.

Mao found himself pushed to the sidelines until 1965, but he was far from finished. In 1965 he began a campaign to return to power. His most important supporters included Lin Biao, the defense minister, and Jiang Qing, a former actress who eventually became the fourth, and last, of Mao's wives. As defense minister, Lin Biao controlled China's army, known as the People's Liberation Army (PLA). As a step to restoring Mao to his old position of dominance, in 1965 Lin had the PLA publish a small red volume of excerpts from Mao's many writings, *Quotations of Chairman Mao*. Soon tens of millions of these "Little Red Books" were in print. Aside from the PLA, Mao's main instrument in his battle against Liu and his supporters was young people, in particular teenage students organized into gangs known as Red Guards. The Red Guards generally were students who had not been successful in China's highly competitive schools and who therefore had little chance of attending a university and achieving a high position in Chinese society. The campaign Mao called the Great Proletarian Cultural Revolution gave the Red Guards a chance to vent their frustrations. Eventually they numbered more than 11 million. Mao was their guiding light and hero. As one newspaper put it:

> Sailing the seas depends on the helmsman, the growth of everything depends on the sun, and the making of revolution depends on Mao's thought. . . . Chairman Mao is the reddest sun of our hearts.[11]

Urged on by Mao's call to "bomb the headquarters," in other words attack party officials who opposed Mao, and backed by the PLA, the Red Guards went on a rampage that tore across China. Party officials, artists, intellectuals, and anyone else who tried to reason with them became their victims. People were beaten and humiliated in huge public rallies, often dying from the injuries and mistreatment they received. The Red Guards attacked anything labeled as foreign, from books to musical instruments to paintings. They destroyed many of China's priceless ancient buildings and works of art because they were linked to the "four olds" Mao had denounced: old ideas, old habits, old thought, and old customs. Some people fought back, especially peasants and workers trying to save their farms and factories. Eventually Red Guard units turned on each other. China was engulfed by a wave of violence worse than anything since the civil war of the 1940s. Liu and many of his supporters lost their positions and were arrested. Liu himself, after a lifetime of brilliant service to the CCP, was denounced as a "renegade, traitor, and scab." He died in 1969 of pneumonia after long mistreatment and neglect.

While this was going on, Jiang Qing led a campaign to purge China's old culture, which was seen as the source of the bad attitudes hindering Mao's effort to build communism in

Chairman Mao Zedong in 1967

China. The old culture was to be replaced by what was called a "proletarian" culture. This meant, among other things, banishing most plays, operas, ballets, and other traditional forms of entertainment, whether Chinese or foreign. They were replaced by a few dreary works Jiang decided had proper revolutionary themes, which consisted mainly of workers and peasants heroically overcoming their oppressors. Meanwhile, in mid-1966, schools were shut down. Elementary and secondary schools remained closed until 1968–1969; colleges and universities did not reopen until the early 1970s. When the schools finally did reopen, traditional educational standards were abolished. Political correctness, which meant loyalty to Mao's ideas, became far more important than academic achievement. The result was that an entire generation of Chinese students finished school unqualified for any kind of serious work. It became known as the "lost generation."

Eventually the chaos of the Cultural Revolution became too great even for Mao. By 1968 he was concerned not only about the disorder it was causing at home but how it was weakening China's international standing. Mao was especially worried about rising tensions between China and the Soviet Union, China's mighty neighbor to the north. In 1969 the PLA was called in to restore order, the Red Guards were sent home, and three years of chaos ended. But not before China had paid a heavy price. Hundreds of thousands of people were dead. Many more careers lay in ruins. Priceless historical records and works of art had been destroyed. The economy had been disrupted, with industrial production dropping by a sixth. Mao's Cultural Revolution had brought havoc and misery to China and its people.

MAO'S LAST YEARS

Although the radical and violent phase of the Cultural Revolution ended in 1969, Mao and his followers ran China until the chairman's death in 1976. They continued many of the same policies, albeit in less extreme forms, they had followed between

1966 and 1969. However, Mao soon found himself at odds with Lin Biao, who, if anything, was even more radical than Mao. The two men had a falling out, which ended with Lin attempting unsuccessfully to overthrow Mao in 1971. That failure cost Lin his life when the airplane in which he was fleeing China crashed in Mongolia.

Meanwhile, Mao found that to repair the damage of 1966 to 1969 and to counter the influence of the PLA, he needed help from the same party officials he had purged and persecuted during those years. Chief among them was Deng Xiaoping, who was restored to a leadership position in 1973. He was joined by thousands of like-minded officials. Thus the need to govern China in an orderly fashion and get back on the track of economic growth forced Mao to bring back the very people he had once accused of betraying his communist ideals.

Mao's death in September 1976 signaled the start of the showdown within the CCP. Once again, the CCP generally was divided between the ideological supporters of Mao Zedong's approach to building communism and the more moderate and pragmatic group that had resisted the Great Leap Forward and opposed the Cultural Revolution. Notwithstanding their deep differences, however, both sides agreed on one thing: They feared and despised the fanatical Jiang Qing and her supporters. Jiang led the most radical faction within the CCP, which wanted to return to the extreme policies of 1966 to 1969. Those who feared Jiang were justified, for her faction was planning a coup to seize power. However, in October, before they could act, Jiang and her three leading associates were arrested. Known as the "Gang of Four," a name Mao had given them, they eventually were tried and sent to prison.

Immediately after Jiang Qing's arrest the main phase of the struggle for power began. The Maoists were led by Hua Guofeng, the man Mao had designated as his successor. Deng Xiaoping, who had been driven from his posts in early 1976, emerged once again as the leader of the moderate anti-Mao faction. It turned out to be a lopsided fight. By 1978, Deng and his supporters were solidifying their control, although they still lacked the strength to introduce far-reaching reforms. Three years later, Hua was forced from office and out of political life, and the path to real change was open.

DENG XIAOPING AND THE MODERNIZATION OF CHINA, 1978–1997

Beginning slowly in 1978 and then at a faster pace after 1980, Deng Xiaoping launched a process of reform designed to reverse the impact of Cultural Revolution and modernize China along rational and systematic lines. These policies quickly led China away from Mao's version of Marxism and, some would argue, ultimately away from Marxism itself.

Deng's program was called the Four Modernizations: modernization of agriculture, industry, science and technology, and national defense. The key to Deng's approach was that CCP policies should be practical and effective, even if they violated certain Marxist or Maoist principles. As Deng once put it, in a phrase that infuriated Mao, "It does not matter if a cat is black or white, as long as it catches mice." In 1978 he put it another way: The time had come to "seek truth from facts." By seeking truth from facts rather than from Marxist ideology, Deng hoped to modernize China's economy with the latest available technology and quadruple its gross national product by the year 2000, raising the standard of living of all PRC citizens in the process.

In effect, modernization of the economy meant introducing elements of free enterprise, or capitalism, into China's socialist economy. Deng began with agriculture, which in the late 1970s still supported about 80 percent of the PRC's population. Over a period of about four years, the CCP dismantled the collective farm system. It was replaced by what was called the household responsibility system (HRS), under which the former collectives were divided into small parcels that were leased (not sold) to individual families. In a word, after being abolished in the 1950s, the family farm was back in China. Each family had to deliver a certain amount of crops to the state; it could do what it wanted with everything above that quota. At first leases were for only one year, but this soon was extended to fifteen years and, in the 1990s, even longer. Peasants also were allowed to hire labor, buy their own farming equipment, and start all kinds of sideline businesses. Mao's egalitarianism was gone, replaced by the popular slogan, "To get rich is glorious." To leave no doubt that the era of Mao Zedong was over, in 1982 the party leadership abolished the post of chairman, the position that had become synonymous with the man who for thirty years was called "Chairman Mao."

The results of Deng's reforms were dramatic, even spectacular. Grain production jumped by a third between 1978 and the mid-1980s. Per capita rural income tripled. One experienced foreign observer noted the change during several visits to southern China:

> When I first visited . . . in 1979, there was virtually nothing in the market. When I went back in 1981, things had started to pick up. But when I went back in 1983, I couldn't believe what I saw. There were hundreds of people selling things. There were tanks of fish, and piles of fruit and vegetables heaped up everywhere. Lots of pigs were being slaughtered for meat—something you rarely saw in the past. You could buy Coca Cola, Budweiser beer, and foreign cigarettes in private shops. The prosperity was impressive.[12]

At the same time, while most peasants saw their standard of living rise, not everyone was successful. Those who did not do well began to leave the countryside for the cities, where unemployment and urban slums grew. After 1985 the government gradually phased out all delivery quotas for farmers. While this further increased incentives to produce, many peasants switched from grain to more profitable crops. Grain production leveled off and even declined a little, leaving China with less grain than it needed to feed its growing population by the end of the 1980s. Meanwhile, as income inequality increased, the number of people living in poverty likewise increased.

Capitalist practices also were an essential part of industrial modernization. In thousands of state-owned factories, managers were freed from constant government supervision, told they could abandon egalitarian wage practices of the past, and informed they were expected to make a profit. These reforms flew in the face of long-established practices and therefore were not very successful. More results were achieved by allowing individuals and groups of people who organized themselves into collectives to take over failing state businesses or set up their own businesses. Many of these businesses did very well and were able to hire some of the workers left unemployed by Deng's other reforms. Most significant for modernization, however, was the policy of encouraging foreign investment in China. This was a huge step that flew in the face of every principle of Chinese socialism. Foreign firms, including leading companies from Japan and the United States, were encouraged to invest in several so-called Special Economic Zones (SEZs), where they were given a variety of financial breaks, including freedom from laws that protected Chinese workers they hired. The SEZs soon had billions of dollars of foreign investment and by the 1990s had turned China into a leading exporter of manufactured goods, including an increasing number of electronics and other high-tech products.

Deng also worked to modernize China's scientific sector and its military. Standards were raised in the schools, tens of thousands of students were sent abroad to study, and the military began to acquire advanced weapons. China's military modernization helped satisfy China's nationalist pride, but it was not good news to its neighbors, nor to the United States, especially since it involved spying to steal advanced U.S. nuclear technology.

China's opening up to the West under Deng was highly selective. It involved allowing capitalist activity, importing technology, and carrying on foreign trade. Meanwhile, the government did what it could to limit the influence of Western ideas in China, especially ideas about human rights and democracy. Ironically, in doing this the Communist Party under Deng in the late twentieth century was following the same basic strategy as China's Confucian scholars and the Manchu dynasty followed in the middle and late nineteenth century. Deng's goal was to bring China's economy up-to-date by borrowing capitalist techniques, not to change the Communist Party dictatorship that controlled the country. Rather, the goal was to use modernization to strengthen that dictatorship. This contradiction was not lost on some Chinese intellectuals. A few of the braver ones began to demand political as well as economic change. In 1979 a twenty-eight-year-old man named Wei Jingshen summed up this sentiment when he demanded what he called the "Fifth Modernization," democracy. The Deng regime did not hesitate. Wei was arrested and sentenced to fifteen years in prison, where he soon was joined by hundreds of other pro-democracy activists. Once in prison, they were badly mistreated. The crackdown continued outside prison, including an "anti-spiritual pollution" campaign to combat Western influences launched in 1983.

On another front, the government had to deal with widespread corruption. China's new freewheeling economy created opportunities for government officials to profit from accepting bribes or getting involved in businesses, which then used their government ties to get special favors. Ordinary people without special connections also took advantage of the new economy to make money outside the law. The regime, despite arrests and harsh sentences, simply lacked the means to control all the new illegal activity. It also struggled to enforce its one-child policy, which was extremely unpopular in the countryside. Aside from couples having more than one child, the problem of female infanticide emerged as a national scandal, reaching all levels of society. In 1983 the *People's Daily*, China's leading newspaper, issued the following report:

[T]he drowning and killing of girl infants and maltreatment of mothers of infant girls . . . have become a grave social problem. These phenomena are found not only in deserted mountain villages but also in cities; not only in the families of ordinary workers and peasants but also in the families of Party members and cadres.[13]

THE TIANANMEN SQUARE MASSACRE

The repressive measures of the 1980s designed to control the spread of democratic ideas and dissent did not do the job. Low-level dissent continued. Then, suddenly, in 1989 it erupted out of control. The trouble began in April, when a student protest involving a few hundred people in Tiananmen Square, the main plaza in Beijing, unexpectedly swelled to a mass demonstration. The hundreds became thousands, and by May, 150,000 students were occupying Tiananmen Square. They demanded democratic reforms, an end to CCP corruption, and a variety of other reforms. The students were supported by many workers and other residents of Beijing, and at one point the total number of demonstrators reached a million. Demonstrations of support for the Tiananmen Square students took place in more than twenty other cities, including in Shanghai, where the crowd numbered 500,000. The students in Tiananmen Square carried placards, often written in English for the benefit of foreign journalists on the scene, with slogans drawn from the politics of the West such as "Give Me Liberty or Give Me Death," "Absolute Power Corrupts Absolutely," and "I Have a Dream."[14] Eventually they built a plaster statue about 30 feet (10 meters) tall closely resembling the Statue of Liberty; they called it the "Goddess of Democracy."

The CCP leaders initially hesitated as they debated what to do. In the end, Deng urged a hard line. In his view the students and their sympathizers had become a threat to the regime. On June 4 the government struck. Thousands of soldiers, backed by tanks and armored vehicles, poured into Tiananmen Square

Students move the statue known as the Goddess of Democracy into Tiananmen Square in May, 1989.

and attacked the demonstrators. The entire world was riveted by one of the most remarkable acts of courage ever photographed: a lone student standing in front of a column of tanks, bringing them briefly to a halt. He stood there until he was dragged away by his friends; his fate remains unknown. The students fought back with the few weapons they had. The death toll is unknown—the government did everything it could to dispose of the bodies—but student leaders and foreign observers have claimed it reached as high as five thousand. In the aftermath of what has become known as the Tiananmen Square Massacre, thousands of student leaders and workers who participated in the demonstrations were hunted down and imprisoned and an unknown number executed.

The CCP dictatorship had survived, but it was not 73
unscathed. At Tiananmen Square the regime had been forced
to use the People's Liberation Army against its own citizens. In
the process, it finished the job of discrediting Marxism, which
already had lost much of its luster in China. The Deng regime
simultaneously lost most of its moral authority in the eyes of the
people.

THE 1990S AND THE END OF THE DENG ERA

In the wake of the Tiananmen Square disaster, Deng Xiaoping
and his supporters busied themselves on two fronts. First, they
cracked down on dissenters across the board. Workers who had
supported the students at Tiananmen were arrested, and many
were publicly executed to drive home the lesson that the CCP
would not permit its dictatorship to be challenged. Intellectuals of all types—artists, teachers, journalists, writers, and others—were fired from their jobs, arrested, or forced into
retirement. Publications promoting what the regime called
"bourgeois liberalism," that is, Western ideas about democracy,
were banned. Satellite dishes were disconnected in order to cut
off foreign news broadcasts. University students were forced to
pass a course that taught them the CCP version of political correctness, which included a list of works by Deng. A huge propaganda campaign told the people that subversives had been
behind the Tiananmen Square demonstrations and that reports
of a massacre after June 4 were untrue. Martial law remained in
effect in Beijing until January 1990.

At the same time, Deng had to shore up support for his
economic reforms within the party leadership. Back in the early
1980s, some important officials had resisted economic reforms
because they feared Deng was undermining state control of the
economy and allowing too many foreign, non-Communist
influences into China. Immediately after Tiananmen Square
these officials succeeded in slowing down or even reversing certain reforms and getting some reformers dismissed from their

THE HANDBOOK OF EAST ASIA

posts. However, Deng remained the single most powerful figure in China, and by 1992 his reforms, especially the effort to bring foreign investment into Chinese industry, again were on track. Deng assured his CCP colleagues who worried the party might lose control that there was no need for concern. He reminded them that the state still controlled the largest industries in the country and added, "More important, political power is still in our hands."[15] Meanwhile, Deng moved a new generation of supporters into key positions. Jiang Zemin became the CCP general secretary (the top party post since the abolition of the position of chairman in 1982) in 1989 and China's president in 1993. Theory was brought into line with practice. Deng's ideas about combining free-market reforms with China's state-controlled economy became official policy under the label "socialist market economy." Still, some opposition to this policy remained. China's prime minister was Li Peng, who mistrusted Deng's market reforms and supported increased central planning and stronger state controls on the economy. But the reformers had their hands on the wheel. Over the next five years they had the numbers as well. Between 1992 and 1997, China's total economy jumped from $369.6 billion to $697.6 billion (while the population rose by less than 3 percent), and foreign trade doubled to more than $277 billion.

By the time Deng Xiaoping died in February 1997 at the age of ninety-two, the men he had put in place to continue his policies were firmly in control of the CCP. Deng's overall program for modernization and reform, known as "Deng Xiaoping Theory," was written into the CCP constitution in September 1997, joining "Mao Zedong Thought," which had been there since the 1940s, as part of the fundamental ideology of the CCP. In 1998, Jiang Zemin was reelected president—by China's CCP-controlled parliament, the National People's Congress, not in a general election—while Zhu Rongli, another Deng protégé, succeeded Li Peng as premier. The party seemed to have its marching orders and its leaders in place, but the path ahead, and China's prospects, were uncertain nonetheless.

At first glance, it seems surprising that China's prospects at the start of the twenty-first century were so uncertain, given its considerable achievements in the second half of the twentieth century. In 1949, China was militarily weak, economically backward, and desperately poor. It had been victimized by foreign powers for more than one hundred years. It had experienced two civil wars in less than a century—the Taiping Rebellion and the Communist/Nationalist struggle of 1946–1949—and during that same period had lost several wars to European powers and one to Japan. China had not had an effective central government in more than a century.

By 2000, China was recognized once again as the most powerful state in East Asia and as a major world power. It had the world's sixth-largest economy and an arsenal of nuclear weapons. In November 2001, fifteen years after first applying, China was admitted to the World Trade Organization (WTO), the world's most important body for promoting international trade. The next month, Beijing achieved another long-standing goal when the United States granted it permanent normal trading status, thereby assuring Chinese products access to the huge U.S. market. Another sign of China's growing international prestige was being selected as the host for the 2008 Summer Olympic Games. But the People's Republic of China faced formidable problems, some of which were approaching the crisis stage, and which altogether could potentially threaten the stability of the regime.

RICH AND POOR IN THE PRC

The Mission Hill Golf Club in Guandong province in southern China cost $250 million to build. It is one of several resorts near the Shenzen special economic zone, where dozens of factories belch smoke into the air as they create products that fuel China's export boom. While about 60 percent of the club's members, who must pay at least $315,000 to join, are from Hong Kong, the balance is increasingly shifting to mainland Chinese who have become rich from the free-market reforms begun under Deng Xiaoping and continued under Jiang Zemin.

More than 1,000 miles (1,600 kilometers) to the north in Hebei province, not simply in another part of China but almost literally in another world, stand the remnants of the Baoding No. 1 paper mill. A model of Chinese socialism for more than thirty years, the factory has been dismantled. Its workers are without jobs, and without futures. Like millions of middle-aged and older workers whose state-owned factories cannot compete in China's part-socialist, part-capitalist economy, pensions and access to medical care disappeared with their jobs. "I never imagined it would get this hard," a seventy-two-year-old woman told a Western reporter.[16] In 2000 she had to live on a pension of $6 per month; in 2001 even that was not paid.

The older workers from defunct factories are not alone in their insecurity. In the countryside, the end of the collective farm system has displaced many young people, especially those without educations. More than 100 million migrant workers wander between their villages and the cities looking for work. Often referred to as China's "floating population," these unfortunate workers survive on low-paying part-time jobs. To their employers, they are "one-day mules." Companies that employ them, mainly foreign but also some that are Chinese owned, have no trouble ignoring laws that limit the workweek and set minimum wages. Safety conditions, especially in privately owned companies, are dreadful, among the worst in the world. Accidents maim and kill hundreds of thousands of workers each year. Government statistics reported that more than 53,000 workers were killed on the job in the first half of 2002 alone, but the real toll certainly was much higher because many accidents go unreported. In fact, factory and mine owners often dispose of workers' bodies to avoid responsibility for accidents. The official CCP-controlled trade union federation rarely helps, and there are no independent trade unions in China. Despite having signed international agreements calling for free labor unions, China's Communist dictatorship does not allow workers to organize themselves. All attempts by workers to set up their own independent trade unions so far have been crushed, the organizers sent to prison or labor camps. Western companies, subject to pressure at home, have sometimes improved working conditions in their Chinese factories; however, this is not the case in factories owned by companies based in Hong Kong, Taiwan, or in mainland China itself. These dreadful conditions are producing thousands of worker protests, spontaneous strikes, and various other forms of protest, but little change for the better.

Nor are China's ordinary people safe in their own homes, at least if those homes are in a thriving city like Shanghai, where unrestrained capitalism is changing the urban landscape. In the summer of 2000, a fifty-five-year-old factory worker named Song Houfu spoke to a Western reporter in his tiny one-room apartment in a half-demolished apartment building near the center of Shanghai. The man already had lost his job to economic change. "I'm a true Communist," he said, but that allegiance to China's ruling party was not helping him.[17] The CCP was doing nothing to save the home he shared with his wife and daughter. Thousands of neighbors shared the man's problems. All of them lived in a working-class residential neighborhood that was being leveled to make way for corporate offices and luxury homes that will cost millions of dollars each. Only one old structure was safe from the wrecking ball: the gray brick building where in 1921 less than two dozen men, among them Mao Zedong, founded the Chinese Communist Party. Yet the birthplace of Chinese communism already was under capitalist siege. A Starbucks was in business one block behind the building, while in the near future a McDonald's was scheduled to open a block in front of it.

These inequalities have not always met with the stoicism shown by Mr. Song. The government could not hide the fact that social protests involving as many as ten thousand people were common in China. Farmers, workers, businesspeople, and even officials and former soldiers were among the protesters. These demonstrations frequently have been militant and even violent, with protesters blocking roads and bridges, storming party or government offices, and destroying property. In 2003, there were almost 60,000 major public protests in China, up 15 percent from just the year before and eight times the number of a decade earlier. Often the police could not control them. In those cases, it has taken martial law and the use of paramilitary troops to restore order.

CRIME, AIDS, AND BODY PARTS

Aside from inequality, the reforms of Deng Xiaoping produced another unwanted result: widespread crime that the government has been unable to control. China's rising inequalities and its growing crime wave have the same underlying cause. From the 1950s through about 1980, most of China's people were closely supervised and unable to move around. In the countryside, they were bound to their communes, which regulated most aspects of their lives. In the cities, factories and other places of work did much the same thing. For example, factories provided their workers with their living quarters, medical care, vacations, and almost everything else. A system of residence permits kept people rooted in one place. These and other levers of totalitarian control virtually stamped out activities like drug use and prostitution, as well as many other criminal activities. Deng's economic reforms allowed people to move around and, by removing the social safety net provided by the state-controlled communes and factories, in fact forced them to strike out on their own. The old system of supervision was fatally compromised, and with so many people suddenly having to rely on their wits to survive, crime almost immediately became and has remained a national problem.

The government's main strategy for controlling crime has been a series of "Strike Hard" sweeps to round up tens of thousands of suspects, rush them through perfunctory and meaningless trials, and execute tens of thousands of people, without concern that many might in fact be innocent. The first Strike Hard campaign, lasting from 1983 to 1986, claimed an estimated 30,000 lives; the regime refuses to say what the actual toll was. One feature of the campaign was public executions in which the convicts received a bullet in the back of the head. Torture commonly was used to extract confessions. A second campaign followed in 1993, and a third began in 2001 and was scheduled to last until 2003. That campaign began in April, and by September about 3,000 people had been executed, as many as 191 in a single day. In addition, at least double that number, and perhaps many more, had been sentenced to death and awaited execution. According to the human rights organization Amnesty International, during the 1990s China executed more people than all the other countries of the world combined.

Huge public rallies attended by as many as a million people witnessed public trials and executions. The police meanwhile were enthusiastic about what they were doing. "There's a strong sense of pride between provinces, and we compare ourselves to each other," one of them told a Western journalist. The public, apparently more worried about criminals than the prospect of innocent people being executed, seemed to support the Strike Hard campaigns. As one college student remarked, "They [criminals] are the termites of society. They deserve the death penalty."[18]

All of this hurt the PRC's international image. Its only concession to world opinion came at the end of 2001, when China's Supreme Court urged officials in the country's largest cities and provincial capitals to begin using lethal injections to carry out executions by the end of the year.

Meanwhile, government officials could take no pride in how they were dealing with AIDS. As in many countries in Asia, Africa, and the former Soviet Union, as the new millennium dawned, AIDS was spreading at an epidemic rate. In China, many factors were at work. Tens of millions of people were on the move in search of work, and they were shockingly ignorant about how the disease is contracted. Intravenous drug use and prostitution were spiraling out of control, spreading AIDS in the process. Greed on the part of unscrupulous people and poverty compounded the problem. The most notorious example of this deadly coupling was a scandal that took place in Henan province in central China. During the 1990s several companies used unsterile methods to collect blood. These companies were collecting blood plasma for making medicines such as gamma globulin and clotting factors. They began by taking blood, usually a pint, from individual donors. The blood from dozens of donors was then pooled and put into centrifuges that separated the desired plasma from the other parts of the blood, mainly red blood cells. The leftover blood the companies did not want, now a mixture of blood from many people, was then divided up into small batches and transfused back into the original donors. This recklessly dangerous procedure limited their blood loss, prevented anemia, and allowed people to give blood more often. It also was a disastrously efficient way of spreading blood-borne diseases, including AIDS, as blood from one sick individual ended up in many different people. The victims were mainly poor farmers in the region trying to earn a little extra money.

Nobody knows how many people in China are infected with AIDS. Educational efforts have finally begun to slow the spread of the disease. However, the government has done more to cover up what is happening than educate the population about the danger it faces. Injections in many rural areas routinely are given with syringes and needles that have not been properly sterilized, a practice that spreads blood-borne infections such as hepatitis as well as AIDS. According to official statistics, as of 2001, 600,000 people were infected with the AIDS virus in China; Henan officials reported 1,495 cases of AIDS in their province. But expert observers estimate that there were 1 million people infected with HIV, the virus that causes AIDS, in Henan province alone. That figure helps explain the grim warning in a recent United Nations report: "China is on the verge of a catastrophe that could result in unimaginable human suffering, economic loss, and social devastation."[19] The Chinese government did not release the report to the public.

Meanwhile, the execution of thousands of prisoners a year, often young and healthy people, has given birth to a new business that reaches from China's execution grounds to doctors' offices in the United States and other countries. In 1998 a Chinese official was arrested in New York, accused of trying to sell organs from executed Chinese prisoners for transplant operations. In fact, since the mid-1980s it has been Chinese government policy to take organs from executed prisoners for transplant operations. Kidneys, livers, lungs, corneas, and other organs are involved. Many of the patients who receive these organs are wealthy Chinese, but foreigners also have been coming to China for these operations. The thousands of dollars these patients pay for their operations—they must pay much more than local patients—has brought Chinese hospitals, especially military hospitals with close ties to government prosecutors, tens of millions of dollars per year. Many new transplant centers have opened, sometimes with special wards for foreign patients who pay top dollar for treatment.

The Chinese government denies that organs are taken from prisoners who have not volunteered to donate them after their deaths, but there is convincing eyewitness testimony to the contrary. Even worse, there is strong eyewitness evidence that organs have been removed from prisoners who have been shot but were in fact still breathing. These practices have in turn created ethical dilemmas for American doctors whose patients received organ transplants in China. Should they treat patients who have received organs under circumstances that violate American medical standards, legal norms, and fundamental assumptions about human rights? As of 2002 more than 78,000 Americans were awaiting organ transplants, and that number was growing rapidly. American doctors, and the United States itself, therefore faces a moral question without an easy answer that will have to be confronted with increasing frequency.

As a great power, China has many foreign policy concerns. China had very tense relations for many years with the former Soviet Union, but during the late 1990s relations with Russia, the Soviet Union's main successor state, improved dramatically. In 1998 a direct telephone link was installed between the Chinese and Russian presidents, and in 1999, after seven years of negotiations, the countries settled their long-standing border disputes. In 2000, Russia's newly installed president, Vladimir Putin, visited Beijing. A year later President Jiang Zemin went to Moscow to sign a Russian-Chinese "friendship and cooperation" treaty.

The improvement in Chinese-Russian relations in part reflected ongoing tension between China and the United States. The PRC has one overriding goal: to "reunify" China by taking control of Taiwan. Most Taiwanese strongly oppose this. Largely because of pressure from Beijing, Taiwan has not formally declared its independence, but the Taiwanese government has resisted all PRC attempts to move toward "reunification." In that Taiwan had been strongly backed by the United States. This is the most serious, but not the only, cause of tension between Washington and Beijing. During the 1990s the United States was critical of Chinese trade practices which protected its markets while Beijing did everything it could to promote exports to the huge American market. These policies helped create an enormous trade imbalance in China's favor between the two countries, which reached $80 billion by the year 2000, topped 100 billion in 2002, and continued to grow in 2003 and 2004. Other tensions between the two countries involved U.S. criticism of Chinese human rights policies, including Beijing's treatment of Tibet, Chinese spying on U.S. weapons programs (between the late 1970s and mid-1990s, Chinese spies stole advanced U.S. nuclear weapons technology), China's sale of nuclear technology to Pakistan, and U.S. plans to build a missile defense system. China's role in promoting the proliferation of weapons of mass destruction went well beyond sales to Pakistan. By the 1990s it had a long record of assisting North Korean missile programs, which had as their goal developing missiles capable of carrying nuclear weapons and reaching the United States. Furthermore, Chinese missile technology and hardware, with Beijing's approval and sometimes with its active participation, passed from North Korea and Pakistan to Iran, Syria, and Libya, all Middle East countries on the United States' official list of nations supporting international terror. In addition, North Korea and Pakistan exchanged their Chinese-based weapons of mass destruction technology. Beginning in 1997, Pakistani technology for building nuclear weapons went to North Korea, while North Korean ballistic missiles went to Pakistan. Given China's relations with both countries, United States intelligence experts argued that neither of these exchanges could have taken place without Beijing's knowledge and approval.

The strain in relations between the United States and China was illustrated in the spring of 2001, when a Chinese jet fighter collided with a United States spy plane flying in international airspace off the Chinese coast. Although the Chinese pilot, who was killed when his aircraft crashed, clearly was at fault, the incident inflamed Chinese nationalist feeling and took months to smooth over.

Yet another source of PRC–U.S. tension has been Beijing's attempt to reach far beyond its borders and control the Chinese-language media in the United States. Beijing's tactics include gaining ownership of newspapers and television and radio stations, using business ties with mainland China to apply pressure, buying broadcast time and advertising space, and assigning government personnel to work in independent media outlets in order to influence what they write or broadcast. It has been a thorough campaign, reaching not only the twelve major U.S. cities in which most Chinese-Americans live but also newspapers and local television and radio stations in smaller communities.

Relations between the two countries took a more positive turn in the fall of 2001, when the PRC announced its support for the American war on terrorism in the wake of the destruction of the World Trade Center in New York City by Islamic militants. That step, while welcome in Washington, grew directly out of China's own needs: its fears of Muslim separatists in Xinjiang province. Another positive development from Beijing's point of view took place in December, when the United States granted the PRC permanent normal trading status.

The PRC's relations with Japan have been clouded by the memory of Japanese aggression during World War II, which most observers agree Japan has failed to confront honestly, especially in history textbooks used in its schools. The two nations also both claim some uninhabited islands in the East China Sea. The PRC's more serious territorial dispute is with Vietnam and four other countries over the Spratly Islands in the South China Sea, which may have significant oil deposits underneath their offshore waters. China and Vietnam also claim the Paracel (Xisha) Islands, which China occupied by force in 1974. Another unresolved border dispute, this one over mountainous terrain along the Tibetan border, remains an issue between the PRC and India.

CHINA IN 2005: A COUNTRY OF CONTRADICTIONS

China at the dawn of the twenty-first century is a land of contradictions. Despite enormous progress since 1980, it has a fragmented economy. One part is modernizing at a rapid rate and becoming increasingly integrated with the rest of the world. That modernized part of China's economy will benefit from China's entering the WTO and gaining normal trade status with the United States. More than half of China's output comes from the thriving private sector. That sector has become a magnet for foreign companies eager to take advantage of cheap labor and lax government regulation to produce goods at the lowest possible cost. They can then export those goods from China to countries all over the world. (Chinese wages are so low that few local people can afford to buy the products foreign companies manufacture in China.) In 2001 half of China's exports were produced by foreign firms, either in their own factories or in joint ventures with Chinese companies. The next year, foreign companies invested an estimated $50 billion in China, a record amount. Between 2000 and 2003, foreign firms opened about 60,000 factories in China. As a result, China increasingly is justified in calling itself the "workshop of the world," a development viewed with concern by several of its neighbors. As foreign investment pours into China, countries like South Korea, Thailand, Malaysia, and Singapore are attracting fewer investors, and their factories are having difficulty competing with low-cost factories in China. Even Japan, East Asia's economic powerhouse, is losing markets to manufacturers based in China. On the other side of the world, Mexico has lost hundreds of thousands of manufacturing jobs to China. Another country adversely affected by China's low-cost export boom is the United States. It has a ballooning unfavorable balance of trade with China, and America's largest companies are investing and creating jobs in China rather than in the United States. And it is losing manufacturing jobs that once paid American workers good wages, more than 2 million between 2000 and 2004. At the same time, the economic presence of the United States in East and Southeast Asia is declining as that of China's grows. Over time that in turn will reduce America's overall influence in that part of the world.

On the other hand, many of China's state-owned industries, which still employ millions of people, are bankrupt. The banking system is plagued by bad debts, and, despite the dismantling of the collective farm system, China's agricultural sector is primitive. Although China's economy has grown rapidly, it still cannot provide for anything close to all its people, more than 200 million of whom were either unemployed or underemployed as of 2002.

If China's economic system has one foot in the present and one in the past, the political system remains largely unchanged: a rigid one-party dictatorship as it was in the days of Mao and Deng. It remains a regime that does not recognize human rights as understood in the West. Even at the village level, where a 1998 law permitted multicandidate elections, in practice the CCP controls the process. As the party's 1999 rules for these elections put it, the village party branches "are the leading core of every organization and every task in the townships and villages."[20] While the press has more latitude than in the past, all newspapers remain under party control. Editors or reporters who stray too far from the party line or probe too deeply into issues such as corruption that the CCP leadership finds threatening, risk their jobs and careers. Academics and anyone else who become too critical of the regime do so at the risk of their freedom. Nor is the Internet free from careful supervision. According to a report issued by a leading U.S. law school in December 2002, China maintains the most extensive Internet censorship in the world, blocking access to more than 19,000 Web sites. They include news, political, and religious sites, as well as entertainment and educational sites.

Nothing better illustrates the regime's determination to maintain an absolute one-party dictatorship than its treatment of the Falun Gong, a spiritual group that may have millions of followers in China. In 1999, Falun Gong shocked the CCP leadership when 10,000 of its members demonstrated in Beijing to demand official government recognition as a religious group. Since then, more than 10,000 of its followers have been arrested and sent to China's brutal labor camps, collectively known as the laogai, where at least 200 have died.

Recently the Chinese Communist Party has made some changes by officially installing a new generation of leaders. The process was done smoothly in two stages, the first during the party's sixteenth congress and the second at a meeting of the National People's Congress, China's parliament. In November 2002, at the CCP's sixteenth congress, Jiang Zemin gave up his post as general secretary, or party leader. Numerous other older party leaders dutifully joined Jiang in stepping down. The new general secretary was fifty-nine-year-old Hu Jintao, a veteran party official with a reputation as someone willing to innovate at times but also strictly a team player prepared to use force to quell any dissent. Hu was the only member of the Standing Committee of the Politburo, the party's top body, to retain his post. Its other six members, among them Le Peng and Zhu Rongji, China's prime minister, all retired. They were all replaced by eight men in their sixties, all members of the party's so-called fourth generation of leaders. (The first generation was Mao's, the second Deng's, and the third Jiang's.)

In reality, the changes were far less than met the eye. Consistent with CCP tradition, Hu was chosen in secret by a tiny group. Hu made his acceptance speech in secret to a small caucus of party leaders. Jiang retained his post as chairman of the party's Central Military Commission, which controls the army, and five of the members of the Standing Committee were his supporters. This meant that Jiang, while no longer officially at the party's helm, remained the most powerful politician in China. Nor did Hu, who made a point of professing his loyalty to Jiang, show any signs of favoring significant changes in policy. If he had any strong convictions about the new policies, they were not known. One former senior party leader compared Hu to the moon, a body that does not radiate its own energy but reflects light or dark depending on the circumstances.

A second round of change, no more meaningful that the first, took place in March 2003 when the National People's Congress, China's rubber-stamp legislature, chose a new group of government leaders. Once again Hu Jintao, until then China's vice president, succeeded Jiang Zemin, this time as president of China. Once again, other government leaders of Jiang's generation, mostly the same men who had given up their party offices in November 2002, followed him into retirement. The legislature also installed a new prime minister, Wen Jiabao, and a new cabinet. Even then, much less had changed than met the eye. Jiang Zemin still was chairman of the Central Military Commission (CMC), the body that controlled the armed forces, and therefore still the most powerful man in China. While Hu was in the best position of China's new generation of politicians, it was possible he could be pushed aside if he did not play his cards right. Finally, in September 2004, Hu succeeded Jiang as Chairman of the CMC, thereby consolidating his position at the top of China's political pyramid. He was there because, as one expert observer put it, he and his ally Wen Jiabao proved they were experts at "Machiavellian infighting and bureaucratic back stabbing."[21] In other words, while the men at the top had changed, China's political system remained very much the same.

Neither Hu Jintao nor the Chinese leadership as a whole played their cards right in late 2002 when a dangerous new viral disease known as SARS (severe acute respiratory syndrome) broke out in the southern province of Guangdong. Instead of acting in the interest of public health and admitting the problem, the regime thought only of maintaning its authority and withheld all information about what was happening. As a result, SARS quickly spread to Hong Kong and beyond China's borders. By March 2003 the new disease was threatening to turn into a worldwide epidemic. Emergency measures by the World Health Organization and medical authorities in many countries including China brought SARS under control by June 2003. However, the SARS scare did not affect the Chinese government's policies regarding its dictatorial control of information. As of mid-2003, Beijing was censoring Chinese newspapers and other media as strictly as ever.

China's young people, at least its current university students, present one of China's more interesting contradictions. To outside observers they seem Westernized. They frequent the discos that have become extremely popular, not only in major cities like Beijing, Shanghai, and Guangzhou but even in less sophisticated parts of the country. They flock to Internet chat rooms (although they cannot reach thousands of Web sites blocked by the government), wear blue jeans and Reebok sneakers, and call each other on cell phones. Yet their attitude toward the West, and especially the United States, is rather different from the outlook of the generation that in 1989 demonstrated so bravely for democracy in Tiananmen Square. The government crackdown since then has had an impact. So has the regime's tireless trumpeting of Chinese nationalism and anti-American propaganda. These campaigns begin in primary school, continue right through college, and are reinforced by the media. China's university students in their early twenties have little knowledge of the Great Leap Forward or the Cultural Revolution, which are largely ignored in the schools. What happened in Tiananmen Square more than a decade ago, when they were at most ten years old, is a vague, distant memory. Current university students appear to agree with the government claim that it is protecting social order when it curbs freedom of expression, represses dissenters like the Falun Gong, and imposes the death penalty on a massive scale. They are interested in the United States, and often want to study there, but they see it as a bully trying to push their country around.

Although the Communist Party still rules in China, a quarter of a century after Mao Zedong's death, the communist ideals that constituted the core of its promises to the Chinese people are as dead as he is. It has a capitalist economy that is growing rapidly but is also characterized by enormous inequality. Aside from the CCP dictatorship itself, nationalism is what holds the country together. That sentiment has considerable strength beyond what it draws from unrelenting government propaganda. Nationalism draws strength from the resentment the Chinese still feel over 150 years of foreign mistreatment after 1800. It is rooted in a history four thousand years old. It is a strong glue. The question is whether it is strong enough to prevent the rifts caused by deep social, economic, and political problems from deepening to the point where they threaten the country's stability.

THREE

THE REPUBLIC OF CHINA

About 100 miles (160 kilometers) east of mainland China, separated from the People's Republic of China (PRC) by the Strait of Taiwan, is the island of Taiwan, home to the Republic of China (ROC). There are few countries in the world whose status is as plagued by uncertainty and riven by contradictions as the Republic of China. It unquestionably was one of the world's most spectacular success stories of the last half of the twentieth century. Having emerged from a background of foreign occupation, civil war, poverty, and dictatorship, the ROC by the mid-1990s was one of the most prosperous nations in the world. It was a leading exporter and trading nation, a center of high-tech manufacturing, a major international investor, and a country that enjoyed one of the world's highest per capita incomes. Political reforms after 1987 had turned it into a genuine democracy by the year 2000.

Yet the Republic of China was an international political outcast. The problem is that the People's Republic of China, which controls the Chinese mainland, claims that Taiwan belongs to it. The PRC demands that Taiwan give up its independent status, which it has had since the end of the Chinese civil war in 1949, and reunify with the mainland. As a result of pressure from the Communist government in Beijing, Taiwan was expelled from the United Nations in 1971 when the People's Republic of China was admitted in its place. It was barred from membership in important international economic organizations, could not compete in the Olympics under its official name but only as "Chinese Taipei," and enjoyed diplomatic recognition from less than thirty countries, mostly small states to whom the ROC provided foreign aid. Even the United States, the ROC's most important political backer, withdrew official recognition in 1979, the year Washington established normal diplomatic relations with the PRC.

GEOGRAPHY, PEOPLE, ECONOMY

The Republic of China has an area of about 13,900 square miles (36,000 square kilometers), almost all of which consists of the island of Taiwan. The ROC also controls a number of smaller islands. They include the sixty-four islands of the Penghu (Pescadores) chain, about 30 miles (50 kilometers) to the west in the Taiwan Strait, and about twenty islands within a few miles of the Chinese mainland, the most important of which are Kinmen (Quemoy) and Matsu. The ROC also is one of several countries claiming sovereignty over about fifty rocks and reefs called the Spratly Islands in the South China Sea. Aside from the Taiwan Strait directly to the west, Taiwan's shores are washed by the East China Sea in the north, the South China sea in the southwest, the Philippine Sea, which blends into the Pacific Ocean, in the east, and the Bashi Channel in the south. South of the Bashi Channel are islands belonging to the

Philippines. The Ryukyu Islands, which belong to Japan, are stepping-stones that begin about 125 miles (201 kilometers) off Taiwan's northeast coast and stretch almost to Kyushu, the southernmost of the four main islands of Japan. Taipei, the ROC's capital and largest city (population 2.6 million people), is in northern Taiwan not far from the coast.

Taiwan is shaped like a giant tobacco leaf. For several centuries it was known as Formosa, or "beautiful island," a name given to it by Portuguese explorers who first saw it in the sixteenth century. The name was well deserved. Taiwan is a lush tropical and subtropical island with spectacular mountain scenery and wide sandy beaches. Millions of years ago, shifting tectonic plates of the Earth's crust and ancient volcanoes pushed what would become Taiwan above the sea, and today a towering mountain range covering two thirds of Taiwan cuts the island in half from north to south. Coral embedded in rock 2,000 feet (600 meters) above sea level testifies to Taiwan's underwater origin. In the east, the mountains rise almost directly out of the sea. Their highest point, Jade Mountain (Yu Shan), is more than 13,100 feet (3,950 meters) above sea level, higher than Japan's famed Mount Fuji. Although all of Taiwan's volcanoes are extinct, hot springs still dot the island. The fault lines between colliding plates of the Earth's crust are still there, which means Taiwan periodically experiences serious earthquakes. The most recent was the disastrous quake of September 21, 1999—known in Taiwan as the "921 quake"—that killed more than 2,500 people and caused extensive property damage.

Taiwan's climate is dominated by annual monsoons. While the climate varies because of the high mountains, Taiwan generally is warm in the fall and spring, hot and humid in the summer, and mild and relatively dry in the winter. Most of the rain comes with the monsoons that sweep over the island from the northeast between October and March and from the southwest between May and September. Although the amount of rain varies according to region, Taiwan as a whole averages about 100 inches (250 centimeters) of rain per year. Its southern cor-

ner is tropical, while snow falls in the winter in the higher elevations of the mountains. Winter winds from inner Asia can
cause the temperature to drop by more than 20°F (10°C) in
just a few hours.

Taiwan is in the path of serious storms similar to hurricanes
called typhoons (the English word comes from the Chinese word
taifeng), which hit the island as they travel northward from the
Indonesian archipelago to their final destination in Japan. Taiwan
experiences about six typhoons per year; every three or four years
a particularly severe typhoon will lash the island with winds of up
to 100 miles (160 kilometers) per hour and torrential rains, causing flooding, landslides, and other damage. In 1968 a typhoon
left much of Taipei under 13 feet (4 meters) of water, forcing
people to get around the city in rowboats.

The western part of Taiwan is a fertile plain where more
than 90 percent of the island's 22.3 million people live. The
island is self-sufficient in rice, its most important crop. Other
important crops include corn, vegetables, and tea. While Taiwan has small deposits of coal and natural gas, its most important natural resources are its fertile soil and lush forests. The
rivers flowing from the mountains to the plain enrich its farmland each year with new soil. These rivers also have created large
tidal mudflats. Because these mudflats make the island difficult
to invade by sea, its rivers not only help feed its people but may
be contributing to Taiwan's defense against the ever-present
threat from the Communist regime on mainland China.

PEOPLE

About 98 percent of Taiwan's 22.3 million people are of Chinese ancestry. Of that, about 84 percent are considered Taiwanese, which means their ancestors came from China before
Chiang Kai-shek and about 2 million of his supporters in the
Nationalist Party retreated to the island in the wake of their
defeat in China's civil war of 1946–1949. The Taiwanese in
turn are broken down into two main groups. About 15 percent

trace their ancestry to the Hakka people, a Chinese group with an unusual history. The Hakka, who speak their own dialect, originated in northern China. Turmoil and warfare at the time of the collapse of the Tang dynasty around A.D. 900 drove many Hakka to migrate to southern China. Most settled in Fujian province directly across the strait from Taiwan, where they were often persecuted by the established Chinese population that formed the majority in the region. Because the newcomers did not assimilate with the majority, they were given the name Hakka, or "guests." Hakka migrants seem to have been the first ethnic Chinese people to reach Taiwan, perhaps as early as 1000. Significant Chinese settlement on Taiwan did not begin until the fifteenth century. This second and far larger wave of immigrants was composed mainly of Fujian (that is, non-Hakka) Chinese, and it continued during the succeeding centuries. As a result, the Taiwanese language spoken by the great majority of the island's population is the same as the Fujian dialect spoken on the mainland side of the Taiwan Strait.

Over time, many Hakka people on Taiwan intermarried with their Fujian neighbors. This has reduced barriers between the two groups and gradually made the Hakka less visible as a minority, although distinctions and some sense of separateness still remain. The main division between people of Chinese ancestry in the ROC is between the descendants of those who arrived before 1945 and those who fled with Chiang Kai-shek to Taiwan in 1949. Although they were a minority, these "mainlanders," as they are often still called, dominated Taiwanese political life for the next fifty years. That domination is reflected in the official language of Taiwan, which is Mandarin Chinese. Today "mainlanders" are less likely than the majority to think of themselves as Taiwanese as opposed to Chinese and therefore less likely to favor independence from mainland China. At the same time, they are slowly shrinking as an identifiable group and as a percentage of the population as the older generation dies and many of the younger generation intermarry with the majority Taiwanese.

A Taiwanese woman makes silk Chinese umbrellas for export.

About 2 percent of Taiwan's population is not Chinese at all. They are the descendants of the original inhabitants of Taiwan, and some of them may have roots on the island that go back ten thousand years. Their origins are still debated, but some may be the descendants of non-Chinese who once lived in southern China. Others clearly are related to Malay and Polynesian peoples who speak what are known as Austronesian languages and who today live in Southeast Asia and on the scattered islands of the South Pacific. Taiwan's aboriginal people suffered at the hands of the Chinese who gradually took over their island. Because they were driven into the mountains by the Chinese population, they were called "mountain people," a term considered insulting. Today, as part of its policy of ending discrimination against these groups, the ROC government officially refers to them as "original inhabitants."

Taiwan's non-Chinese people are divided into ten tribes, each with its own language. In recent years they have become more politically active in defense of their rights, and popular attitudes toward them are changing and becoming more positive. Since the 1990s there has been a growing appreciation for aboriginal arts and crafts as well as popular enthusiasm for their singers and dancers. Perhaps the best-known aboriginal performer is the pop singer A-mei, whose soulful music, heavily influenced by rhythm and blues, won her a huge following throughout the Chinese world, including mainland China. In 2000 she was chosen to sing the national anthem at the inauguration of Chen Shui-bian as the ROC's new president.

With a population of more than 22 million and an area of only 13,900 square miles, Taiwan is one of the world's most crowded countries. In recent years, government efforts to encourage family planning have helped reduce the population growth rate to less than 1 percent per year, and that rate continues to fall. About 70 percent of Taiwan's people live in urban metropolitan areas. The largest of these, home to about 6 million people, is the metropolitan area centered on Taipei and the nearby city of Keelung in northern Taiwan. The Koahsiung metropolitan area in southern Taiwan contains about 2.6 million people, while the Taichung-Changhua metropolitan area along the western coast in the middle of the island is home to about 2 million people. More than 90 percent of Taiwan's people follow a mixture of Buddhist, Confucian, and Daoist religious beliefs. About 4.5 percent of the population is Christian, including many aboriginal people.

ECONOMY

Decades of hard work, careful planning, and individual initiative have made Taiwan an economic powerhouse. Whereas in the past agriculture and then labor-intensive industries were the basis of its economy, today Taiwan produces a range of high-tech products. Computer chips, chemicals, monitors, computer motherboards, CD-ROM drives, cell phones, and other technologically advanced products are exported to countries throughout the world. Taiwan has a large trade surplus and the world's second-largest foreign exchange reserves, more than $100 billion, trailing only Japan. Its Hsinchu Science Industrial Park, founded in 1981, has been called the Silicon Valley of the East. Taiwan also is a leading investor in emerging Asian economies, including mainland China, where Taiwanese businesses have invested an estimated $60 billion (some estimates are as high as $100 billion). To increase competitiveness, the government role in the economy is being reduced and some government-owned banks and industries privatized. By 2000, Taiwan had a per capita GNP of more than $13,000, a figure about half that of the United States and the advanced countries of Europe but far higher than most Asian countries. One statistic is especially remarkable, given the history of inequality in China before the Communist revolution and the growing inequality on the mainland since the reforms of Deng Xiaoping: In 1999 only 1 percent of Taiwan's population was living below the poverty line.

THE HISTORY OF TAIWAN

Until the seventeenth century, Taiwan was an unknown territory largely cut off from the outside world. Portuguese sailors had briefly visited the island in the sixteenth century, but they soon withdrew and made Macao their base in East Asia. Other outsiders, both Chinese dynasties on the mainland and European adventurers, generally stayed away because of dangerous seas, treacherous sand shoals, typhoons, malaria, and hostile natives. The Dutch came to Taiwan in the 1620s. They established a trading settlement on its western coast and, having beaten off both Spanish competitors and Japanese pirates, maintained a colonial outpost until the early 1660s. It was the brief Dutch presence on Taiwan that began to draw Chinese immigrants from the mainland. Eventually, the Dutch on Taiwan were overwhelmed by the upheaval taking place on the mainland, where the invading Manchus were completing their destruction of the Ming dynasty. They were driven from Taiwan in 1662 by a Ming loyalist known as Koxinga, who had fled the mainland with 35,000 troops and four hundred ships. Koxinga continued to fight the Manchus, as did his son and grandson. In effect, Koxinga and his immediate descendants ruled over an independent Taiwan whose population grew rapidly as tens of thousands of Chinese fled there from the mainland. Not until 1683 did the Manchus finally capture Taiwan.

At first the Manchus made Taiwan a county of Fujian province. In 1887, as immigration from the mainland swelled Taiwan's population to 2.5 million, it became a separate province. In reality, Manchu control over Taiwan was not very effective. A frontier atmosphere prevailed on the island, and local officials, safe from central supervision, used their positions to enrich themselves. This situation changed in 1895, when Japan annexed Taiwan after defeating China in the Sino-Japanese War of 1894–1895. Taiwan's population resisted Japanese control, rebelling in 1895 and declaring their independence. Their Formosan Democratic Republic was the first republic in Asian history. It survived for only half a year, from May to October, before a Japanese army of 12,000 crushed it; more than 7,000 Taiwanese died in the fighting. Japan then ruled Taiwan as a colony for the next fifty years.

JAPANESE RULE, 1895–1945

Japanese rule in Taiwan was harsh, although probably not as brutal as it was in Korea. The Japanese had two goals in Taiwan: to use Taiwan's farmland and natural resources for the benefit of the home economy, and to break Taiwan's links to China and assimilate its population into Japanese culture. Tokyo took the first steps toward modernizing Taiwan's economy, building roads and railroads, establishing new industries, building dams and reservoirs to improve agriculture, and building hospitals and schools. It promoted assimilation by making Japanese the language of instruction in the schools, and eventually by forcing Taiwanese to take Japanese names and forbidding the use of Taiwanese. The people of Taiwan were further forced to eat Japanese food, observe Japanese religious ceremonies, and wear Japanese-style clothing. The Taiwanese resisted Japanese rule as much as they could, and in 1915 a major rebellion broke out that took seven months to suppress. During World War II, tens of thousands of Taiwanese young men were drafted into the Japanese army; many never returned home. Although the Japanese built a number of major industries in Taiwan in the early 1940s to support the war effort, by the end of the war Taiwan's economy was in ruins.

Japan's defeat in 1945 restored Taiwan to Chinese sovereignty, but the Taiwanese quickly found that they had little to celebrate. Brutal and efficient Japanese colonial rule was replaced by corrupt and inefficient GMD rule. Massive protest riots in early 1947—known in Taiwan as the February 28th incident of 1947—were suppressed with the loss of at least 10,000, and possibly as many as 28,000, Taiwanese lives. Then, in 1949, having been defeated on the mainland, the GMD retreated to Taiwan. The island, previously just a small Chinese province, became the Republic of China.

GMD RULE, 1949–2000

Chaing Kai-shek's Guomindang (GMD) government survived on Taiwan largely because of the United States, which protected his regime militarily from the PRC and provided economic aid that helped promote economic growth. The GMD regime on Taiwan was a dictatorship. As it ruled over the Taiwanese people, it continued to maintain the fiction that the Republic of China was the legitimate ruler of the mainland and some day would displace the Communist regime there. That claim was undermined in 1971, when the ROC lost its U.N. seat to the Communist regime in Beijing. Chiang himself died in 1975, just a year before his bitter adversary Mao Zedong. Three years later his son, Chiang Ching-kuo, became the ROC president. By then Taiwan's economy was growing and industrializing rapidly, even though U.S. economic aid had stopped in 1965. Political change began to catch up to economic change in 1986, when Chiang Ching-kuo allowed the formation of the Democratic Progressive Party (DPP), the country's first opposition party. In 1987 the younger Chiang lifted martial law, which had been in effect since 1949. It was an enormous step, as under martial law the GMD government had systematically suppressed Taiwanese language and culture, a policy that included banning the Taiwanese language from popular music, news broadcasts, television, and the movies.

Ending martial law opened the road to genuine democracy. When Chiang Ching-kuo died in 1988, he was succeeded by Lee Teng-hui, the first Taiwanese to hold the post of ROC president. For the first time, Taiwan had a president who was more comfortable speaking Taiwanese than Mandarin. Under Lee's leadership, there were further democratic reforms in the early 1990s, including genuine parliamentary elections. In 1996, Taiwan's voters for the first time received the right to vote directly for their president. (Previously, presidents were chosen by the ROC's National Assembly.) When Lee Teng-hui won in a four-man race with 54 percent of the vote, he became the first Chinese leader in history elected directly by the people he was governing. Even more significant change took place in the 2000 elections, when Chen Shui-bian of the DPP was elected president in a race with three major candidates in which the GMD candidate finished a distant third. The ROC had its first non-GMD president and a firmly established democratic system.

None of these developments took place without close scrutiny from grim-faced Communist Party observers in mainland China. What worried Beijing's leaders was that two things were going on at once: As Taiwan was becoming more democratic, it also was becoming more Taiwanese, and therefore moving away from the idea of a united China and toward the idea of formal independence. Since 1949 the GMD and CCP, bitter enemies on almost every issue, had at least agreed on one thing: There was only one China and Taiwan was part of it. With the decline of the GMD in China, and, even more, with the passing of the old GMD generation, that idea was rapidly losing ground on Taiwan. By the 1990s, even some leading GMD politicians, including Lee Teng-hui, were distancing themselves from the idea of reunification. Beijing's response was to threaten to use force against any Taiwanese attempt to declare formal independence. Thus in early 1996, just before the presidential elections, the PRC conducted missile tests in which they fired missiles that landed in coastal waters close to Taiwan. Beijing also conducted live artillery exercises in the Taiwan Strait.

The threats did not have their intended effect. Lee not only was reelected but in 1999 infuriated Beijing when he announced that the PRC and ROC should conduct relations on a state-to-state basis and that reunification could only take place when mainland China had become a democracy, not a likely development under any foreseeable circumstances. Meanwhile, the United States announced its support for Taiwan should Beijing attempt to use force to seize the island. The Taiwanese people moved even further from the idea of one China in March 2000, when they elected DPP candidate Chen Shui-bian as president. In December 2001 the DPP, which formally supported independence from mainland China, won a decisive victory in Taiwan's legislative elections, completing the political fall of the GMD that had begun with the 2000 presidential election. Adding to the GMD defeat, Chen's DPP also had the support of a new party, the Taiwan Solidarity Union, led by Lee Teng-hui, who had quit the GMD because its old guard remained committed to reunification. By 2001, opinion polls showed that no more than a fifth of Taiwan's population had any interest in reunification, even far down the road. At the same time, Taiwan was vulnerable to pressure from Beijing, and this weighed against efforts to move in the other direction. Taiwan's economy was increasingly becoming entwined with that of the mainland as Taiwanese investment in China and the two-way trade across the strait separating the two countries continued to grow. Meanwhile, Beijing was threatening to use military force if Taiwan dared to officially change its political status. Over the next several years, these factors influenced many Taiwanese and put the brakes on the movement toward independence. In March of 2004, Chen Shui-bian was reelected president, but only by a tiny margin. This kept him in office but left him weakened politically. In December, Chen and his supporters suffered a defeat in legislative elections when his DPP and Taiwan Solidarity Union failed to win a majority. Instead, the GMD and its allies won a very narrow but still significant victory. The election showed that most Taiwanese were not willing to accept the risks involved in changing their uneasy but tolerable relationship with the mainland.

MODERN TAIWAN AND TAIWAN'S PAST

As it begins the twenty-first century, Taiwan is a society very much in tune with the modern world and also in touch with its past. The end of martial law, increased prosperity, and the impact of thousands of young Taiwanese who have studied abroad have created a vibrant cultural scene. Taiwanese films are very much up-to-date, and some of its directors have achieved international reputations. Notable among them are Hou Shian-hsien, the most famous of Taiwan's "new wave" generation of directors, and Ang Lee, the most famous member of the "second new wave." Taiwanese pop music reflects both Western influences and a merging of electronic instruments with long-neglected local folk traditions. The island's tradition of glove-puppet theater is enjoying a revival and is increasingly popular, in part because of a successful full-length feature movie called *Legend of the Secret Stone* (1999), which attracted large crowds of both the young and old. The movie was produced by the High Energy Puppet Theater, whose cable TV channel broadcasts only glove-puppet dramas. Taiwanese enjoy a wide range of dance troupes. The Taipei Dance Circle, drawing its inspiration from the Western modern dance tradition, is a defiantly cutting-edge troupe whose oiled, near-nude, squirming dancers have caused their share of controversy. At the same time, song and dance shows based on the traditions of Taiwan's non-Chinese aboriginal peoples also are extremely popular.

Taiwan continues to live dangerously in the shadow of the People's Republic of China. By 2002 the PRC had deployed three hundred long-range ballistic missiles along the coast capable of reaching Taiwan, and was adding to that force at the rate of fifty per year. Taiwan has attempted to balance that threat with arms purchases from the United States, the most recent of which were announced in April 2002 and included submarines, surface warships, and modern aircraft. Late in 2001, Taiwan took an important step forward in terms of its international standing when it was admitted to the World Trade Organization (WTO), gaining membership one day after the PRC. Meanwhile, it seems fair to say that during the past half century, Taiwan has modernized both economically and politically *and* preserved traditional Chinese arts and culture better than the Communist mainland. Taiwan's ability to enjoy the fruits of its successes will depend heavily on how it manages its relations with its huge, powerful, and ambitious neighbor across the strait. As a retired Taiwanese geology professor put it, summing up both his country's past and what it can expect in the future, "We have to struggle for whatever independence we can get."[1]

FOUR

JAPAN

At the edge of East Asia, where the world's largest landmass meets the even vaster expanse of the world's largest body of water we call the Pacific Ocean, stands the island nation of Japan. A country of great physical beauty, Japan is also a country of many historical contrasts and contradictions. Its written history dates from about 1,500 years ago, but that makes it young by East Asian standards. During the first thousand years of its history, Japan consciously borrowed much of its civilization from abroad—from Chinese writing and philosophy to Korean art and ceramics to a religion, Buddhism, whose origins lay in India; then, for several centuries beginning shortly after 1600, it followed a policy of self-imposed isolation, cutting most of its ties with the outside world. After expelling almost all Westerners from its shores in the early seventeenth century, Japan did an about-face in 1868; in the decades that followed, Japan became the first non-European country to modernize many of its economic and political institutions according to Western models. While modern science has debunked traditional racial myths, many Japanese still cling tenaciously to the belief that they are somehow unique among the peoples of the world. Art and beauty are central to many aspects of Japanese life, but Japan's culture also is deeply infused by militarism and the cult of the warrior. Today, Japan is in many ways ultramodern, yet traditional customs still strongly influence many aspects of Japanese life. And perhaps most ironically, a society that for centuries taught that it was glorious to die to preserve the future of the Japanese people today has a birthrate so low that it faces a serious population decline and, as a result, an uncertain future.

JAPAN AND THE UNITED STATES

A central feature of Japan's recent history is its intense and complex relationship with the United States. It was the United States, having sent a small naval flotilla under Commodore Matthew Perry into Tokyo Bay in 1853, that finally forced the Japanese to end its policy of isolation that had lasted for more than two centuries. The Japanese leaders were not enthusiastic about opening their country to foreign trade and influence. When the first American government representative arrived in the country a few years after Perry's visit, a crowd of thousands of people welcomed him with total silence. Still, the Japanese understood the foreigners from across the sea had advanced technology that gave them overwhelming military power, and that without this technology Japan would always remain at risk. They were well aware of the crushing defeat Britain had dealt China in the First Opium War of 1839–1842. So in the late 1860s the Japanese systematically began to learn from the West, especially with regard to mastering its modern technology. As it industrialized and modernized its military, Japan gradually received recognition as a great power from the Europeans and Americans. Serious problems with the Western powers began in the 1930s. Japan sought expansion abroad, and its attempt to dominate East Asia eventually brought it face-to-face with the United States and its Allies. This confrontation led to events that neither side can remember without feeling pain, nor is likely to forget.

By the late 1930s, Japan's leaders had concluded that their expansionist ambitions required an end to American power in East Asia. This in turn led to the decision to attack Pearl Harbor in Hawaii, the headquarters of the U.S. Pacific fleet, on December 7, 1941. Japan's surprise attack, made without a declaration of war, killed almost three thousand U.S. soldiers and civilians and brought the United States into World War II. Japan and the United States fought bitter battles during the war, as Japanese soldiers on island after island in the Pacific consistently chose to fight to the death rather than surrender. The Japanese often treated American prisoners of war brutally, a situation that was known in the United States even while the fighting was going on. Although by early 1945, Japan's leaders

The explosion of the U.S.S. Shaw *in Pearl Harbor. The Japanese planner of the attack, Admiral Yamamoto, is reported to have said afterward, "I fear we have awakened a sleeping giant, and filled him with a terrible resolve."*

understood the war was lost, they refused to surrender until the United States attacked the cities of Hiroshima and Nagasaki with atomic bombs in August of that year. Japan to this day remains the only country that has ever suffered a nuclear attack.

The United States did not take revenge on its defeated enemy. American forces occupied Japan until 1952, introducing political and economic reforms. One of the most important reforms was a new democratic constitution that officially took effect in 1947. These reforms helped pave the way for Japan's remarkable prosperity and growth during the second half of the twentieth century. Meanwhile, Japan and the United States, once bitter enemies, became close allies and trading partners. They did not, to be sure, agree on every issue. Still, Japan became the most important American ally in East Asia during the Cold War, the tense forty-five-year struggle between the world's democratic nations led by the United States and the world's Communist nations led by the Soviet Union that began after World War II and lasted until 1990.

The close U.S.–Japanese relationship continued after the Cold War has lasted into the twenty-first century. Over the course of the century and a half since Commodore Perry entered Tokyo Bay, American influence on Japan has been far reaching. Modern technology, democratic political institutions, American baseball, English loanwords, and other aspects of American culture all have become part of daily Japanese life.

GEOGRAPHY, NATURAL RESOURCES, CLIMATE, AND ENVIRONMENT

AN ISLAND NATION

Japan is an archipelago that forms an arc about 2,000 miles (3,200 kilometers) long along the coast of East Asia from Russia's Sakhalin Island almost to Taiwan. It includes four main islands, which make up about 98 percent of Japan's land area, and more than three thousand smaller ones. A Japanese legend tells that this archipelago was formed by the tears of a goddess, each of which turned into an island as it splashed into the Pacific Ocean. Another legend has two gods, one male and one female, standing on the rainbow bridge of heaven, dipping a spear into the Pacific Ocean. As they lift the spear out of the water, drops from the tip of the spear fall into the ocean and change into the sacred islands of Japan. In actuality, Japan's islands were built over millions of years from the bottom up by colliding and buckling plates of the Earth's crust and uncounted volcanic eruptions of molten lava surging irresistibly upward from beneath that thin crust. Japan actually sits on the edge of an underwater cliff. Just to the east is the Japan Trench, where the ocean floor suddenly plunges to a depth of 5 miles (8 kilometers) below sea level. The deepest point in the Japan Trench is more than 34,000 feet (10,375 meters) below sea level.

If Japan's four main islands—Hokkaido, Honshu, Shikoku, and Kyushu—were superimposed on the eastern United States, Hokkaido in the north could cover much of New Hampshire, Vermont, and northern New York; while Kyushu in the far south would stand astride the Georgia-Alabama border. A few smaller islands just south of Kyushu would be sprinkled across the panhandle of northwestern Florida. The Ryukyu chain farther south, whose largest island is Okinawa, would stretch across the Gulf of Mexico approximately to Mexico's Yucatán Peninsula.

The islands of Japan have an area of about 145,884 square miles (377,837 square kilometers), about the size of Montana and slightly smaller than California. Their craggy and indented shores give the country a coastline of more than 18,490 miles (29,750 kilometers). Honshu, the largest Japanese island and the seventh-largest island in the world, alone accounts for almost two thirds of that area, about 89,175 square miles (230,965 square kilometers). It also is home to just over 100 million people, about 80 percent of Japan's population. Honshu looks very much like a mirror image of California, its southern section tilting westward while California's tilts eastward. On the map mentioned above, Honshu would stretch from the southeast corner of New York State all the way to Atlanta, Georgia. Tokyo, Japan's capital and largest city, is on Honshu. So are Yokohama (the country's most important port, which serves the Tokyo region), Osaka, and Nagoya, Japan's next three largest cities. Three other important cities on Honshu are Kyoto, Japan's ancient capital; Kobe, the country's second most important port, which serves the Osaka industrial region; and, in the far southwest, Hiroshima, the first city ever to suffer a nuclear attack.

Hokkaido, Kyushu, and Shikoku are respectively the world's twenty-first, thirty-second, and forty-seventh largest islands. Hokkaido, the northernmost island, is separated from Honshu by the Tsugaru Strait. It accounts for about a fifth of Japan's area but is home to only 5 percent of its population. Although the first Japanese settlers probably reached the island in the thirteenth century, it remained a frontier area for centuries afterward, as open to settlement and control by Russians as by Japanese. Hokkaido was not formally made part of Japan until the 1870s, and the Japanese did not fully occupy the island until after World War I. Hokkaido was and remains the last refuge of the Ainu, Japan's indigenous people, who over many centuries have been pushed northward and displaced by the Japanese. Despite its cold climate, the thinly populated island produces more food than any other part of Japan, mainly wheat, potatoes, corn, rice, and dairy products. Hokkaido's forests are a source of lumber and paper pulp, while the sea surrounding the island enables many local people to make a living as fishermen. In recent years, tourism has played a growing role in the island's economic life. Hokkaido's mountainous terrain is broken by the valley of the Ishikari River, Japan's longest, which flows north to south on the western part of the island. Hokkaido is connected to Honshu by the Seikan Tunnel, which runs almost 800 feet (244 meters) underneath the Tsugaru Strait. Completed in 1988 and 33.5 miles (53.8 kilometers) long, it is the longest tunnel in the world (although the Euro-tunnel, which links Great Britain and France, runs under the sea for a longer distance) and one of the great engineering feats of the twentieth century. Sapporo, Hokkaido's largest city, was the site of the 1972 Winter Olympics.

Kyushu, the southernmost island, is where about two thousand years ago the Japanese people first established them-selves in what would become their homeland. Lying across the Korea/Tsushima Strait from Korea and the Kanmon Strait from Honshu, the island was the main entry point for Chinese and Korean culture in the centuries that followed. In the thirteenth century, the northern coast of Kyushu was the battleground where the outnumbered Japanese twice held off huge invading Mongol armies until storms destroyed their invasion fleets. In 1945, Kyushu's southern coast was where the United States was planning to invade Japan during the last months of World War II. Although that attack never took place, the event that finally ended the war did occur on Kyushu when Nagasaki, a city on the island's northwest coast, became the second, and the last, city on which an atomic bomb was dropped.

Shikoku, the smallest island, remains largely rural, with a population of barely 4 million. It was the last of Japan's three smaller main islands to be linked to Honshu by bridge, an event that did not occur until 1988, after ten years of construction. The Seto Ohashi, the bridge that finally did the job, actually is a series of six bridges using five small islands as stepping-stones. The bridge took ten years to build and cost more than $1 bil-lion (more than 1 trillion yen, the Japanese currency). Its dou-ble-decker structure has four lanes for cars and dual tracks so trains can travel in both directions at once and is the largest combined road and rail bridge system in the world. The sus-pension bridge at the southernmost end of the Seto Ohashi bridge has a 3,609-foot (1,100-meter) center span, the tenth longest in the world. However, automobile traffic on the Seto Ohashi bridge remains light, in part due to the $50 toll—one way!—cars must pay to cross the bridge.

Two other routes link Honshu and Shikoku, both involving bridges that are the largest of their type in the world. Certainly the most spectacular is the Akashi Kaikyo Bridge, the longest suspension bridge in the world. Opened in 1998 in a glittering ceremony complete with fireworks and the presence of Japan's crown prince and his wife, its center span, with a length of 6,529 feet (1,990 meters), is more than 1,150 feet (350 meters) longer than any other in the world. It is almost 1,970 feet (600 meters) longer than the center span of the Verrazano-Narrows Bridge, the largest suspension bridge in the United States (and the sixth largest in the world), and almost twice as long as the span of the majestic George Washington Bridge. The third Honshu–Shikoku route, opened in 1999,

The beautiful Akashi Kaikyo Bridge in Hyogo, Japan

includes the Tatara Bridge, an elegant structure whose center span of 2,920 feet (890 meters) makes it the longest cable-stayed bridge in the world.

All of these bridges are built to withstand heavy winds and, most menacing of all, earthquakes. The Seto Ohashi Bridge is designed to withstand winds of up to 146.26 miles (235 kilometers) per hour and earthquakes of magnitude 8.5 on the Richter scale. The Akashi Kaikyo Bridge is built to similar specifications. Its construction had to be halted in 1995 when an earthquake of 7.2 on the Richter scale—an earthquake of 8.5 is over ten times more powerful than a 7.2 quake—devastated the city of Kobe, which stands on the Honshu side of the bridge. The bridge rests on foundations fixed 230 feet (70 meters) beneath the seabed, but the Japanese seem to be leaving nothing to chance: When the bridge was opened Buddhist priests were on hand to bless it. Similar precautions went into building the Tatara Bridge, which withstood a powerful typhoon during the most difficult part of the installation of its center span. For brave souls who seek an adventure, the Tatara Bridge includes lanes for bicycles, motorbikes, and pedestrians.

The bridges and tunnels that connect the islands of Honshu, Kyushu, and Shikoku span the Inland Sea, a shallow inlet of the Pacific Ocean that winds its way among the three islands. It is connected to the Sea of Japan by the narrow Kanmon Strait that separates Honshu from Kyushu. The strait is so narrow that at one point pedestrians can walk from one island to the other in about fifteen minutes via an undersea tunnel less than a half mile long. The Inland Sea stretches about 260 miles (419 kilometers) from east to west and varies in width from about 3 to 32 miles (5 to 52 kilometers). About one thousand islands dot its calm waters, which cover an area of 3,700 square miles (9,583 square kilometers). Although major industrial cities and ports along its shores have created pollution problems, the Inland Sea remains a place of remarkable scenic beauty, relatively unspoiled islands, and rich fishing grounds. In 1934 it became the site of Japan's first national park.

Aside from the four main islands, Japan's most important possession is the Ryukyu archipelago, a chain of more than seventy islands that extends southwesterly for 450 miles (724 kilometers) from Kyushu to within 125 miles (201 kilometers) of Taiwan. Like Hokkaido, the Ryukyus were not incorporated into Japan until the 1870s. The largest island in the chain is Okinawa, a long, irregularly shaped subtropical island of volcanic origin. Okinawa, which has an area of 454 square miles (1,176 square kilometers), was the scene of the last major battle of World War II, and one of the most terrible for both the Japanese and the Americans. About 103,000 Japanese soldiers died in that two-month battle out of a garrison of 120,000, as did more than 12,000 American fighting men of the army, Marines, and navy. Okinawa was the bloodiest battle in the history of the United States Navy, which lost almost 5,000 sailors to Japanese suicide pilots called kamikazes, who deliberately crashed their planes into American warships.

As an island nation, Japan is bordered by seas and straits. To the east and southeast the border is the Pacific Ocean. The Sea of Japan forms Japan's western border and separates it from the coastlines of Russia, North Korea, and South Korea. In the southwest, a 500-mile (800-kilometer)-wide section of the East China Sea lies between Kyushu and the People's Republic of China. The Sea of Japan and the East China Sea in turn are connected by the Korea/Tsushima Strait, the 120-mile (190-kilometer)-wide waterway that also separates the islands of Honshu and Kyushu from Korea.

To Japan's north, across three different bodies of water—two straits and one sea—is Russia. The Soya Strait directly north of Hokkaido separates Japan from the Russian island of Sakhalin, just 28 miles (45 kilometers) away. In the northwest the Numuro Strait flows between Hokkaido and Russia's Kurile Islands, a long chain of more than thirty small islands (and many tiny ones) that extends northeastward for about 775 miles (1,250 kilometers) to the Kamchatka Peninsula. Between 1875 and 1945 the Kuriles belonged to Japan, but the Soviet

Union took them after World War II, and they are now part of Russia. Japan still claims several other Russian-occupied islands that are not part of the Kuriles chain—Etorofu, Kunashiri, Shikotan, and the Habomai group—just off Hokkaido's extreme northwest tip, which it calls its Northern Territories. This territorial dispute remains a source of tension between the two countries. Between the Soya and Numuro straits, and broadening like a huge fan as it extends northward to Russia's frigid northeast, is the huge Sea of Okhotsk.

The islands of Japan were not always cut off from the Asian mainland. More than 20,000 years ago, Ice Age land bridges linked Hokkaido with Siberia and the western tip of Honshu with the Korean Peninsula. The Sea of Japan, cut off from the ocean by land that today lies beneath the sea, was a gigantic lake. These land bridges provided the routes by which the first human beings reached Japan at least 30,000 years ago.

Japan and its relationship to the Asian mainland has often been compared to that of Britain, another island nation, and Britain's relationship to Europe. Both are island nations close enough to a great continent to benefit and be enriched by mainland cultural influences while also enjoying a degree of geographic protection and isolation that allowed them to develop in their own ways. Both depended on the sea for food and to trade and used the skills they developed as sailors to become naval powers. In modern times, both focused on becoming manufacturing societies, which enabled them to trade for the food they needed to feed their populations. However, the English Channel between Britain and France is only 21 miles (34 kilometers) wide, barely a sixth of the width of the Korea/Tsushima Strait. As a result, Japan's interaction with the Asian mainland to its west has never been as close as Britain's with the European mainland to its east. In addition, Britain was exposed to the cultures of many countries, while in Japan's case one country, China, dominated the cultural development of the region.

The Japanese archipelago is in a dangerous geological neighborhood. It sits atop the Pacific Ring of Fire, a gigantic arc of faults in the Earth's crust that surrounds the Pacific Ocean on three sides (east, north, and west) and includes three quarters of the world's active volcanoes. Japan itself has two hundred volcanoes, about a quarter of which are active. It experiences about 1,500 earthquakes per year, most of which are minor. A major quake occurs about every five years, and some are terribly destructive. The Great Kanto Earthquake that hit Tokyo and Yokohama in September 1923 killed more than 140,000 people and destroyed more than a half million houses. The earthquake that hit the city of Kobe in 1995 killed 6,400 people, left more than 300,000 homeless, and destroyed gas mains (which supposedly were earthquake proof), highways, and railway lines. Today Japan spends millions of dollars trying to predict earthquakes but without significant success. This is of particular concern because the Tokyo area generally has a major earthquake every seventy years. Since the last quake was in 1923, Tokyo is now a decade overdue.

Offshore earthquakes or underwater landslides far from Japan also can be destructive when they cause tidal waves known as tsunamis. These waves can skim across the ocean surface at speeds of more than 500 miles (800 kilometers) per hour, as fast as a jet airliner. As tsunamis approach land, they slow up and grow in height until they can tower 100 feet (30 meters) in the air by they time they crash onto the shore, causing destruction and great loss of life if they land near populated areas.

Volcanic eruptions are far less frequent than earthquakes but still make their presence felt. In 1792 a volcanic eruption on Kyushu caused an avalanche and tsunami that between them killed 14,500 people. More recently, in 1986, a volcano on the small island of Oshima near Tokyo erupted, forcing thousands of people to flee their homes. An eruption on Kyushu several years later ruined many square miles of farmland, and a volcano on Kyushu regularly pours ash, and sometimes large boulders, onto the nearby city of Kagoshima.

A LAND OF MOUNTAINS

Japan's most important volcano, and its highest mountain, is Mount Fuji, about 60 miles (97 kilometers) southwest of Tokyo. Mount Fuji's almost perfect cone—which is capped with snow from the late autumn until spring—rises 12,388 feet (3,776 meters) above sea level. Mt. Fuji has long been a sacred place and has inspired generations of Japanese poets, writers, and artists. Paintings and photographs of snowcapped Mt. Fuji have made it the most recognizable symbol of Japan throughout the world. Climbing Mount Fuji is something of religious pilgrimage for the Japanese, and for centuries women were forbidden to make that climb. That barrier was not broken until a British woman ignored the local taboo and climbed the sacred mountain in 1867. Currently more than 400,000 people of both sexes climb Mount Fuji each year, including many foreign tourists, some of whom stay overnight to watch the sun rise from its peak. Mount Fuji's aura is enhanced by the mists and clouds that surround it and often block it from view. Mount Fuji last erupted in 1707, covering Tokyo (then known as Edo) with ash.

While Mount Fuji is Japan's best-known volcano, the country also has the world's largest volcanic crater, Aso-san, in central Kyushu. The crater, created in a gigantic eruption about 100,000 years ago, has a circumference of about 48 miles (77 kilometers). Although there are five smaller active volcanoes within its rim, the crater contains several towns and villages. There are small eruptions in Aso-san every two or three years, and toxic gases regularly spew from crevices within the crater rim. Although the Aso-san eruptions are small, they can be deadly; one in 1959 killed twelve people, and another in 1979 took three lives.

Whatever the dangers Japan's volcanoes pose, they have given the country numerous hot springs, or *onsen*. Bathing in

冨嶽三十六景
凱風
快晴

A colored woodblock print of Mt. Fuji by Katsusika Hokusai (1760–849), an influential and revered Japanese artist

hot springs has been a part of Japanese culture for centuries, but the tradition is even older than Japan itself. For example, there is evidence that people have been bathing in one hot springs region in western Shikoku for three thousand years, longer than anywhere else in Japan. The region is mentioned in the *Record of Ancient Matters (Kojiki)* Japan's oldest written record, which dates from the year 712, and a poetry anthology called the *Collection of Myriad Leaves* (*Manyoshu*), which was compiled about fifty years later. A resort region on Kyushu's northeastern coast draws more than 13 million tourists per year to its 3,795 hot springs. It is also known for its "hell ponds" of boiling mud, one of which is 400 feet (122 meters) deep.

Japan's volcanoes are part of a mountainous terrain that covers about 80 percent of the country. Less than 20 percent of Japan's territory, including terraces painstakingly carved out of hillsides, is suitable for agriculture. While all of Japan's islands are mountainous, the country's highest mountains, known as the Japanese Alps, form the backbone of Honshu. Hokkaido has three distinct mountain ranges, and most of Shikoku and the eastern two thirds of Kyushu are rugged as well.

By far the largest and most important flat area in Japan is the 5,000-square-mile (13,000-square-kilometer) Kanto Plain on the east coast of Honshu. It is both a major agricultural region and Japan's most important industrial and urban center. The Kanto Plain fronts on Tokyo Bay, on whose northern shore the capital city of Tokyo stands. Tokyo, with a population of almost 12 million, is the core of an enormous urban complex 50 miles (80 kilometers) wide that since World War II has spread and engulfed several other cities, among them Yokohama and Kawasaki. With a total population of more than 34 million, the Tokyo megalopolis is the largest urban concentration in the world. The Kanto Plain by itself produces almost a third of Japan's gross domestic product. There are two other important plains on Honshu, each only about a tenth the size of the Kanto Plain: the Nobi Plain around the city of Nagoya and the Kansai Plain around the city of Osaka. Nagoya is an important industrial city on the northern tip of Ise Bay, an inlet of the Pacific, about 170 miles (270 kilometers) southwest of Tokyo. Just west of the city is Lake Biwa, Japan's largest lake. Osaka faces the Inland Sea and the island of Shikoku. It once served as Japan's capital and for more than three centuries prior to the rise of Tokyo was the country's leading commercial and industrial center.

CLIMATE

Although Japan is not a large country in terms of land area, it is a long one that stretches across about 20 degrees of latitude. Its climate therefore ranges from cold and continental in the north around Hokkaido and northern Honshu to subtropical in the south around Kyushu, Shikoku, southern Honshu, and Okinawa and the Ryukyus. A second factor determining Japan's climate are monsoon winds, which come from the west and Asia in the winter and from the east and the Pacific Ocean in the summer. Finally, the high mountains that form the spine of Honshu block many winds and create differences in climate between Japan's western coast along the Sea of Japan and its eastern coast on the Pacific Ocean.

In winter, frigid winds from Asia pick up moisture over the Sea of Japan before reaching northern Japan, which results in heavy snowfall on Hokkaido and on the northern part of Honshu. Annual snowfall in these regions can reach 10 feet (3 meters). On the western side of the mountains, protected from these winds, winters are drier but still very cold. Winters are much milder in the south, which is why farmers on Kyushu can grow a winter crop. The south is further warmed by what is known as the Japan Current, an ocean current that washes Japanese shores with warm water drawn from the tropical regions of the Pacific.

In March, as the Asian landmass warms, the direction of the winds reaching Japan changes. Warm moist winds from the Pacific give most of Japan uncomfortably warm and humid summers. During August and September, winds coming up from the south bring heavy rains and typhoons. Japan usually experiences about three or four typhoons per year, which are powerful enough to destroy houses and uproot trees. Most of the typhoons hit the southern or Pacific parts of the country. Summers in most of Japan are hot and humid. The main exceptions, aside from high mountain areas, are Hokkaido and northern Honshu, which are cooled by northern ocean currents.

Japan's climate is excellent for agriculture. The growing season is long, especially in the south, and there is plenty of rain for crops. Southern Japan receives more than 80 inches (200 centimeters) of rain per year, which is well suited for growing rice. Japan's farmers are able to raise two crops of rice from the southern part of the country as far north as the 36th degree of latitude, about the latitude of Tokyo. However, typhoons, if they are strong enough, can ruin the rice crop.

An important event that marks the change from winter to spring is the flowering of Japan's cherry blossoms. Cherry trees, which grow wild in the mountains, are planted all over Japan. They flower on southern Kyushu in late March, and are greeted each year with a festival the Japanese call *hanami*, or blossom viewing. The flowering of the cherry blossoms gradually moves northward until it reaches Hokkaido during the second week in May. As with many things beautiful, the flowering of the cherry blossoms is short lived. They fall from the trees after only a week, after which they are blown away by strong southerly winds. This is the signal that the rainy season is about to start. While few Americans get to enjoy cherry blossoms in Japan, they can see the same thing on thousands of trees in Washington, D.C., along the Potomac River and on the grounds of the White House. These trees are the result of two gifts made by the Japanese government to the United States, the first in 1912 and the second in 1965.

NATURAL RESOURCES AND THE ENVIRONMENT

Japan has few natural resources. It must import most of its raw materials, including oil and coal for producing energy. The country does have many fast-running rivers, many of which have been dammed, enabling Japan to meet about 12 percent of its energy needs from hydroelectric power. Nuclear power provides almost 32 percent of Japan's electricity. About two thirds of Japan's territory is covered by forests. While the majority of these forests are natural, about 40 percent are tree farms planted by companies that harvest trees for timber and other commercial purposes. Because the Japanese have been exploiting their forests for centuries, the only place to see forests that have not been changed in some way by humans is in the most remote mountain regions. Some of the forests in southern Japan are bamboo, a plant that grows widely in Asia and is turned into everything from construction scaffolding, ladders, fence railings, and walls to musical instruments, paper, food, and even—in pulverized form—medicine. Farther north are evergreen deciduous forests that include species such as fir, spruce, beech, oak, and maple. Japan has suffered from deforestation in the past and today tries much harder than before to protect its forests. Even so, tree farms often are clear-cut, leaving barren hillsides where heavy rains often cause landslides. In order to preserve its own forests, Japan prefers to import lumber from the United States, Canada, and Southeast Asia. The Southeast Asian imports have concerned many environmentalists, as it has led to extensive clear-cutting of rain forests and serious environmental destruction in places like Borneo, Burma, and Thailand.

Ocean currents that mix warm water from the south with colder water from the north have created rich fishing grounds around Japan. However, over the centuries these areas have been overexploited, and large Japanese fleets now fishing in international waters take almost 15 percent of the world's total fish catch. The Japanese have been criticized for ignoring international conservation programs by continuing to hunt whales—which, of course, are mammals, not fish—a practice that threatens to drive several species of these magnificent animals to extinction.

Aside from problems caused by deforestation, Japan's environment has suffered serious damage from industrial pollution. One problem was that the first item on Japan's domestic agenda after World War II was economic recovery and growth. The environment was left to fend for itself. Environmental pollution issues finally became both a Japanese and an international story in the 1960s, when it became known that thousands of people in the Kyushu fishing town of Minimata were suffering from severe mercury poisoning. Wastes from a plastics factory discharged into Minimata Bay had been absorbed by fish, which the local people then ate. Many people died, others were disabled, and babies were born with severe birth defects. The Minimata disaster raised awareness about the extent of pollution in Japan, where most of the population lives in a coastal region only about 400 miles (640 kilometers) long that has been heavily industrialized and increasingly polluted. Freshwater resources also have suffered from pollution from Japanese industries. Valuable species of fish such as trout and salmon largely disappeared from Japan's polluted rivers and lakes. The crested ibis and the Japanese crane, two birds closely associated with Japan, are almost extinct.

Local governments began passing environmental laws in the late 1960s, and a national law to protect the environment was passed in 1972. Japanese companies eventually became world leaders in limiting pollution from factories, building energy-efficient products (including cars), and generally using energy efficiently. In its effort to use energy efficiently, Japan led the way in the development of modern electrified trains. In particular, in the 1960s, Japan developed the high-speed *shinkasen*, or "bullet trains" as they are called outside Japan, which provide the fastest train service in the world. Running at an average speed of about 100 miles (160 kilometers) per hour and reaching much higher speeds on some lines, the bullet trains leave Tokyo every fifteen minutes and connect the capital with every major Japanese city. For example, the 310-mile (500-kilometer) trip from Tokyo to Osaka, including stops in Nagoya and Kyoto, takes only three hours. Each train on the Tokyo–Osaka line has sixteen cars, is 1,300 feet (400 meters) long, and can carry 1,300 passengers. It requires forty motors to move it through sixty-six tunnels, the longest of which is 5 miles (8 kilometers) long. From its top speed of 170 miles (274 kilometers) per hour, the train needs 3 miles (5 kilometers) to come to a complete stop.

THE REMARKABLE JAPANESE ECONOMY

Japan's economy is the second largest in the world, trailing only the United States in total size. It also is one of the world's most advanced industrial economies, certainly the most advanced in Asia, comparable to that of the United States and far more advanced than China's. On a per capita basis, Japan ranks among the world leaders, although behind the United States, and exceeds China by a ratio of six to one (that is, the average Japanese produces goods and services with six times the value of the goods and services produced by the average Chinese). Japan also ranks second to Canada as a U.S. trading partner and third behind the United States and Germany in total trade of goods and services. The United States is Japan's most important trading partner. Japan exports more of its goods to the United States than to any other country, and imports more goods from the United States than from any other country. Japan has consistently exported more than it imports for many years, both in its dealings with the world as a whole and in its dealings with the United States.

Agriculture accounts for barely 2 percent of the country's gross domestic product. Japan's main crops are rice, potatoes, cabbages, sugar beets, and citrus fruits. Although Japan's farmers are extremely efficient, there simply is not enough local farmland, and the country must import about half its food, especially meat and grains. The importance of imported food has increased as the Japanese diet has moved beyond the traditional staples of rice, fish, and potatoes. The Japanese people today eat more meat, bread, and other foods they must buy from abroad. Because Japan has so few mineral resources, mining is even less important than agriculture in the economy, accounting for two-tenths of one percent of the economy and employing one-tenth of a percent of the workforce.

It is industry—manufacturing, construction, and utilities—that is the core and driving force of Japan's economy. Japan is an ultramodern industrial giant. As any American consumer knows, Japan produces cutting-edge, high-quality electronic equipment, from computers to videocassettes, televisions, stereo equipment, and video-game machines, and software. Japanese cameras, motorcycles, and cars rank with the very best in the world. Japanese corporations are leaders in fields such as electronic miniaturization and robotics: More than half of the world's robots used in manufacturing are in Japan.

Japan's recovery from the devastation of World War II was one of the great economic achievements of the postwar era. The Japanese worked hard, reinvested their profits, and brought government and industry together to promote development. Japan also had the advantage of enjoying American military protection; this has allowed it to spend very little on defense and concentrate on building up industries that produced for the consumer market. At first the Japanese produced inexpensive goods for a mass market, but careful planning enabled them to switch to high-tech and high-quality products and sell them all over the world. The Japanese economy grew by a spectacular 10 percent per year during the 1960s, by 5 percent per year during the 1970s, and by 4 percent per year during the 1980s. Growth slowed during the 1990s, and a recession that began early in the decade continued to grip the economy into the new century. By 1999, Japan had an unemployment rate of more than 5 percent for the first time since World War II. Economic growth had ground to a halt. Still, the country remained an overall economic powerhouse second only to the United States.

THE PEOPLE OF JAPAN

Almost 127 million people live in Japan, making it the world's seventh most populous country and about a tenth the size of China, its great rival. About three quarters of all Japanese live in urban areas, the largest of which are on Honshu. As of mid-2001, more than 34.7 million people lived in the Tokyo metropolitan area, about 17.8 million in the Osaka metropolitan area, and about 5.1 million in the Nagoya metropolitan area, all on the island of Honshu. More than 99 percent of Japan's population is ethnically Japanese, making it ethnically the most homogeneous large country in the world.

Japan's population grew rapidly for much of the nineteenth and twentieth centuries. It jumped from 30 to 65 million between 1868 and 1930, reached 100 million in the late 1960s, and passed 120 million by 1990. By then, under the impact of urbanization, modern birth control methods, and other social changes, the rate of population growth was declining quickly. Today, Japan's population is virtually steady: It increased by less than two-tenths of a percent in 2001 and in the coming decades will start to decline. With a current birthrate of only 1.34 per woman (versus 2.08 in the United States), far below the minimum replacement rate of 2.1, Japan's population is expected to peak in the very near future and then fall to 120 million by 2025 and to 101 million in 2050. And many of those 101 million will be old. This is because Japan combines one of the world's lowest birthrates with the world's longest life expectancy. The average Japanese lives 80.7 years, with women living an average of 82.1 years and men an average of 77.6. By 2015, Japan will not only be the oldest society in the world but, with a median age of 45, the oldest in the history of the human race. By 2025, fully one quarter of all Japanese, as opposed to 15 percent today, will be over 65. Precisely who will be working to support them all in their retirement years is one of Japan's greatest worries. Demographers predict that within twenty years Japan will be unable to afford its pension taxes and health care costs. And the situation will only get worse: By 2050 Japan will have a workforce of only 55 million people, barely half the population.

In some places, this gray future has already arrived. For many years, young people have been migrating from rural areas to the cities, leaving the countryside with a shrinking and aging population. This is most obvious with farmers, who across Japan average sixty years of age. On Oshima, an island in the Inland Sea, half of the population is over sixty-five.

JAPANESE AND NON-JAPANESE

Anthropologists generally agree that the Japanese people of today arose from several waves of migration that began in about the third century B.C. The Japanese language, which seems to be related to Korean and other Altaic languages, suggests that the main source of migrants was northeast Asia and Siberia. These migrants then merged with groups that probably arrived earlier from South China and elsewhere in southern Asia. In addition, later centuries saw further migration from the north Asian mainland, in particular from the Korean Peninsula. These links with Korea continued well into historical times. Korean migration was significant when the first Japanese state was developing in the fifth and sixth centuries, and it continued into the ninth century. The importance of Korean migration and its impact on Japanese culture is illustrated by the composition of the ninth-century Japanese aristocracy, a third of which seems to have been of Korean origin.

The Japanese, then, have diverse origins, and clearly have long-standing historic ties to the people of Korea. Yet these facts are not accepted by many nationalistic Japanese. Rather than see themselves as a distinct people with their own history and culture, an outlook that is common throughout the world, the Japanese have tended to see themselves as unique, both racially and culturally. The idea of "Japaneseness," which in many cases turns into overt racism, has been the topic of many best-selling books for more than a hundred years. These books focus on any number of factors that supposedly make the Japanese "unique," from language to brain functioning to methods of raising children. In the 1980s the government got into the act when the agricultural ministry insisted that American beef was unsuited to the special digestive systems of the Japanese. The argument of uniqueness has even been stretched to include physical characteristics of Japan itself, such as several decades ago when the claim was made that French skis were unsuited to Japan's supposedly unique snow. The need to prove Japanese uniqueness is also the reason why some militant Japanese nationalists deny that over centuries many of the people who settled Japan came from Korea, despite overwhelming evidence of that migration.

Given this background, it should not be surprising that it is not easy to be anything other than Japanese in Japan. Ethnic

Koreans are Japan's largest non-Japanese minority. They are, in fact, the only significant minority in terms of absolute numbers, about a million people, or eight-tenths of a percent of Japan's population. Most are descendants of Koreans who came to Japan to escape harsh conditions in their homeland after Japan made it a colony in 1910, or the hundreds of thousands brought to Japan as forced laborers during World War II. Ethnic Koreans are subject to widespread discrimination in many areas of Japanese life. Even if they were born and raised in Japan and speak only Japanese, most Koreans are still denied Japanese citizenship. Although marriage between ethnic Koreans and Japanese has increased, Japanese families still often oppose these marriages. It is not unusual for them to investigate a suspicious or uncertain background to make sure their children are not marrying someone of Korean ancestry. Interestingly, many Korean families, bitter at their mistreatment by the Japanese, also oppose mixed marriages.

Another ethnic group that in practice qualifies as a minority, at least in terms of being subject to discrimination, are the Burakumin. The Burakumin, who probably number about 3 million, are in fact ethnically Japanese. The problem is that their ancestors worked in professions that are considered unclean because of their association with death, such as butchering, working with leather, and handling corpses, and therefore were treated as outcasts by the rest of society. Today discrimination against Burakumin is illegal, but that has not helped in many areas, including employment. Perhaps most painful, Burakumin face severe discrimination when it comes to marriage. Japanese families do not hesitate to investigate any potential son-in-law or daughter-in-law whose background raises any suspicions of Burakumin ancestry.

A third ethnic group that has struggled with its status as a minority in Japan are the Ainu, who today probably number less than 20,000. They arrived thousands of years before the earliest ancestors of today's ethnic Japanese crossed over from the Asian mainland about 2,300 years ago. In the centuries that

An Ainu couple prepare for the first salmon ceremony of the season.

followed, the Ainu were forcibly displaced, much like the native peoples of North America. The Ainu were driven from their lands by people with a more advanced technology and gradually were pushed northward. Today a small remnant of that ancient population live on Hokkaido, where they survive by hunting and fishing or by entertaining Japanese tourists by posing for pictures dressed in their native costumes.

Japan's gloomy long-term population prospects have brought about a few changes in policy regarding immigration, which the Japanese have traditionally opposed. The immigrants Japan is allowing in are people of Japanese descent whose ancestors migrated elsewhere during the course of the twentieth century, primarily Brazil. By the late twentieth century, Brazil had about 1.3 million people of Japanese descent, most of whose ancestors had arrived beginning in 1908 to work on coffee plantations. In 1990, in order to attract workers for its assembly lines, Japan for the first time allowed Brazilians of Japanese descent and their spouses to come to Japan on a temporary basis. Most came just to take advantage of high Japanese wages and then go home. Then, in the mid-1990s, many decided to stay. The Japanese government responded by offering them permanent visas, and by 2001, Japan's Japanese-Brazilian population had reached 254,000.

While the government has worked to integrate the new arrivals into Japanese society, that transition often has not been easy or smooth. Children of Brazilian immigrants are not culturally Japanese. They often lack the study habits of native Japanese or a sufficient mastery of the Japanese language to succeed in Japanese public schools. In fact, only about a fifth of Japan's 35,000 school-age children of Brazilian immigrants attend Japanese public schools. Many attend private Brazilian schools, and many others have dropped out of school altogether. This is a disaster in a country like Japan, where education is essential for getting ahead, and is also a cause of delinquency and crime. Sometimes social pressures and cultural clashes drive Japanese-Brazilian children from school. As one fourteen-year-old dropout explained, "They [Japanese children] treat you differently. The Japanese don't like to hang out with Brazilians."[1] Cultural differences cause all sorts of misunderstandings and awkward situations. For example, in the fall of 2001 at a meeting to discuss social problems involving Brazilians, a Brazilian school put on a show for an audience that included the mayors of thirteen Japanese cities. The show began with teenage girls from the school, dressed in bikinis and feathers, performing the samba, a rhythmic dance popular in Brazil. As the schoolgirls shimmied seductively across the stage, the black-suited Japanese men in the audience stared straight down at their feet.

Since they are not legal citizens, Japanese-Brazilian children do not benefit from Japanese laws that mandate school attendance and provide health coverage. Still, there are success stories like that of Edson M. Tamada. He arrived in Japan at age seventeen after dropping out of high school in Brazil and today runs a food company with annual revenues of $16 million.

There is also a determination on the part of both Brazilians and Japanese to work together, driven by the undeniable reality that both sides need each other.

RELIGION

The overwhelming majority of Japanese observe both the Shinto and the Buddhist religions. While this might seem impossible to most Americans, the Japanese have no trouble combining these two religions. Shinto, "the Way of the Gods," is the indigenous religion of Japan. Its exact origins are unknown. Shinto does not have a holy text like the Bible or even a systematic set of beliefs, yet it influences most aspects of Japanese life. It is grounded in a reverence for nature that extends from the sun, water, and trees to mountains, unusual rock formations, and even sounds. According to Shinto, these and other natural phenomena, whether alive or not, have a spiritual side or god (*kami* in Japanese). Shinto includes ancestor worship and the belief that, as spring follows winter, the dead will be reborn in this world. It also includes myths about the origins of Japan and the Japanese people. It is an upbeat religion lacking any moral sense of guilt or sin. Consistent with the belief in the beauty and bountifulness of nature, Shinto shrines often are in places of great natural beauty. Worship ceremonies are simple, usually little more than bowing, clapping hands, and leaving a small offering of food, rice wine, cloth, or strips of paper tied to sacred branches. Shinto stresses the importance of purification before entering sacred shrines. Festivals at these shrines are joyous affairs, among the few occasions when the usually reserved Japanese become boisterous in public. Sumo, the Japanese form of wrestling, was founded on the basis of ancient Shinto rituals, perhaps as long as two thousand years ago.

Modern life has not separated the Japanese from their traditional Shinto practices. Infants are taken to Shinto shrines to be blessed either thirty or one hundred days after they are born, as are children ages three, five, and seven. Young people cele-

brate reaching adulthood when they reach the age of twenty
according to Shinto beliefs. Almost all marriages in Japan are performed according to Shinto ritual. New cars are blessed to prevent driving accidents, and Shinto purification rites often are performed at the sites of new buildings. When the buildings are completed, they receive another Shinto blessing. Some Shinto beliefs, however, have been abandoned. Until 1945, Shinto tradition held that Japan's emperor was a divine being. This idea was repudiated as part of the democratic reforms the United States imposed on Japan after World War II.

Buddhism, Japan's other major religion, originated in India and arrived in Japan via China and Korea in the sixth century A.D. Buddhism was part of the huge wave of Chinese influence that swept over Japan during the next several centuries, affecting government, education, art, literature, crafts, and many other aspects of Japanese life. It was the arrival of Buddhism that led the Japanese to give the name Shinto to their native beliefs to distinguish them from Buddhism. Buddhism is based on the idea that desire causes all the world's pain and that the way to escape from that pain is to overcome desire and reach a blissful state called *nirvana*. It requires multiple lifetimes to reach nirvana, and in each lifetime, according to the idea of *karma*, is based on what one has done in the past. As they would do again many times, the Japanese imported or borrowed a foreign cultural trait, in this case Buddhism, and over time changed it to fit their established traditions. Buddhist temples were built near Shinto shrines, and Japanese worshipers visited both. As Japanese beliefs penetrated Buddhism, the new religion became very different from what was practiced in China or elsewhere in Asia. For example, Japanese Buddhists often say that the dead go to paradise, an idea alien to mainstream Buddhism. Some scholars have questioned whether Japanese Buddhism really is Buddhism at all. In a typical compromise, trees chopped down to build Buddhist temples were not used for several years to allow the Shinto spirits inside the trees time to leave. Today there are more than fifty versions of Japanese Buddhism. The best known is called Zen Buddhism, which actually got its start in China in the seventh century and became established in Japan two hundred years later.

Christianity is not unknown in Japan, but its presence has never been very large. It was introduced to Japan by Catholic Jesuit missionaries from Portugal in the mid-sixteenth century. At first they met with success, reporting to Rome in 1582 that they had established more than two hundred churches and made 150,000 converts, a number that doubled over the next twenty years. Some Christian converts occupied high positions in Japanese life. However, by the late 1580s the most powerful military leader in Japan banned Christianity, possibly because he believed the foreign faith threatened his country's unity. In the late 1590s persecution began when twenty-six Christians were crucified near the city of Nagasaki. Christianity nonetheless continued to win converts, especially on Kyushu and several smaller islands just offshore, which led to more intense and systematic persecution after 1612. Finally, a revolt in 1637–1639, which began as a result of high taxation but then became a Christian rebellion, was crushed with great loss of life. This broke the back of Christianity in Japan. Although a few Japanese Christians continued to practice their faith in secret, they remained a tiny group. After 1868, Christian missionaries again were allowed into Japan. They built churches and hospitals, but did not win many converts. Today there are about a million Christians in Japan, less than 1 percent of the population.

GOVERNMENT

Japan is a parliamentary democracy. The emperor, stripped of his divine status by the United States after World War II, is the head of state. Under the Constitution of 1947 written by the United States, legislative power is vested in a two-house parlia-

ment called the Diet. The lower house, the House of Representatives, has 480 members elected to four-year terms. Three
hundred are elected from single-seat constituencies, as in the
United States, and 180 are elected by party according to a system of proportional representation. The 252 members of the
House of the Councillors are elected to six-year terms. One
hundred members are elected by proportional representation
and 152 from multiseat districts. Half of the House of Councillors is elected every three years. Japan's executive power lies
with the cabinet. The cabinet is appointed by the prime minister, who is designated by the Diet but officially appointed by
the emperor. The prime minister in turn appoints the rest of the
cabinet. Japan is divided into forty-seven units called prefectures, each run by elected governors. Japan has universal suf-
frage for all adults over the age of twenty.

DEFENSE

Japan's constitution has an unusual feature imposed after World
War II by the United States. It is Article 9, under which Japan
renounced war and the use of force, though not self-defense. In
1951, when Japan's sovereignty was restored and the United
States ended its occupation, the two countries signed a mutual
security treaty. That treaty, which was modified by a treaty of
mutual security and cooperation in 1960, put Japan under
American nuclear protection. In 1954, Japan set up a Self-
Defense Force of 150,000 soldiers. It included army, navy, and
air force units, but its mission was strictly limited, as was military spending. By the 1980s, the tables had turned a bit. Japan
had prospered by devoting its resources to civilian rather than
economic needs, while heavy Cold War defense expenses were
straining the United States and hurting its economy. Washington began to pressure Japan to increase its military spending. In
1992, Japan sent troops abroad for the first time since World
War II when the Diet voted to participate in U.N. peacekeep-
ing missions. The first of these troops went to Cambodia that

year. Others went to Mozambique in 1993 and the Rwanda-Zaire border in 1994. These commitments notwithstanding, Japan's defense spending remained less than 1 percent of its gross domestic product.

AN ARTISTIC CULTURE

Art and aesthetics have always played a central role in Japanese life. The Japanese traditionally did not distinguish between art (or fine art) as understood in the West and what people in the West consider crafts. In fact, before 1868 the Japanese used one word—*kogei*, which means "craft"—as a term that covered all the arts. Art was not something confined to museums or the homes of the wealthy. Form, beauty, refinement, and ceremony often were as important as function in many of the products Japanese people used in their daily lives. The Japanese sense of beauty as it developed over centuries has been strongly influenced by the ideas of Zen Buddhism. It stresses a reliance on simplicity and the creation of an atmosphere of tranquility. It also includes an efficient use of limited space, that is, the ability to use a small area to its fullest, but always in a way that maximizes beauty and taste.

A prime example of this blending of art and everyday life is the Japanese folded screen, or *byobu*. Often exquisitely painted, these screens were used for all sorts of practical purposes, from blocking off areas in a home or providing backdrops at outdoor festivals to serving as ceremonial furniture in Buddhist temples or government buildings. The same was true about woodblock prints, or *ukiyo-e*, a Buddhist term that means "pictures from the floating world" and suggests the impermanence of the physical world and short-lived nature of human pleasures. Woodblock printing in Japan dates from the seventeenth century. At first these prints were black-and-white, but during the eighteenth century, Japanese artists and craftspeople mastered the technique of color printing. Woodblock art covered a wide spectrum of subjects. Many artists focused on the sensual and seedy entertainment district of the city of Edo (present-day Tokyo). This was Japan's "Floating World," where money ruled and the strict social rules and hierarchy that dominated most aspects of Japanese life did not apply. The subjects depicted on these woodblocks ranged from famous actors in their best-known roles to erotic scenes and portraits of prostitutes. Landscapes, including scenes of Mount Fuji, also were subjects of woodblock art.

For a long time, woodblock prints did not have a high status in Japan. Traditional Japanese art experts who admired classical Chinese painting considered them vulgar. Woodblock prints were associated with popular culture and enjoyed by the merchant class. In particular, they were used to create a popular type of adult storybook that resembled a comic strip or cartoon. Art experts in the West tended to view these prints more favorably than their counterparts in Japan. After Western sailors and traders brought them home, Japanese woodblock prints became extremely popular and influential in late nineteenth-century avant-garde European art circles, particularly among artists associated with the Impressionist and Postimpressionist movements.

Art and function also merged in other Japanese crafts. Japanese lacquerware has won admirers throughout the world. The Japanese have been using lacquer, a resin made from tree sap, to decorate wood, leather, and textiles for about 1,500 years. The process that produces Japan's extraordinary lacquer bowls, trays, dishes, small boxes, and furniture requires as many as fifteen layers of lacquer, literally dozens of steps, and the skills of many artists and craftspeople. Japanese artisans also create highly admired ceramics using techniques originally imported from China and Korea. Among the most-prized Japanese ceramics are tea bowls. They are an essential part of Japan's traditional tea ceremony, a delicate and elaborate centuries-old ritual that itself is considered a work of art by many Japanese. The serene and formal Japanese garden, in which trees and shrubs are carefully and meticulously arranged, often around a pond, is yet another place where art and practical use meet. So is traditional Japanese architecture, with its emphasis on light, utilizing limited space as much as possible, and blending buildings into surrounding gardens and landscapes. The Japanese also have tried to beautify their world through the craft of flower arranging, whose origins date from the fifteenth century. Even today, flower arranging is widely studied in special schools and is considered a skill likely to improve a young woman's marriage prospects.

TRADITIONAL THEATER AND LITERATURE

Japan has a rich history in the performing arts. Perhaps the best-known traditional Japanese form of theater in the West is *kabuki*, an intricate combination of drama, music, and dance that dates from the seventeenth century. Kabuki's performers originally were women, but in 1629 they were banned from the stage by authorities who considered their presence a threat to public morality. Since then all kabuki performers have been men, who play both male and female roles. Kabuki actors must master a wide variety of extremely difficult skills, and training therefore begins in early childhood, sometimes as young as age three. Often, these skills are passed on from generation to generation in the same families. Somewhat older than kabuki is *bunraku*, Japan's traditional puppet theater. These two art forms are related, and many kabuki plays were originally written for bunraku. It takes great skill, and as many as three people, to manipulate bunraku puppets, which are about two-thirds life size. A crucial component of bunraku is a three-string instrument similar to a banjo known as the *shamisen*, which came to Japan from the island of Okinawa in the sixteenth century.

One interesting feature of traditional Japanese literature is the role played by women, especially Murasaki Shikibu, a lady-in-waiting to Japan's empress about a thousand years ago. Her enormous novel about court life, *The Tale of Genji*, which appeared around the year 1008, is considered one of the greatest works of Japanese literature. A form of Japanese poetry that has become increasingly familiar in the West is the *haiku*, one of the world's shortest poem forms. A haiku is a seventeen-syllable poem that has three lines containing five, seven, and five syllables respectively. The first acknowledged master of the haiku was Matsuo Munefusa, known as Bashō (1644–1694), who began his professional life as a soldier and then became a poet after the death of the feudal lord he served. It is uncertain how many haiku he wrote, but more than one thousand are known to us.

AN OUTLINE OF JAPANESE HISTORY

BEGINNINGS TO 1192

While Japan has been inhabited for tens of thousands of years, its earliest identifiable residents were Stone Age hunter-gatherers and fishermen who made a distinctive type of rope-patterned clay pottery. This Jōmon pottery has given its name to an era that lasted from about 10,000 B.C. to about 300 B.C. The first Jōmon pottery is generally considered to be the oldest pottery in the world. After 300 B.C. new arrivals from the Asian mainland brought a culture based on the cultivation of rice in irrigated fields. Known as the Yayoi culture after an archaeological site in Tokyo, it included weaving, the use of the potter's wheel, and technology for producing both bronze and iron. By A.D. 100 the people of the Yayoi culture had established themselves in most of Japan, with the exception of northern Honshu and Hokkaido. The Yayoi culture lasted until about 300, after which a people who built large burial mounds called *kofun* became the dominant group in Japan. The Kofun period (300–710) saw the emergence of increasingly powerful clans. Eventually a clan from the Yamato Plain on southern Honshu united that region under its rule, creating Japan's first recognizable state in the process.

The founding of what would become the Yamato dynasty marked a significant step in the formation of the Japanese nation. The present imperial family is its descendant, and today's Japanese still often refer to themselves as the "race of Yamato." The Kofun period also saw the arrival from Korea of Buddhism, which by the end of the sixth century was firmly established at the emperor's court. In 607 the first official mission from a Japanese ruler arrived at the court of the emperor of China. The Japanese diplomats carried a letter to the Chinese emperor that began with the salutation, "From the Emperor of the sunrise country to the Emperor of the sunset country."[2] By its wording the letter implied that Japan was equal to its mighty neighbor on the mainland. That notion violated China's Confucian view of the world, and the Japanese soon had to abandon it in their official contacts with the Middle Kingdom. But they held fast to the notion of their country as "the land of the rising sun," a phrase that has been applied to Japan ever since and is reflected in its national flag, a bright red sun set against a white background. Meanwhile, Chinese influence grew as Chinese classical writings, including those of Confucius, became available. Japanese rulers, deeply impressed by the power, wealth, and splendor of China's Tang dynasty, also attempted to copy Chinese ruling techniques, including strengthening the power of the emperor and central government at the expense of local clans.

Centralization reached a new level after 710, when the imperial court built Japan's first permanent capital—previously the capital was moved at the death of each emperor—at Nara in southern Honshu near the Inland Sea. Nara was modeled on the magnificent Tang capital of Changan, probably the largest and grandest city in the world at the time. The Nara period (710–794) was a time of growth and cultural development in Japan, in large part as a result of Chinese influences. Japan's first written records, really ancient Shinto legends, were compiled in the *Record of Ancient Matters* (*Kojinki*), published in 712, and the *Chronicles of Japan* (*Nihohshoki*), published in 720. They were written in Chinese characters, although the writers of the

Kojinki used those characters phonetically to represent the sounds of the Japanese language, a decision that makes the work extremely difficult to read and understand. In about 760, an anthology of more than 4,500 poems appeared called the *Collection of Myriad Leaves* (*Manyoshu*).

At the end of the eighth century, the court moved slightly northward to a new site that eventually became the city of Kyoto. It would remain Japan's official capital for more than one thousand years. Once again, Japan's capital was built on the Chinese model, but Japan was coming of age, changing what it learned from China and adapting it to local traditions and needs. The next four hundred years (the Heian period,

A classic Japanese garden, with cherry trees arching over a running stream

794–1185) saw the flowering of what is considered classical Japanese culture. An important development along that line was a new system of writing using phonetic symbols (*kana*) to indicate the sounds of the Japanese language. It became the vehicle for a new distinctly Japanese literature whose outstanding work was Murasaki Shikibu's *The Tale of Genji*. A distinctive Japanese style of painting also emerged, taking its inspiration from popular legends and tales (including *The Tale of Genji*) and famous scenic places and the changing seasons. The artists of the Heian period painted their works, known as the Yamato pictures, on long scrolls. Eventually they added poems to these works, thereby combining in their creations three art forms: painting, poetry, and calligraphy. Temples and palaces built during this period have characteristics, such as open pavilions set in carefully designed gardens, that reflect an emerging Japanese style of architecture.

Cultural development did not translate into political unity. By the eleventh century, central power had weakened dramatically, and for most of the twelfth century, Japan was riven by civil war. As lawlessness and banditry spread, provincial landowners operated more and more like feudal lords, using their own military forces to defend their territories and expand their power at the expense of rivals. Their armies were made up of a new warrior class, the *samurai*, who operated according to a strict code of honor and absolute loyalty to their lords. Finally, between 1185 and 1190, a military leader named Minamoto Yoritomo (1147–1199) routed all of his major opponents and brought most of the country under his control. He established his headquarters in the coastal town of Kamakura, just south of present-day Tokyo. In 1192 the emperor granted Yoritomo the military title of *shogun*, which means "barbarian-subduing general." In theory, the shogun was the emperor's chief military adviser. In practice, he was the ruler of Japan while the emperor sat powerless on his throne in Kyoto. Although the emperor officially still ruled Japan, for the next 676 years, until 1868, Japan would be ruled by a military dictatorship under the shoguns.

The era of shogun rule is divided into four major periods, each named after a shogun regime: the Kamakura period (1185–1333); the Muromachi period (1333–1568), when the Ashikaga shoguns ruled from Kyoto; the Momoyama period (1568–1600), when Japan was unified after a long period of feudal disorder and civil war; and the Edo period (1600–1868), when the shoguns ruled from the city of Edo, which later was renamed Tokyo. The Kamakura shogunate managed to maintain relative peace and order for about a century beginning in the early 1220s. However, for most of the shogun era prior to the Edo period, Japan knew little internal peace. It resembled feudal Europe, with a weak central government and feudal lords with private armies struggling with each other for power.

The most dramatic event of that long unstable period occurred in the thirteenth century, when the Mongols, builders of the greatest land empire in history, tried to conquer Japan. The Mongols made their first attempt in 1274, when a fleet of nine hundred ships landed 25,000 soldiers at Hakata Bay on northern Kyushu, the part of Japan closest to Korea. The Mongols, the world's best cavalry fighters, had weapons far superior to anything Japan's samurai warriors could muster. But fierce samurai resistance kept the invaders on the beaches—it helped that the Mongol horses were weakened from seasickness and therefore useless—until a typhoon destroyed many of their ships and forced them to retreat to Korea.

In 1281 the Mongols were back, this time with an army of 140,000 men transported by more than four thousand ships. It was the largest naval attack force in history prior to World War II. The Japanese had prepared well. They had assumed correctly that the Mongols would again land on northern Kyushu and had built a massive stone defensive wall around Hakata Bay. Heroic samurai resistance again kept the Mongols from getting off the beaches in a battle that raged for two months, while at sea, small Japanese ships attacked the larger but less maneuverable Mongol vessels. Once again the weather came to the rescue.

On August 1 an enormous typhoon struck and tore through the Mongol fleet. Again the Mongols had to retreat to the mainland, never to return. The Japanese called that great storm the kamikaze, or divine wind. It became a part of their country's lore and faith in their invincibility. More than 650 years later, in the closing days of World War II, the Japanese again would call on the kamikaze, this time in the form of young, poorly trained pilots flying suicide missions into American warships, to thwart yet another invasion. This time, however, not even the kamikaze could save them from military defeat.

The shogun government that defeated the Mongols collapsed within a half century of its historic victory. A new shogunate was established in the 1330s at Kyoto, but it never established an effective government. In 1542 the Portuguese, the first Europeans to reach East Asia by sea, landed on Kyushu. Their baggage included muskets, powerful new weapons the Japanese quickly learned to copy and use. Seven years later the Jesuit missionary Francis Xavier brought the Catholic religion to Japan. Meanwhile, a century of constant warfare that started in 1467 caused the shogunate to collapse in 1568. Political turmoil continued until a general named Toyotomi Hideyoshi finally unified the country under his rule in 1590. Despite his great achievement—it was the first time any government had controlled all of Japan—Hideyoshi had even larger ambitions: He intended to conquer China. That project began with a disastrous failed invasion of Korea in 1592 and ended with Hideyoshi's death in 1598.

Yet another general, Tokugawa Ieyasu, now emerged as Japan's strongman. After defeating his main rivals, in 1603 he had the powerless emperor in Kyoto designate him as shogun. Ieyasu then moved his capital to the village of Edo, a collection of about a hundred huts overlooked by a crumbling castle, and began a process of construction and development that would turn it into one of the world's great cities. Far more important, he had established the Tokugawa shogunate, the first durable national government in Japanese history. His main goal, and that of his successors, after centuries of disorder, was stability,

and that goal was achieved. One means of achieving it was to cut off Japan almost completely from the outside world. This was done with a series of decrees aimed at eliminating Christianity and foreign traders from Japan. Christianity was suppressed by the late 1630s, and by the early 1640s the only foreigners allowed to trade in Japan were Chinese and Dutch merchants confined to the port of Nagasaki under strict rules.

During the next two centuries Japan enjoyed unprecedented stability and unbroken peace. Along with the building of roads and other measures such as standardizing coinage, this newfound order promoted trade, the development of a wealthy merchant class, and a measure of prosperity. These conditions also promoted cultural and artistic development. Wealthy merchants eagerly bought lacquerware, ceramics, and fine textiles produced by craftsmen whose skills and techniques improved to supply a growing market. Japanese kabuki and bunraku puppet theater thrived, as did the writing of haiku poetry and the production of woodblock prints. Many of these developments were most clearly in evidence in Edo, which by the eighteenth century had grown into a vibrant city with a population of more than a million.

At the same time, there was also a costly downside to Tokugawa isolationism. Japan remained a feudal society, dominated by a rigid class structure divided according to occupation. Samurai warriors, who alone had the right to bear arms, stood at the top of this social order. The samurai were Japan's nobility and included wealthy lords down to ordinary soldiers. They were followed in descending order by three groups of commoners: farmers, artisans, and merchants. Any samurai offended by a commoner could cut him down and leave the body where it fell. Meanwhile, Japan successfully kept out European influences, but only at the price of falling behind Europe economically and technologically. Already by the late eighteenth century, some Japanese scholars were well aware of Western scientific and technological advances and criticized the shogunate's isolationist policies as counterproductive.

THE HANDBOOK OF EAST ASIA

The American arrival in Tokyo Bay in 1853 brought the Japanese face-to-face with these problems. It was impossible to deny that the policies of the Tokugawa shogunate had weakened rather than strengthened Japan vis-à-vis the "barbarians" from across the sea. The imposing American "black ships," as the Japanese called them—they were steam-powered warships with black hulls—could sail against the tide and were armed with weapons the Japanese could not match. The shogunate lost authority at home when it had to back down to foreign threats and sign treaties with the Americans and then with several European powers that imposed unfavorable conditions. Domestic opposition swelled. In 1868 rebel forces captured Kyoto, seized the emperor, and declared the restoration of imperial rule. The Tokugawa shogunate collapsed. The event that returned the emperor to power after almost seven centuries takes its name from the newly empowered emperor and is known as the Meiji Restoration. It marks the beginning of the history of modern Japan.

THE MEIJI (1868–1912) AND TAISHO (1912–1926) ERAS: JAPAN MODERNIZES AND BECOMES A GREAT POWER

The slogan that guided the Meiji reformers was "Enrich the Country, Strengthen the Military." It was a slogan they did much to turn into a reality. Japan, in contrast to China, had an advantage in dealing with the West: a long tradition of borrowing from other cultures and adapting what it learned to its particular needs and traditions. Now, rather than borrow as in the past from China, the Japanese borrowed from the West. The Charter Oath, issued in 1868 in the emperor's name, pledged that Japan would "seek knowledge throughout the world" in order to strengthen the country. The Japanese sent missions to Europe and the United States to study foreign technology, industrial and business practices, education, and methods of government. At home the imperial government used that knowledge to overhaul the country's educational system. The new system provided compulsory education for both boys and girls and included new universities. The Meiji reformers encouraged economic development and industrialization, in particular the growth of key industries such as iron, steel, railroads, shipbuilding, and arms manufacturing. Military reforms laid the basis for a modern army and navy. A new constitution issued in 1889 established a Western-style parliamentary system, but only on the surface. After all, the Meiji reformers wanted an economically and militarily powerful Japan based on its traditional values, not a democratic Japan based on Western ideas. The electorate under the new constitution consisted of wealthy male property owners, about 1 percent of the population; the emperor, who had the power to dissolve the parliament, was declared "sacred and inviolable"; and the military had an influential role in the government. The Meiji reformers also actively countered Western democratic ideas by trumpeting Japanese nationalism and traditional values, especially in the schools. Meanwhile, most ordinary Japanese worked long, hard hours at low pay and under strict discipline; they remained poor so that their country could grow rich and finance its military buildup.

The results of the Meiji soon could be measured in concrete demonstrations of Japanese power. Japan defeated China in the Sino-Japanese War of 1894–1895 and annexed the island of Taiwan as its victory prize. It then shocked Europe by defeating Russia in the Russo-Japanese War of 1904–1905, the first such victory of an Asian state over a European power in modern times. That victory gave Japan the southern half of Sakhalin Island and increased its economic presence in both China and Korea. In 1910, Japan annexed Korea, beginning a harsh occupation of its neighbor that lasted until 1945. It exploited both Korea and Taiwan as sources of raw materials and food to support its industrial development and feed its growing population. Japan then sided with the Allies in World War I (1914–1918), getting the best of both worlds. It stayed out of the horrendous fighting in Europe, took over German outposts in China and elsewhere in Asia, pressured the weak Chinese government for favorable concessions, and profited and developed economically from trade with the Allies and access to new markets in Asia. After the war, Japan joined the League of Nations and was invited to participate in a major Great Power conference on naval warships whose goal was to prevent an arms race.

In just two generations, Japan had transformed itself from a weak and technologically backward nation into a modern industrial and military power. Its population had almost doubled from 30 million in 1868 to 55 million in 1920, and that population probably was the most literate in the world. It had built an empire, albeit a small one, beyond its four main islands. Japan's program of modernization, combined with China's decline and continued weakness, had brought about a historical first: The Middle Kingdom had been replaced as the most powerful state in East Asia by the Land of the Rising Sun. The implications of that change extended beyond East Asia, for Japan now was a major world power.

MILITANT NATIONALISM, AGGRESSION, AND WORLD WAR II: 1926–1945

In 1926, upon the death of his father, Hirohito became emperor of Japan. His long reign (he ruled until his death in 1989) is known as the Showa period, which means "Enlightened Peace." It turned out not to deserve the name. The Showa period would see Japan aggressively expand its territory to the greatest extent ever and then suffer catastrophic defeat in World War II. Only afterward would it rise from the ashes of that defeat to become an economic powerhouse second only to the United States.

Despite its successes, Japan in the 1920s remained a society where most of the wealth and political power was in the hands of a tiny minority. This caused social unrest and political

instability that grew in intensity after the onset of the Great
Depression in 1929, which had started in the United States and
then spread worldwide. This in turn increased the influence of
powerful extreme nationalist groups and their allies in the military, who saw territorial expansion as both the solution to current problems and the key to Japan's future security. The first
step was to seize Manchuria, a huge and tempting target rich in
natural resources. In late 1931 the Japanese army used a
trumped-up incident to conquer Manchuria, which was
detached from China and turned into a puppet state the Japanese called Manchukuo.

Japan reacted to international criticism of its aggression by
withdrawing from the League of Nations. In 1937, Japan
launched a full-scale invasion of China and immediately began
committing acts of horrible brutality in a futile attempt to crush
Chinese resistance. When they seized the Chinese capital of
Nanjing at the end of the year, Japanese troops began a two-
month-long reign of terror, now generally known as the Rape
of Nanjing, in which they murdered an estimated 300,000 civilians. As the invasion of China blended into World War II, the
Japanese would commit further atrocities throughout East Asia,
including the use of biological weapons against civilians and
prisoners of war. These actions have left a legacy of bitterness
among Japan's neighbors that has not dissipated even with the
passage of six decades.

When World War II officially began on September 1, 1939,
with Germany's invasion of Poland, East Asia already had been
at war for more than two years. In 1940, four years after its first
treaty with Nazi Germany, Japan signed a military alliance
called the Tripartite Pact with Germany and Italy. The United
States came into the war when Japan bombed Pearl Harbor on
December 7, 1941, a surprise attack that destroyed a large part
of the U.S. Pacific fleet. Japanese victories continued into 1942,
by which point they controlled much of East and Southeast Asia
and a series of tiny islands in the Pacific Ocean. The tide of battle turned with the decisive American victory near Midway

Island in the Pacific in June 1942, in which American planes sank four Japanese aircraft carriers. But more than three years of bloody fighting lay ahead. U.S. forces had to push the Japanese back island by island in fierce battles that often involved hand-to-hand fighting. By early 1945, U.S. bombing attacks on Japan's home islands were taking a heavy toll. Still, the Japanese government, dominated by military hard-liners who believed they could beat back an American invasion, refused to surrender. Finally, in August 1945, the United States destroyed the cities of Hiroshima and Nagasaki with atomic bombs. Stunned by the terrible power of the new American weapons, Japan surrendered on August 14. When Emperor Hirohito announced the surrender to his people on August 15, it was the first time ordinary Japanese had ever heard his voice. The official surrender ceremony marking the end of World War II took place in Tokyo Bay on the battleship USS *Missouri* on September 2, 1945.

POSTWAR JAPAN: 1945 TO THE 1990S

World War II left Japan in ruins. Its economy had collapsed, its major cities had been bombed into rubble, its overseas empire was lost, millions of people were dead or maimed, many millions more were homeless and hungry, and Japan was under United States occupation. The U.S. occupation of Japan was headed by General Douglas MacArthur, the overall commander of American forces that had defeated the Japanese in World War II. The Japanese, who had been brutal as occupiers during the war, expected a harsh occupation in defeat after the war. Instead, in 1946 the United States began shipping hundreds of thousands of tons of emergency supplies of food to Japan to prevent mass starvation. Many Japanese soon found they approved of the reforms imposed on their country by the Americans, policies that were turning Japan into a more democratic country and encouraging its economic recovery. Nor were they necessarily unhappy to see the removal of the military leaders who had led their country to disaster. That process included putting twenty-five leading government officials on trial for war crimes. Seven were hanged and the rest sentenced to long prison terms. Emperor Hirohito remained on the throne, mainly because American authorities believed they needed his cooperation to govern Japan. But he ruled strictly as a figurehead and in 1946 publicly renounced his supposedly divine status.

American reforms included introducing a democratic constitution (which went into effect in mid-1947), implementing land reform to give land to tenant farmers, and breaking up many of the huge holding companies that dominated much of the Japanese economy. The education system was overhauled, in part to promote the teaching of democratic ideas. New laws granted workers the right to organize trade unions and to strike. By 1951 the United States and several dozen other nations had signed a peace treaty with Japan. In 1952, Japan's independence was restored and the occupation of the four main islands came to an end. (The United States continued to control Okinawa until 1972.) Japan and the United States also signed a security treaty under which some American troops remained in Japan as a protective shield. Notwithstanding Article 9 of its new constitution under which Japan renounced war and pledged never to rearm, as early as 1950, Japan, with strong U.S. approval, established an armed force it called the National Police Reserve. In 1954 it became the Self-Defense Force, which by the 1960s was a modern military organization complete with tanks, warships, and aircraft.

Meanwhile, Japanese political life under the new constitution became more democratic, although not fully democratic, at least by American standards. The prime minister for seven out of the first eight and a half years after Japan's first postwar elections in 1946 was Shigeru Yoshida, whose method of rule often was called "one-man government." In 1955, two conservative parties merged to form the Liberal Democratic Party (LDP), which controlled the government without a break into the 1990s. The LDP was closely tied to powerful interest groups, including Japan's largest industrial, financial, and trading firms.

Japan certainly had fair and often lively elections and active, well-organized opposition parties. Yet behind the scenes many key decisions were made beyond the control of the voters by the so-called "establishment," an insular network of LDP politicians, businessmen, and government bureaucrats.

One result of this system was corruption. Beginning in the 1970s, Japan was rocked continuously by scandals involving bribery, tax evasion, and other illegal activity by leading politicians. A stock market scandal in 1989 led to the resignation of three government ministers, those of finance, justice, and economic planning. These scandals continued into the 1990s and finally cost the LDP control of the government in 1993. A series of electoral reforms followed in 1994, the same year the LDP returned to power. However, the reforms did not stop the corruption. New scandals involving both government officials and businessmen emerged throughout the rest of the 1990s and led to the resignation of more ministers, among them a prime minister, a justice minister, and a minister of finance. The bribery and corruption scandals spilled over into the new century. This caused several resignations by government officials, the most serious being the resignation of the minister of state for economy, industry, and information technology in early 2001.

Japan's economic success was its most dramatic postwar story. It was helped in that effort by American aid immediately after the war and by military protection in the decades that followed. Whereas at times Japan had spent as much as 60 percent of its total output on military-related expenses, after World War II that figure dropped to less than 1 percent. Yet most of the credit for the Japanese economic miracle certainly must go to the Japanese people. Japan had an educated workforce willing to work hard. Most Japanese were willing to save a large portion of their rising income, which then found its way into new industrial investment.

The key was to export. The Japanese government worked with business to identify key industries and overseas markets on which to focus to promote industrial growth, while at the same time protecting its home markets from foreign competition. This was done with tariffs, and also with a web of complex regulations and bureaucratic red tape that frustrated foreign companies trying to sell in the Japanese market. Japan also limited public welfare benefits in order to control taxes and thereby enable businesses to keep more of their profits, which were then available for investment.

As in Germany, industrial companies in Japan built new factories to replace those destroyed during the war. This gave them an edge on foreign competition, including American companies, because their new factories made use of the most advanced technology. By 1951, Japan had recovered from the war and reached production levels of the 1930s. During the next twenty-five years, fueled by exports, Japan's economy grew at a record rate. Both income and output tripled. Japan became a leading producer of high-quality steel, electronics, cameras, consumer appliances, automobiles, ships, and other products. These products were exported all over the globe, from the United States and Western Europe to the People's Republic of China.

By 1967, Japan was the second-largest economy in the non-Communist world. By the mid-1970s, Japan was the world's leading automobile exporter: More than 60 percent of all imported cars sold in the United States were made in Japan. In 1980, and for about the next fifteen years, Japan produced more cars and trucks than the United States. During the 1980s the Japanese economy became the second largest in the world, ahead of the Soviet Union. By the 1980s, Japan had one of the highest standards of living in the world. Its leading companies had profitable investments in many foreign countries. Although Japan had a small group of extremely wealthy people, it had become a largely middle-class society with an extremely low poverty rate. Japan also had the highest life expectancy in the world.

Japan's success as an exporter of industrial goods caused resentment abroad, including in the United States. Many

American industries were badly hurt or destroyed altogether by Japanese competition, including the automobile industry. Meanwhile, Japan often continued to protect its home markets when its industries could not compete with foreign competition. The Americans also pointed out that Japanese consumers paid very high prices for Japanese products, which enabled Japanese companies to sell their products cheaply abroad, sometimes at a loss, and win market share. In the face of American pressure, in 1981 Japan agreed to accept what were called "voluntary" limits on exports of automobiles to the United States. At the same time, the leading Japanese manufacturers announced they would build factories in the United States to produce some of their cars there. While these restrictions helped to save the U.S. auto industry, they did not affect the overall balance of trade between the two countries. Japan's exports to the United States continued to run far ahead of imports from the United States. In fact, the imbalance grew worse. In 1983, Japan exported about $20 billion more to the United States than it imported. By 1991 that figure reached $38 billion, and by 1999 it had swelled to more than $120 million. Almost a quarter of all Japanese exports were going to the United States.

CONTEMPORARY JAPAN

RECESSION AND OTHER PROBLEMS: THE 1990S AND BEYOND

In 1989, Emperor Hirohito died; his reign of sixty-two years was the longest in Japanese history. His son and the new emperor, Akihito, gave his reign the name Heisei, which means "attainment of peace." The reign got off to a difficult start. In the early 1990s, after four decades, the Japanese economic miracle finally ran into trouble. Part of the problem was recession in industrialized countries that were Japan's most important export markets. At home, a fall in real estate prices caused huge losses for banks as loans they had made based on highly inflated real estate prices went bad. Between late 1989 and early 1992, the Japanese stock market lost more than half its value. Industrial output shrank by 12 percent during 1991–1992 alone.

Japan suffered another shock in January 1995, when a powerful earthquake hit the city of Kobe, killing 6,400 people and leaving more than 300,000 homeless. Elevated expressways and railroad lines collapsed, as did gas mains that were supposed to be earthquake proof. Just a few months later, a local fanatical religious cult called Aum Shinrikyo released deadly nerve gas in the Tokyo subway, killing 12 people and injuring more than 5,000. This act of terrorism shook Japan more than any earthquake. The Japanese took great pride in the order and safety of their society, and suddenly a tiny group had shown how easily both could be undermined. Making matters worse, this attack had not been carried out by foreigners with some score to settle but by Japanese whose motives seemed incomprehensible. These events were followed in the summer by yet another banking scandal. In 1996 came more unnerving news, this time about public health. There had been a cover-up of leaks at a nuclear power plant, unhygienic school lunches caused food poisoning in thousands of children, and hundreds of hemophiliacs had been given infusions with HIV-infected blood. The image of a violence-free Japan was tarnished again in June 2001 when a drifter with a history of mental illness entered an elementary school near Osaka and stabbed eight children to death. He also wounded fifteen other people. It was the first such incident in Japan's history. Some schools reacted by arming teachers with deterrents like noise alarms and canisters of tear gas and conducting self-defense demonstrations that included mock stabbings. When some observers suggested the school officials might be overreacting, an official in the ministry of education, reflecting the unease spreading in a country unaccustomed to public violence, commented, "They are necessarily overreacting."[3]

Meanwhile, Japan remained mired in recession. Although it continued to sell huge quantities of automobiles, electronics, and other high-tech products abroad, total exports of merchandise declined steadily from the mid-1990s through 2002. At the same time, low consumer demand—automobile sales dropped by 25 percent between 1990 and 2001—and lack of spending by businesses at home kept the economy in the doldrums. Another problem was that the entire Japanese economy was not as efficient as the ultramodern world-class factories that turned out Japan's automobiles and high-tech electronics. In fact, in 2001 overall Japanese productivity was only 72 percent of that of the United States, a figure 2 percent lower than the year before. The year 2000 saw the highest unemployment since World War II and a 30 percent decline in the stock market. In 2001 unemployment climbed still further, reaching an official figure of 5.5 percent. This statistic was not high by American or European standards. However, it did not count people who had become discouraged and stopped looking for work. One American economist estimated that the real figure was at least 8.5 percent, while a Japanese trade union official argued that unemployment was "at least double official figures."[4] Making matters worse, decades of government spending on huge construction projects had left Japan with an enormous public debt. By 2001 it was about 140 percent of the country's gross domestic product (GDP), the highest ratio of any industrialized country.

Japan's economy finally turned around during 2002. It grew that year and in 2003 and 2004, in large part because of strong exports of electronics to the United States and China and investment in new factory equipment by large electronics and automobile companies. Unemployment fell and by mid-2004 was at a four-year low. Many Japanese companies, having cut workers and paid off debts, once again became profitable. Still, there were new and formidable economic challenges ahead. Japanese manufacturers face intensified competition abroad. In particular, on the western horizon is a new industrial giant, the People's Republic of China, the country with the world's largest low-wage economy. Billions of dollars of investment by foreign companies, including major Japanese companies like Sony, Sanyo, Fujitsu, and Toshiba, have turned the PRC into a manufacturing powerhouse. Factory wages in China are only 5 percent of those in Japan. In the spring of 2001, Toshiba stopped making televisions in Japan. Other Japanese companies, seeking low-wage workers, are moving the production of products like cell phones, motorcycles, and buses from Japan to China. Japan is likely to remain a center for research and development and the manufacture of certain high-precision and high-tech products, but many more manufacturing jobs are going to be lost to low-wage countries, especially China.

LIVING WITH THE PAST

During the summer of 2001, two events in Japan infuriated two of its neighbors, China and South Korea. The issue raised in both cases was how Japan was remembering, or, more accurately, not remembering, its actions during World War II. In July the government announced it was accepting a new middle school history textbook. A month later, newly installed Prime Minister Junichiro Koizumi visited a Shinto shrine honoring 2.5 million Japanese dead from World War II. Among those honored at the Shinto shrine are convicted war criminals, including Hideki Tojo, Japan's prime minister from 1941 to 1944. For their part, the new textbooks either totally ignored or barely mentioned Japanese war crimes for which Tojo and others were convicted. The crimes include the 1937 Rape of Nanjing and other massacres of civilians; forcing tens of thousands of Asian women, mainly Koreans, to provide sex for Japanese soldiers; the horrible medical "experiments" performed on prisoners of war, including Americans; and the use of biological weapons against the Chinese. The textbooks also whitewashed Japan's brutal occupation of Korea between 1910 and 1945. Prime Minister Koizumi made a small concession to critics by not visiting the shrine on the anniversary of Japan's surrender, as originally planned. As for the new textbooks, most of Japan's school districts said they would not use them. Neither of these gestures satisfied the Chinese or South Korean governments or millions of people throughout East and Southeast Asia. As they saw it, with great justification, Japan had yet to come to terms with the aggression and crimes it committed during that war.

CHANGING CUSTOMS AND ATTITUDES

One of the most significant qualities about contemporary Japan is that attitudes which have endured for centuries have begun to change. One positive development concerns treatment of the disabled. Japan has long demanded strict conformity to social norms, and anyone who would or could not conform to those norms was an embarrassment and often hidden away at home. That has changed, in part because of the increase in the number of elderly, and hence in the number of people who need special assistance. Modern technology, which helps the disabled to perform more tasks, has also played a role in changing perceptions of them. Whatever the reasons, efforts are being made to enable the disabled to participate actively in society. The popular media now portray the disabled functioning in society. One disabled person, who today runs a business with the help of a special wheelchair that enables him to stand, observed that what has happened in recent years is "not nearly enough, but still a great improvement has taken place."[5]

Another notable change involves growing numbers of young people, perhaps 3.4 million, known as "freeters." The word, which implies being up-to-date, is a combination of the English "free" and the German "Arbeiter," which means worker. Freeters are young people who have rejected the seventy-hour workweeks of their parents' generation and the total loyalty their fathers had to the companies that employed them. Instead of building a career at one company or in a single field, they hop from job to job and, when it suits them, take time off.

In part this new attitude has evolved because Japanese companies can no longer guarantee lifetime employment to today's workers, as those companies did to their parents. In part it is a result of young people watching their fathers devote all their energy to work, with little left over for personal interests, including their families. Young people in their late teens and twenties, freeters work at temporary jobs, make some money, live at home to save money, and then use the money to enjoy themselves. "My boyfriend and I spent a month in Hawaii. Now we are saving up for Indonesia," a nineteen-year-old freeter told an American journalist.[6]

However, as Japan's freeters enjoy life without too much thought for the future, other Japanese worry. They are concerned with the growing gap in wealth between the older and younger generations and about who is going to support Japan's aging population in the coming decades. This does not bother the freeters. As one magazine editor noted, "They think: 'Look at Americans. They job hop. They seem to be free. That's the way we want to live.'"[7]

Probably the most far-reaching change in Japanese attitudes concerns the thinking of millions of women. Women in Japan are demanding more control over their own lives and faster progress toward equality with men. Married women, breaking with tradition, are asserting their independence. In rural areas, where the tradition of two or even three generations living together still persists, some middle-aged women, after decades of marriage, are refusing to defer to their mothers-in-law any longer. As one woman who had just moved out of her mother-in-law's house explained, "I thought this is my own life and I have to live it before it's crushed."[8] Another emerging trend is wives refusing to honor the tradition of being buried alongside their husbands. "For most of my marriage I wasn't allowed to decide anything," a sixty-one-year-old woman commented. "I finally got fed up and told my husband to have himself buried alongside his mother, and I bought my own grave."[9] This particular change has come quickly. Ten

These girls attending an impromptu concert in a Tokyo park are going to lead quite a different life than their mothers did.

years ago married women who wanted to be buried alone could not find a cemetery that would take them; today more than four hundred will.

Much more far-reaching in terms of Japan's future is what young women are thinking and doing. Currently, half of all women thirty and younger are not married; the figure in the United States is only 37 percent. "If I were married, I'd have to worry about what my husband thinks, about cooking for him, cleaning. And if I have kids . . . . Child rearing takes up so much time," a woman in her late twenties explained.[10] While many of these young women plan to marry someday—"around the age of 30, but I can't think about that until I get a stable position in a company," a university student told a journalist—others seem uninterested in the prospect altogether. "My immediate goals are to become self-reliant, to have a career and to live alone," a twenty-year-old trade school student noted.[11]

Nor does getting married seem to change attitudes on some important matters. The fastest-growing segment of Japan's population is couples without children, a group that by 2015 will be 40 percent larger than it was in 1995. One result of all this is already evident: Japan's plunging birthrate, which is well below replacement level. To traditionalists these young women are spoiled: They are called "Parasite Singles," after a Japanese horror film called *Parasite Eve*. They also are referred to by the word *wagamama*, meaning selfish and willful. But there are other things at work, at least regarding the reluctance to have children. Japan's long economic downturn has created an atmosphere of pessimism among the young. As a magazine editor in her mid-thirties, who is single and lives with her parents, explained, "We didn't create all these problems with the economy . . . where women have no hope for the future. . . . It's difficult to have dreams when the economy is so bad."[12]

The search for solutions to economic problems, as well as frustration with endless scandals, finally led to a shakeup in the leadership of the governing LDP. In April 2001 the charismatic Junichiro Koizumi, who had pledged to push through far-reaching economic reforms, won the contest for LDP party leader and became Japan's new prime minister. In July he led his party to a decisive victory in parliamentary elections. Koizumi, whose photogenic dynamism was such a refreshing change from the bland bureaucratic personalities of his predecessors, began his term as the most popular prime minister in Japan's postwar history. A year later, that image was tarnished by Koizumi's inability to turn the economy around. Koizumi himself did not seem discouraged. He pointed out that in the 1980s Japan had been overconfident. "It's not good to be overconfident," he said, "but also not good to lose too much confidence. I have not lost confidence in the potential for Japan."[13]

One thing Koizumi and other leading Japanese do seem to have lost confidence in is Japan's ability to guarantee its future security with its current defense forces. Some politicians from Koizumi's Liberal Democratic Party wanted to amend Japan's constitution to allow Japan to field a regular army, rather than its limited defense force. Others were going further still. Worried by China's growing nuclear strength and North Korea's weapons program, influential Japanese political figures, including a top aide of Koizumi's, a leading opposition figure, and the major of Tokyo, all suggested that Japan should consider building nuclear weapons. While Koizumi did not publicly endorse those statements, he pointedly did not repudiate them either. In late March 2003, Japan launched its first two military spy satellites to monitor North Korean activities. The North Korean government immediately called the launch a hostile act and warned Tokyo that it is heading for "self-destruction." Undeterred, in June parliament passed a series of laws giving the government much greater powers in a military emergency. Plans also went forward to upgrade Japan's antimissile defense, in cooperation with the United States. All this added up to yet another significant potential change looming on the horizon in the Land of the Rising Sun.

FIVE

NORTH KOREA AND SOUTH KOREA

Choson, the ancient name for Korea, means "Land of the Morning Calm," a phrase that does not suit Korea's history. It has been Korea's fate to be pressured by more powerful neighbors-- mainly China, the giant of East Asia. In the thirteenth century, Koreans faced a new menace in the Mongols, who overran them in a brutal military campaign. These conquerors of China and vast additional parts of Eurasia held Korea in their grip for a century. Another threat emerged in the late sixteenth century when a newly united Japan tried to conquer the peninsula, albeit without success. In the late nineteenth century, as China weakened, the Russian Empire challenged Japan for control of Korea. The Japanese won that struggle in the Russo-Japanese War of 1904–1905. Japan then annexed Korea in 1910, exploiting and often brutalizing its people until the end of World War II.

161

In 1945, liberated from Japanese colonialism, Korea immediately was caught in the great emerging Cold War struggle between the world's new superpowers—or, as the Korean proverb might have it, super-whales—the United States and the Soviet Union. Their struggle with each other literally tore Korea in half. By 1948 a supposedly temporary division at the 38th parallel near the middle of the peninsula had become permanent. North of that parallel was the Soviet-sponsored Democratic People's Republic of Korea (North Korea); to its south was the American-supported Republic of Korea (South Korea). The devastating Korean War of 1950–1953 that followed left the entire peninsula in ruins. After that long violent night came a remarkable recovery, especially in the south, but not a morning calm. There was no peace, only an armistice. Two hostile states and tens of thousands of soldiers glared at each other across a narrow demilitarized zone that became a legal border. The Korean Peninsula became, and a half century later remains, one of the world's most heavily militarized and tensest pieces of real estate in the world.

NORTH KOREA AND SOUTH KOREA

NORTH KOREA

The fundamental political fact about the Korean Peninsula is its division into two countries, North Korea and South Korea. While both countries are ethnically Korean, they are radically different types of societies. North Korea, officially the Democratic People's Republic of North Korea, has been a rigid and brutal Communist dictatorship ever since its establishment in 1948. Its leader and dictator from 1948 until his death in 1994 was Kim Il Sung. Kim in fact was in charge even before the official founding of the state, making him the only political leader to head a country from the first day of the Cold War until the last. His ambition to unite all of Korea under his, and

Communist, rule was the primary cause of the Korean War. At Kim Il Sung's death in 1994, power passed to his son, Kim Jong Il. It is unlikely that the younger Kim is as powerful as his father, who ruled North Korea for forty-six years as an absolute dictator.

North Korea has a highly centralized socialist economy on the model of the former Soviet Union. All economic assets are state owned, and almost all economic activity is state controlled. Farmers work on state-run collective farms. State-owned factories produce almost all the country's manufactured goods. Following the example of the Soviet Union, after 1948, North Korea's Communist regime focused on developing the country's heavy industrial base and military power. It built factories to produce steel, other metals, cement, and military hardware. Military spending had first call on all resources, from raw materials to manufactured goods. North Korea developed ballistic missiles, and sold missiles or missile technology to Middle Eastern countries such as Syria, Iran, and Libya. These countries, along with North Korea itself, have been leading supporters of international terrorism. It also developed biological and chemical weapons and, of even greater concern to its neighbors and the United States, established a program to build nuclear weapons.

Massive military spending to support an army of more than a million soldiers drained resources from the civilian economy. North Korea lost further ground in the late 1980s when the Soviet Union, itself in deep economic trouble, stopped sending aid. By the 1990s the North Korean economy was in crisis. Its chronically inefficient collective farm system had left the country with widespread food shortages. Between 1995 and 1998 a series of natural disasters—floods followed by drought—turned those shortages into catastrophic famine. Although North Korea received $1 billion worth of food and other aid from abroad, mass starvation occurred. It is clear the North Korean regime did not pass on the food aid to the general population. Most expert observers agree that between one and three million people in North Korea died of starvation during the late 1990s. None of the suffering affected the Communist Party elite, who continued to live well amid the general misery.

SOUTH KOREA

South Korea, or the Republic of Korea, followed a very different path. Its economy was based on private enterprise, although beginning in the 1960s the government worked closely with private companies to promote industrial growth and expand export markets. Most of the help went to a small group of huge family-run conglomerates known as the *chaebol*, whose owners had close ties to leading government officials. These companies also benefited from tax concessions and government-subsidized bank loans. Meanwhile, imports were restricted so local industries could control the market at home, and wages were kept low to make Korean products more competitive abroad. Foreign aid and borrowing, mainly from the United States, also helped, especially in the difficult early days when the country had not fully recovered from the Korean War. South Korea first developed relatively labor-intensive consumer industries such as textiles, but it soon moved to industries such as shipbuilding, automobiles, and electronics. The economy grew extremely quickly, following the pattern established in Japan about a decade earlier. During the 1980s, South Korea's economy grew at the remarkable rate of 9.5 percent per year and from 1990 through 1997 at 7.2 percent. By the mid-1990s, South Korea had a modern industrial economy and one of the world's highest standards of living. The late 1990s saw Korea experience an economic crisis that included major bankruptcies and rising unemployment. But these problems, however serious, in no way invalidated the enormous achievement of the previous four decades.

South Korea's political development has been a bit rockier but still radically different and vastly preferable to what occurred in North Korea. Although in form a republic that held regular elections, in fact for almost four decades after 1948 South Korea was an authoritarian country in which presidents held dictatorial power. Between 1948 and the 1980s, there were two military coups and several periods of martial law. Genuine democratic reforms finally were introduced in the late 1980s and gradually took root during the 1990s. In 1997, Kim Dae Jung, a former dissident who in the 1970s was in prison under sentence of death, was elected president of South Korea. He took office in early 1998, signaling South Korea's entrance into the world's democratic group of nations.

GEOGRAPHY AND PEOPLE

The Korean Peninsula extends due south from the Asian mainland for about 620 miles (1,000 kilometers) and is between 134 and 150 miles (216 and 240 kilometers) wide. Its total area is slightly more than 85,000 square miles (220,150 square kilometers), a bit more than the state of Minnesota. The peninsula is bordered by the Yellow Sea in the west and the Sea of Japan, which Koreans prefer to call the East Sea, in the east. To the south, the 120-mile (190-kilometer)-wide Korea/Tsushima Strait separates the Korean Peninsula from the main islands of Japan. North Korea, with an area of about 47,300 square miles (122,500 square kilometers), slightly smaller than the state of Pennsylvania, occupies the northern half of the peninsula. Two rivers, the Yalu in the west and the Tumen in the east, form North Korea's long northern border with China. An 11-mile (18-kilometer) stretch of the Tumen River in the northeast marks North Korea's border with Russia. South Korea, occupying the southern part of the peninsula, has an area of 38,291 square miles (99,173 square kilometers), slightly larger than the state of Indiana. South Korea's only land border is the demilitarized zone (DMZ) that separates it from North Korea. The DMZ runs close to the 38th parallel and has an area of 487 square miles (1,262 square kilometers).

About three quarters of the Korean Peninsula is mountainous, leaving only a small lowland area suitable for farming. Most of that is a coastal plain on the western side of the peninsula stretching from near the Chinese border in the north to the peninsula's southern tip. It is home to most of the population of both North and South Korea and to their respective capital cities, North Korea's Pyongyang (population 3.1 million) and South Korea's Seoul (population 10.2 million). The Taebaek mountain range forms a spine that runs most of the length of the peninsula along its east coast, with spurs branching out toward the west. It contains many scenic peaks, including an especially majestic group called the Kumgang (Diamond) mountains just north of the 38th parallel. Koreans always have appreciated the rugged beauty of their peninsula, describing it as *kumsu kangsan*, or "rivers and mountains embroidered in silk."[1] Korea's rugged natural beauty is a theme repeated often over the centuries by Korean poets and painters.

Mount Paektu (White Mountain) on the border between North Korea and China—where it is called Baitou Shan—is the Korean Peninsula's highest point. Standing 9,000 feet (2,740 meters) above sea level, it is an extinct volcano crowned with a huge crater lake called Cheonji (Lake of Heaven). The lake is one of the deepest of its kind in the world. Both the Yalu and Tuman rivers, the peninsula's longest, rise on Mount Paektu.

The Korea Peninsula's smooth eastern coast has few harbors. The jagged western and southern coasts have many bays, inlets, and numerous natural harbors. These coasts also are dotted with about 3,400 offshore islands. The largest island is egg-shaped Chejudo, about 100 miles (160 kilometers) off South Korea's southern coast. Once called the "Island of the Gods" by an American newsmagazine, Chejudo is a semitropical jewel whose landscape ranges from beautiful beaches to spectacular volcanic peaks and craters.

Korea generally has a temperate climate with four seasons. Most rainfall occurs between June and September when monsoon winds blow in from the ocean. During the winter there are

Lake of Heaven

heavy snows in the north, while some parts of the south get no snow at all.

The Korean Peninsula's natural resources are not distributed evenly between north and south. South Korea has the majority of the arable land, which helps explain why its population, about 47.9 million, is more than double that of North Korea (about 22.9 million). North Korea has more mineral resources, including large deposits of soft coal, iron, and magnesium; extensive hardwood and softwood forests; and fast-running rivers that provide two thirds of its electrical power. South Korea has small deposits of coal and iron. Its forests are smaller than those in the North, although they are expanding as a result of one of the world's largest reforestation efforts. Ten nuclear plants provide almost 40 percent of South Korea's electricity needs, which, reflecting its modern industrial economy and high standard of living, are about nine times larger than those of the North.

Rice is the most important crop in both North and South Korea. South Korea, however, produces over three times more than the North. Other important crops are root crops, barley, vegetables, and fruits in the South and corn, potatoes, and soybeans in the North. Fishing provides another important source of food in both countries. Again, the South is far more productive: Its total catch from year to year (including fish farming) averages about eight times that of the North.

THE KOREAN PEOPLE

The Korean people are the descendants of tribes that migrated to the peninsula from Central and northern Asia. The strongest evidence for this is the Korean language, which belongs to the Altaic group of languages that probably originated in Central Asia. Over time, various groups of migrants merged into one people, and today Korea is one of the world's most ethnically homogenous nations. There are no minority ethnic communities of any significant size in either North or South Korea.

South Korea, like Japan, has a rapidly aging population. As of 1999 its fertility rate had fallen to 1.4 births per woman, well below the replacement rate. Although life expectancy in South Korea had risen dramatically in the second half of the twentieth century—from only 47 years in 1955 to 76.2 years for women and 69 years for men in 1998—its population is still increasing slowly, at a rate of less than 1 percent per year. The slow pace is good news to many observers since South Korea already is one of the world's most densely populated countries. The problem will emerge in the decades ahead when the country does not have a large enough labor force to support a growing elderly population that is no longer working.

Another population problem in South Korea is who is being born. Over the centuries Korea absorbed Confucian values from China, and those values retain their influence today, even among people who consider themselves up-to-date. These values, which favor boys over girls, have created serious difficulties because most young South Korean couples want only two children. One of each sex is considered ideal, and two boys are fine. But having two girls

is not acceptable. There will be no child to carry on the family
name or perform ancestor worship ceremonies, which can only be
properly done by males. Since under Confucian traditions married
daughters become part of their husbands' families, a couple without sons will not have anyone to care for them when they are old.
To forestall these eventualities, many young couples are taking
advantage of modern medical techniques to learn the sex of their
unborn children and aborting female fetuses. The trend is ominous. Currently 111 boys are being born for every 100 girls, and
there are 113 boys for every 100 girls under the age of fifteen.
According to one estimate, in the near future there will be 128
men of prime marrying age—between twenty-seven and thirty—
for every 100 women. The social consequences of this are uncertain, and some could be disruptive. Pessimistic predictions range
from rising prostitution and kidnapping to secure a bride to a
"baby bust" and a rapidly falling population.

RELIGION IN KOREA

One important way in which North and South Koreans differ
from each other is in their religious beliefs. During the nineteenth century, Christian missionaries had unusual success winning converts in Korea compared with most other countries in
Asia. As a result, about 49 percent of all South Koreans are
Christians. About 47 percent are Buddhists, while most of the
rest profess Confucianism or follow ancient folk religious traditions. Korea's folk religious beliefs do not constitute an organized religion with a scripture or temples. They are based on the
activity of shamans, people who supposedly serve as intermediaries between this world and the spirit world. Shamanism is the
indigenous faith of the Korean people and dates from when the
ancestors of today's Koreans still lived in northern Asia.

North Korea's Communist regime views religion as a backward superstition and antirevolutionary and therefore has systematically repressed most religious observance. A reasonable
estimate is that two thirds of North Koreans do not consider

themselves as having any religious faith. An estimated 15 percent of the people follow traditional shamanist religion. A slightly smaller number follow a faith called Chondogyo (Religion of the Heavenly Way), a nineteenth-century sect that combines traditional shamanist beliefs with other religious traditions and is tolerated by the Communist regime.

THE KOREAN LANGUAGE SINCE 1945

The Korean people have been divided by one of the world's most sealed borders since the end of the Korean War. That long separation, aside from hurting millions of individuals kept apart from their families and friends, has had an impact on the Korean language. Accents and vocabularies have changed and diverged over the course of a half century as the Korean spoken north of the 38th parallel was influenced by Chinese and Russian, while the Korean spoken to the south was influenced by Japanese and English. In South Korea, more than eight thousand words have been borrowed from Japanese and English. Specific vocabularies commonly used in the North and South, such as words used to discuss economics and politics, have become noticeably different. One result is that Koreans from north and south who do manage to meet and talk are having trouble understanding each other.

AN OUTLINE OF KOREAN HISTORY

BEGINNINGS TO 1953

While local legends put the founding of the first Korean state in 2333 B.C., that event probably took place on the northwestern part of the peninsula about two thousand years later. The Koreans came under Chinese pressure almost immediately and their state, Chosøn, was conquered by the Middle Kingdom in 108

B.C. It took several centuries for the Koreans to drive the Chinese out. Korea then was divided among three rival kingdoms until the seventh century A.D., an era known as the Three Kingdoms period. During this period, Korea developed under the sway of Chinese cultural influences that included Buddhism, Confucianism, and Chinese forms of art and architecture. Korean became a written language for the first time through the use of Chinese characters. Meanwhile, as China influenced Korea, Korea in turn had a strong influence on Japan, usually as a transmitter of Chinese culture and technology.

Late in the seventh century, one of the Three Kingdoms, Silla, united the entire peninsula under its rule. That unification would last through good times and bad until 1945, a period of almost 1,300 years. The bad times included the Mongol conquest of Korea, which lasted for more than one hundred years during the thirteenth and fourteenth centuries. After the Mongols were driven out, the Yi dynasty was founded in 1392. More bad times came when the Japanese attempted to conquer the peninsula in the 1590s. It was during that struggle with Japan that Korea produced its greatest military hero, Admiral Yi Sun-shin. He is credited with inventing ironclad warships, called turtle ships because of their protective layer of overlapping metal plates, that sank hundreds of Japanese vessels in a series of battles. Aided by China, the Koreans eventually drove out the Japanese, but six years of fighting between 1592 and 1598 caused enormous destruction and hardship. The Manchu conquest of China in the mid-seventeenth century and the expansion of Chinese power that followed during the next century brought Korea closer into the Middle Kingdom's orbit. Contact with nations other than China was severely limited, so much so that Korea was called the "Hermit Kingdom." Japanese pressure and declining Chinese power eventually forced Korea's doors open in the 1870s, a process that resulted in Japan annexing Korea in 1910. With this, the five-hundred-year Yi dynasty ended.

The Japanese occupation of Korea was extremely harsh. The Koreans were kept under tight police control. The Japanese tried to suppress Korean culture and forced Korean students to learn Japanese. The Japanese occupiers did promote economic development and modernization, but only to exploit Korea's natural resources and labor for the benefit of Japan's economy. Life under Japanese rule became even more difficult during World War II. Hundreds of thousands of Korean workers were taken to Japan to work in mines and factories. Others were drafted into the Japanese army. Far worse, thousands of Korean women were taken to the war zones, where as "Comfort Women" they had to provide sexual services to Japanese soldiers.

The end of World War II brought more hardship to Korea. In 1945 the country was divided at the 38th parallel as a temporary measure. The United States' plan was that Japanese soldiers north of that line would surrender to Soviet troops, and those to its south would surrender to American troops. Once peace was restored, Korea would then be reunified as an independent country. However, once the Japanese soldiers were removed from Korea, events did not proceed according to plan. As the Cold War began, the temporary occupation zones were turned into two countries: Communist North Korea backed by the Soviet Union and non-Communist South Korea backed by the United States. By 1949 all Soviet and American troops had left the peninsula. However, the Soviet Union supplied the North Koreans with weapons to build a powerful army. In 1950, with Soviet backing, North Korea attacked South Korea. The United States, backed by a United Nations Security Council resolution, sent troops to defend the outgunned South Koreans. In November, after the tide of battle had turned against the North Koreans, the PRC intervened on the North Korean side. The war dragged on until 1953, eventually ending near the 38th parallel, almost where it began. The fighting ended with an armistice, not a peace treaty. Millions of Koreans were dead or homeless, and most of their peninsula was in ruins.

The history of North Korea until 1994 is largely the history of Kim Il Sung. Few men ever dominated a country more completely. Statues and pictures of him were everywhere, his word was considered the absolute truth, schoolchildren sang hymns to his glory. Kim Il Sung was not only the Great Leader; he was, among many other things, Our National Father Who Shines Like the Sun, the Ever-Victorious Marshal (even though his forces were routed during the Korean War and had to be saved by Chinese troops), the Fatherly Leader of All Koreans, and, of course, the Greatest Genius the World Has Ever Known. Kim was a fanatical Communist and bitterly anti-Western. In 1968 he caused a serious confrontation with the United States when North Korean forces seized the American intelligence ship *Pueblo* sailing off their coast in the Sea of Japan and held its crew prisoner for eleven months. Generally, North Korea's Great Leader did everything he could to keep his country isolated from the rest of the world. A rare exception occurred in 1991, when North Korea and South Korea, as separate countries, joined the United Nations. When Kim Il Sung died in July 1994, North Korea observed an official mourning period that lasted three full years. When the official mourning finally ended, the government announced that North Korea would use a new calendar whose first year would be 1912, the year of Kim Il Sung's birth.

There seems to have been a power struggle of some sort after the Great Leader's death as it took three years for his son, Kim Jong Il, to emerge officially as his father's successor. By then, North Korea was suffering from famine and mass starvation. North Korea was also entangled in a serious dispute with the United States over Pyongyang's nuclear weapons program. By 1994 the United States, with good reason, had concluded that North Korea was about to produce weapons-grade plutonium that would enable it to build several nuclear bombs. In October 1994, after tense negotiations during which the two countries came dangerously close to war, the United States and

North Korea concluded what was called an Agreed Framework. It turned out to be a very bad deal for the United States. North Korea agreed to stop its effort to build nuclear weapons and dismantle its nuclear facilities in return for a massive American-led multinational aid program. The largest portion of that aid was two modern light-water nuclear reactors whose fuel would be very difficult to convert to nuclear weapons use. However, by the late 1990s, the United States determined that North Korea had secretly continued its nuclear weapons program. In January 2002 the U.S. Central Intelligence Agency reported that "North Korea had produced enough plutonium for at least one, and possibly two, nuclear weapons."[2] Three months later the United States officially announced that North Korea was not in compliance with the 1994 agreement, in effect placing the aid program on hold.

The simmering crisis boiled over in October when the United States announced that North Korea, confronted with U.S. intelligence reports, had admitted it had violated the 1994 agreement by restarting its nuclear weapons development program. The latest North Korean effort was based not on plutonium but on producing enriched weapons-grade uranium. Because the United States was watching for secret North Korean efforts to reprocess spent nuclear reactor fuel into weapons-grade plutonium, this new approach helped North Korea evade U.S. intelligence gathering efforts for several years. Key help, mainly in the form of technology to develop complex gas centrifuges to enrich uranium, came from Pakistan, supposedly an American ally. Beginning in the late 1990s, Pakistan supplied this technology in return for North Korean help in developing ballistic missiles. The 2002 crisis this caused became even worse in December when the North Koreans announced that they were activating their five-megawatt nuclear reactor at Yongbyon, which produces enough plutonium to make one or two nuclear weapons per year. The next day they added they were removing international surveillance cameras and seals from a storage facility where spent nuclear fuel rods were stored. Those rods contain enough enriched plutonium for several bombs. On January 10, 2003, North Korea withdrew from the Nuclear Nonproliferation Treaty. On February 12, the International Atomic Energy Agency, helpless to do anything to stop what was happening, announced that North Korea was in violation of atomic safeguards and referred the case to the U.N. Security Council. Two weeks later, the United States confirmed that North Korea has indeed reactivated the Yongbyon nuclear reactor.

Matters went from bad to worse. In August 2003, talks began involving six nations—the United States, China, Russia, Japan, North Korea, and South Korea—to discuss North Korea's nuclear program and seek a way to end the North Korean-American confrontation. The talks ended without any progress. Meanwhile, the North Koreans boasted that they already had what they called a "nuclear deterrent." In October 2003, the Pyongyang announced that it had reprocessed 8000 spent plutonium fuel rods, a claim that if true—there was no way to prove or disprove it—meant they had enough for six nuclear bombs. In June 2004 a new round of the six-nation talks broke down as soon as they began.

The continuing U.S.–North Korean confrontation was all the more urgent in light of North Korea's development of ballistic missiles. In 1999 it tested a new missile, the Taeopodong-1, with a range of 900 to 1,200 miles (1,500 to 2,000 kilometers). A more advanced missile reportedly under development, the Taeopodong-2, might have the potential of reaching the United States and remains a major concern in Washington, Tokyo, Seoul, and other international capitals. A further concern is that North Korea is planning to work with Iran, a militant Islamic power with a long record of support for international terrorism, on long-range missile development.

As the new century began, North Korea opened up ever so slightly to the outside world. In June 2000, Kim Dae Jung became the first South Korean leader to visit Pyongyang, where he met with his counterpart Kim Jong Il. The North Korean government also began to encourage a little foreign investment, and by 2002 more than 125 South Korean firms were doing business in the North, although not always successfully because of government interference. But the overwhelming emphasis remained on keeping the North Korean people isolated from the outside world, and especially from finding out about how much better life is in South Korea. The North Korean government continued to jam foreign radio broadcasts and ban mail and telephone links with the South. Although a few years earlier it had permitted a South Korean company to open a tourist resort for South Koreans at Onjung-ri just north of the 38th parallel in the scenic Kumgang (Diamond) mountains, it went to enormous lengths to make sure the South Korean tourists and local North Korean villagers never got close to each other, much less met. Of course, North Koreans knew conditions were better elsewhere. That was why by early 2002 between 100,000 and 300,000, at great risk, had fled across their county's northern border (it's impossible to get across the DMZ into South Korea) into China, where they live illegally under constant risk of deportation back to North Korea. That is also why North Korea's prison camp system held about 200,000 inmates, mainly dissenters of various kinds or people who had tried to flee the country into China but had been forcibly returned by PRC authorities.

Although most North Koreans were silenced by their government, the evidence was overwhelming that North Korea's experiment with communism was a cruel failure. It therefore came as no surprise to many observers when in July 2001 the American newsmagazine *Newsweek* called North Korea the worst country in the world. North Korea topped *Newsweek*'s list of the world's ten worst countries, ahead of second-place Afghanistan, then ruled by the fanatical Taliban, and well ahead of tenth-place Iraq, then ruled by the tyrannical Saddam Hussein. A *Newsweek* correspondent who had recently visited North Korea wrote in an article called "The Worst of the Worst" that North Korea represented "the worst combination of absolute despotism and utter breakdown—a weird coincidence of totalitarianism and state failure." The correspondent added:

> No food and no culture. No future and no past. Just an unbearable present, both predictable and unbearable. It can't get any worse than this, except that it will.[3]

SOUTH KOREA: FROM 1953 INTO THE TWENTY-FIRST CENTURY

South Korea recovered slowly from the Korean War. The government under Syngman Rhee was dictatorial, corrupt and inefficient, and much American aid was wasted. The large influx of refugees from the North that had arrived between 1945 and 1953 added to South Korea's economic and social difficulties. In 1960, Rhee was elected to a fourth term in elections marred by massive and obvious fraud. In April of that year, student protests led to an upheaval that forced Rhee from office and into exile. Free elections followed, but the government chosen in that election lasted only a year. In May 1961 a junta led by General Park Chung Hee seized power and put South Korea under military rule.

Direct military rule lasted until the fall of 1963, when Park retired from the army, permitted presidential elections, and, to nobody's surprise, won the election. He would be elected again in 1971 and, after a return to martial law and an extension of the presidential term to six years, elected yet again in 1974. Park ruled as a dictator but also eased some controls as he became entrenched in power. He remained South Korea's president until he was assassinated in 1979.

Whatever Park's faults as a political leader from a democratic point of view, his policies for promoting economic development and industrial growth were enormously successful. The government built transportation and communications networks to bind the country together. It worked with large companies, which benefited from their close ties to the regime, to develop new industries and find export markets abroad. Meanwhile, high tariffs kept foreign products out and allowed South Korean companies to control the home market. During Park's first five years in office, South Korea's gross national product (GNP) grew by 8.5 percent per year, a very impressive figure, and exports jumped by 41 percent per year, a phenomenal figure. Between 1972 and 1976, South Korea's GNP grew at an annual average rate of 11.2 percent. By the late 1970s, South Korea was producing modern ships, automobiles, and consumer electronics and was well on the road to industrialization and prosperity.

After Park was assassinated by his own intelligence chief, the military in effect took control of the country. South Korea was under martial law from May 1980 until January 1981, after which another former general, Chun Doo Huan, was elected president. A period of social unrest followed, fueled in part by corruption scandals that from the early 1980s through the late 1990s became a regular part of South Korean public life. At the same time, during the mid-1980s political reform inched forward. In 1987 that process received a big push. A series of huge demonstrations by students, workers, and even Buddhist monks forced the regime to introduce reforms. The reforms lifted restrictions on the press, established direct election of the president by the voters, and generally protected human rights. The presidential election of 1987 was fair, although a split among opposition political parties allowed a member of the political establishment, yet another ex-general named Roh Tae Woo, to win the presidency. He took office in 1988, the year South Korea achieved some welcome international prestige by hosting the Summer Olympics in Seoul. The presidential election of 1992 marked yet another step forward with the election of Kim Young Sam, who upon taking office in February 1993 became the first nonmilitary man to serve as South Korea's president since 1960.

Kim Young Sam's presidency witnessed a serious attempt to combat the deeply rooted corruption that arose from close ties between South Korea's government and the country's largest business conglomerates. It was also a time of calling to account politicians who had participated in corruption and political repression. In 1996, two former presidents, Chun Doo Huan and Roh Tae Woo, were sentenced to long prison terms for a variety of crimes. Chun initially was sentenced to death, but the sentence was commuted to life in prison. Actually, neither stayed in prison very long. They received presidential pardons from Kim Young Sam in December 1997. By then, concerns about corruption were sharing the stage with economic problems. Several months earlier, East Asia's economic downturn had reached South Korea. Many large businesses, which had gone deeply in debt to finance expansion, found themselves in serious trouble, as did the banks that had loaned them billions of dollars. Still, political history was made in December 1997, when Kim Dae Jung, the former dissident who had once sat in prison under sentence of death, was elected president.

Upon taking office in 1998, Kim Dae Jung attacked his country's economic problems. He refused to prop up failing companies and banks and worked hard to attract foreign investment. Previously, South Korea had not permitted foreign companies to invest in key local industries such as autos or electronics. This changed in the late 1990s and helped the South Korean economy, but serious problems remained. During 2000, economic difficulties contributed to a shocking jump in major crimes, which rose by a third over 1999. During 2001 there were new corruption scandals that badly hurt Kim Dae Jung's popularity and reputation. Daewoo Motor Company, one of South Korea's most important firms, was declared bankrupt with more than $47 billion in debts. Still, South Korea was in better shape than many of its neighbors and beginning to show signs of recovery. Despite its difficulties, South Korea's economy grew by 6.2 percent in 2002 and 2.8 percent in 2003.

As for President Kim Dae Jung, he was widely praised internationally for his "sunshine" policy of encouraging new ties and attempting to ease tensions (often without success) with North Korea. For these efforts and for his contributions to democracy and human rights, in October 2000 he was awarded the Nobel Peace Prize.

However, by 2002, as his term was drawing to a close, much of the glow surrounding Kim had faded, mainly because of corruption scandals that landed two of his sons in prison. North Korea's betrayal of its 1994 promise to end its nuclear program was another setback for Kim. Still, in December 2002, Roh Moo Hyun, the candidate of Kim's Millennium Democratic Party, won a hard-fought presidential election. One of the main issues in the election was how South Korea should deal with the North, with Roh supporting a continuation of Kim Dae Jung's sunshine policy and his opponent advocating a much harder line, in coordination with the United States. The difficulty Roh would face in making the sunshine policy a success was graphically illustrated when he was inaugurated in February 2003. A week before the inauguration, North Korea threatened to abandon the 1953 armistice that had ended the Korean War if the United States continued its military buildup in the region. The day before, North Korea test-fired a land-to-ship missile into the Sea of Japan. The day after the inauguration, the United States announced that North Korea had restarted its five-megawatt nuclear reactor capable of producing weapons-grade plutonium in Yongbyon. A month after that, the North Korean Army announced it was withdrawing from regular armistice meetings (not abandoning the armistice itself) with U.S. military authorities. These events constituted a daunting beginning for any presidential term, especially that of a new president lacking any experience in international affairs.

Roh's presidency did indeed get off to a rocky start. A series of policy disputes caused him and his supporters to leave the Millenium Democratic Party. They formed a new political party called the Uri Party, which means "our party." In March 2004, a month before scheduled parliamentary elections, the

South Korean parliament voted to impeach Roh for collecting campaign funds illegally. He had to leave office while his case was decided. With its leader on the sidelines, in April the Uri Party placed first in the elections. The political party behind Roh's impeachment lost more than a fifth of its seats. A month later, Roh's impeachment was overturned by South Korea's supreme court, and he returned to office. South Korea had its president back, but continued disputes over foreign policy and economic problems that included a national pension fund crisis hurt Roh's popularity.

NORTH KOREA VERSUS SOUTH KOREA: A FEW STATISTICS AND A COMPARISON

A half century after the Korean War, South Korea, with the world's thirteenth-largest economy, has a per capita income of more than $13,300; North Korea's per capita income is $757. There are nine million passenger cars in South Korea, 3,000 in North Korea. South Korean workers produce as many cars in two eight-hour shifts as North Korean workers produce in an entire year. In late 2001 and early 2002, to help stem continued serious food shortages still causing starvation, South Korea sent North Korea 100,000 tons of corn, 200,000 tons of fertilizer, and 300,000 tons of rice. In February 2002, just before he arrived in Seoul for an official visit, President George W. Bush summed up the difference between the two countries on the opposite sides of the 38th parallel in Korea:

> On the one [north] side of a parallel, we've got people starving to death, because a nation chooses to build weapons of destruction. And on the other [south] side there's freedom.

SEVEN

MONGOLIA

Mongolia is a large, sparsely populated, land-locked country wedged between Russia and China, Asia's two giants, along East Asia's arid northern tier. It is best known as the homeland of the Mongols, the nomadic people who in the thirteenth century terrorized and conquered much of Eurasia and built the largest empire in history. It is not surprising that this land produced a tough and hardy people capable of conquest. Mongolia is a hard, unforgiving place of extreme heat and cold whose awesome emptiness and hardscrabble landscape always demanded strength, endurance, and ingenuity from the people who live there. At the same time, it has also impressed both natives and visitors with its stark beauty. Mongolia has long been known as the "Land of the Blue Sky," an apt moniker for a country of seemingly endless horizons where the sun shines in a cloudless sky for more than 260 days per year.

Geography, People, Economy

THE HANDBOOK OF EAST ASIA

Mongolia's area of about 604,830 square miles (1,566,500 square kilometers) makes it slightly larger than Alaska. It is shaped like a gigantic ark, somewhat like the one described in the biblical story of Noah. Located deep in the interior of Asia, Mongolia has only two neighbors: China to the south, west, and east, and Russia to the north. Most of the country is a high plateau; overall it is one of the highest countries in the world, with an average elevation almost 1 mile (1.6 kilometers) above sea level. The Altai Mountains stretch across the western and southwestern parts of the country and reach elevations of more than 14,000 feet (4,000 meters). Their highest peak, and the highest in Mongolia, is Tavanbogd Uul in the far western corner of the country, where Mongolia, Russia, and China converge. The huge glacier that crowns Tavanbogd Uul towers over all three countries. A lower mountain range is in the central and north central sections of the country. Still lower mountains in the northeast extend eastward from the capital of Ulan Bator (population 773,000). About 80 percent of Mongolia is a dry steppe grassland. The steppe's most productive pastures are in the north, where the rainfall averages between 10 and 20 inches (25 and 50 centimeters) per year. The bulk of Mongolia gets less than 10 inches of rain per year. That means much of Mongolia's steppe grasslands is really a semidesert. In the far south, the steppe gives way to the arid, rocky landscape of the Gobi Desert, which runs along about half of Mongolia's southern border with China. There are a few areas of forest covering less than 10 percent of the country, mainly a region of Siberian taiga in the north and forests on the slopes of the Altai Mountains. Less than 1 percent of Mongolia is suitable for agriculture.

Mongolia has many lakes in the valleys between its mountain peaks. The largest is a salt lake in the northwest called Uvs Nuur. The country's second-largest lake is Hövsgöl Nuur in the far north. Hövsgöl Nuur, a long, thin body of water 84 miles

(136 kilometers) long and only 19 miles (30 kilometers) wide lying on an almost direct north/south axis, is the deepest lake in the region and contains two thirds of Mongolia's surface fresh water. Mongolia's main rivers also are in the north. Most are swift-flowing streams that freeze in winter and often dry up during periods of drought.

Far from any moderating sea breezes, Mongolia has a severe continental climate. Winters are intensely cold and long; some lakes stay frozen into June. Summers are short and hot, at least in the daytime. Temperatures drop quickly when the sun sets and the summer nights therefore are cool. Shifting winds also cause drastic temperature changes, especially in the fall and spring. Depending on whether the wind is from the north or south, the temperature on a given day can vary by as much as 70°F (35°C).

Mongolia has plentiful wildlife, including deer, lynx, gazelles, wild camels, donkeys, wolves, and other animals. The Altai Mountains shelter the rare snow leopard. Among the most interesting animals are the *takhi*, Mongolia's wild horses. They actually went extinct in the late 1960s but recently were restored to the wild in certain areas using animals formerly in zoos. The takhi are unique because they are a distinct species. They are genuinely *wild* horses, not domesticated horses that returned to the wild, like the mustangs of the western United States or wild horses elsewhere in the world. Mongolia's most important mineral natural resources are coal, iron, gold, uranium, oil, copper, molybdenum, and several other metals.

PEOPLE

About 85 percent of the country's 2.65 million people are ethnic Mongols, mostly a group known as Khalkha Mongols. The largest single minority are Kazaks, who account for about 7 percent of the population. There are smaller numbers of Chinese, Russians, and several other groups. More than 95 percent of the population follow a Tibetan form of Buddhism known as Lamaism. There are small communities of Christians, Muslims, and people who follow shamanist folk religions.

About 55 percent of the current inhabitants of this traditionally nomadic country live in urban or suburban areas, while about 45 percent live in rural areas and follow the old nomadic lifestyle. However, even city dwellers have not abandoned some of the old ways. Most Mongolians, even those in urban areas, still live in traditional temporary structures called *gers*. A ger is a round structure held up by a collapsible wooden frame. Its skin usually consists of two or more canvas layers—depending on the season—surrounding an insulating layer of felt. A stove in the center provides both heat and a place to cook. The brightly painted door of a ger always faces south. A ger usually can be assembled in one to three hours.

Mongolia was under Communist rule for seven decades from 1921 until 1991. One of the few benefits of that experi-

Shelters called gers are home to the herders grazing their sheep on a Mongolian steppe.

ence was a comprehensive ten-year public education system in which eight years' attendance was compulsory. Today about 97 percent of the population over the age of fifteen is literate. However, since the fall of the Communist system, government funding for education has declined.

ECONOMY

Mongolia is a poor country. In 2000 it ranked 161st (or 164th, depending which statistical system is used) among the world's nations in per capita income, close to the bottom of the list. Turning Mongolia into a prosperous country is made more difficult by its decades of Communist rule. As with other former Communist countries, it has not been easy for Mongolia to make the transition from a state-controlled Communist economy to a free-enterprise capitalist one. During the Cold War, Mongolia depended on aid from the Soviet Union, the world's leading Communist country at the time. That aid, which accounted for almost a third of Mongolia's economy, disappeared overnight when the Soviet Union collapsed in 1991. Meanwhile, there was a tremendous amount to do to get a free-market economy up and running. The Communist regime had taken over the entire economy; even nomad animal herders were forced to join state-controlled collectives called *negdels.* The process of privatization, as elsewhere in the former Communist bloc, involved corruption as people well-placed under the Communist regime used their connections to get their hands on valuable economic assets. For most of the population, the 1990s were a difficult time. During the first years of privatization, social inequality and the number of people living in poverty increased. Real wages fell by 50 percent. During 1990–1998, per capita income fell at an average of 1.5 percent per year.

Still, change that may provide the basis for future growth did take place. During the Communist era the state owned every cow, sheep, horse, goat, and camel in the country. By the mid-1990s, more than 90 percent of all livestock was privately

owned. Although as of 2002, Mongolia's largest businesses, **187**
including important mines and factories, were still under state
control, the state overall controlled only about 30 percent of
the country's economy.

Currently, raising livestock in the traditional nomadic fashion by moving herds from pasture to pasture across the vast
steppe remains Mongolia's main economic activity. Livestock
raising employs almost half of the labor force and accounts for
about 30 percent of Mongolia's overall economy. Sheep, cattle,
horses, goats, and camels are the most important livestock. The
number of goats doubled (to 11 million) during the 1990s as a
response to the rising international demand for cashmere, a soft
wool. Horses, long the basis of Mongolia's nomadic way of life,
still play an important role in herding livestock, and today there
is about one horse for every person in Mongolia. Livestock
herders suffered a very hard blow during the winter of
1999–2000, which was long and bitterly cold even by Mongolian standards and killed several million animals. Large numbers
of animals continued to die into 2001.

Most Mongolian industrial enterprises, aside from power
stations and some mines, are small and devoted mainly to producing food products or goods such as cashmere, leather, clothing, and carpets. Cashmere is an important export. Mongolia is
the world's second-largest producer of cashmere wool. The
country's most valuable export in terms of earnings is copper,
which comes from a large mine near the northern city of
Erdenet. This joint Russian-Mongolian enterprise, which also
produces the metal molybdenum, accounted for more than half
of Mongolia's industrial output during the mid-1990s. Copper
and gold together are responsible for half the country's export
earnings. Many of Mongolia's three hundred mines produce
coal, the fuel that produces most of the country's electrical
power. Oil was discovered in Mongolia relatively recently, the
first production beginning in 1997.

Mongolia's abundant mineral resources give it some economic potential, but realizing that potential will be expensive.

Tapping the country's natural resources more effectively will require large amounts of foreign technology and investment. Roads, bridges, and railroads will have to be built to tie this vast and undeveloped country together. Care will have to be taken to make sure that growing livestock herds do not over-graze and destroy the pastures upon which they depend. During the 1990s, only large amounts of foreign aid, of which the United States provided $1.5 billion, prevented economic collapse. Today, foreign aid accounts for a third of Mongolia's economy. Additional reforms will be necessary to make better use of that aid. Corruption is still widespread, as is tax evasion. Unemployment is also a serious problem. The official estimate of urban unemployment is 20 percent, but unofficial estimates range as high as 50 percent. Simply put, Mongolia's road to prosperity is likely to be long and very hard.

AN OUTLINE OF MONGOLIAN HISTORY

The Mongols have their origins in the nomadic groups who moved their livestock herds across the vast steppe of Central and eastern Asia for many centuries before they were mentioned in Chinese records more than two thousand years ago. It was to defend against these nomads that the Chinese undertook their centuries-long labor of building and rebuilding their Great Wall in the third century B.C. There may have been Mongols among the Huns, the nomadic plunderers who ravaged northern China for several centuries beginning in the first century A.D. and terrorized the Roman Empire in Europe three centuries later.

In any event, the Mongols generally lived as disunited tribes who fought mostly each other until unified by Genghiz Khan (1162–1227) in the early thirteenth century. They then went on to conquer much of Eurasia from eastern Europe and the Middle East to the Pacific Coast. The key to Mongol success was their extraordinary skill as mounted warriors. The fast-moving Mongol cavalry, equipped with bows with a range twice that of European bows, was the most devastating fighting force the world had ever seen. Another Mongol weapon was terror. The Mongols were merciless, destroying entire cities and leaving a path of destruction littered with millions of dead as they ranged across Eurasia. Cities that resisted them were wiped out, which is why towns often surrendered without a fight. Some cities in Central Asia along the Silk Road never fully recovered from the devastation of the Mongol conquest. Russia took centuries to recover. Nor were the Mongols deterred by strong resistance: It took them more than sixty years of bloody fighting to conquer China, a campaign they began under Genghiz Khan and finished in 1279 under his grandson, Kublai Khan (1215–1294).

The Mongol conquests, by establishing a single empire that stretched from East Asia to Europe, brought the civilizations of those regions into direct and steady contact for the first time. It was the China of Kublai Khan that the famous Italian traveler Marco Polo visited between 1275 and 1292. The Mongols ruled China as the Yüan dynasty, but their power lasted less than a century. They were driven from China in 1368. In the following centuries, unity once again eluded them, except for a brief period in the sixteenth century, the same time that most Mongols became converted to Buddhism. By the late seventeenth century the territory where Mongols lived—an area much larger than today's Mongolia—had been absorbed by either the Russian or the Chinese empires. Mongolia itself was part of the Manchu-ruled Chinese Empire.

When the Chinese Empire collapsed in 1911, Mongolia declared its independence under a Buddhist religious leader, whose title was the "Living Buddha," who was declared the "Holy King." A decade of turmoil followed that in the end opened the door to a group of Mongol Communists. They received support from the newly established Communist regime in Russia, which itself had seized power in 1917. With that crucial outside help, the Mongolian Communists took control of the country in 1921. In 1924, when the "Holy King" died, they proclaimed the founding of the Mongolian People's Republic (MPR), a one-party dictatorship under the Mongolian People's Revolutionary Party (MPRP).

The MPRP followed the example set by the Soviet Union and its dictator Joseph Stalin in its effort to turn Mongolia into a modern socialist society. That example involved great violence and brutality. In the early 1930s the Communist regime under Khorloogiyn Choibalsan met stiff resistance when it tried to collectivize the country's livestock. Millions of animals were killed, often by herders unwilling to give them up. The net result was famine, a series of uprisings, and, finally, a temporary retreat from the policy. (The government finished the job of collectivization in the 1950s.) The 1930s also witnessed the beginning of two decades of purges that claimed tens of thousands of lives, including those of most of the country's leading writers, scientists, and thinkers. There also was a systematic attack on Buddhist religious institutions. This plan to "liquidate the lamas" included thousands of arrests and the closing of seven hundred monasteries; only four were left open as museums.

Life in Communist Mongolia became easier after Choibalsan's death in 1952 and Stalin's a year later. Mongolia sided with the Soviet Union in its contest with the People's Republic of China for leadership of the Communist world that began in the 1960s. The decline of Soviet power in the late 1980s was paralleled by the decline of MPRP power in Mongolia. The party responded by swimming with the tide. It introduced constitutional reforms that abolished its one-party dictatorship, announced it was an "ex-Communist party," and managed to win free elections in 1990. A new constitution was adopted in early 1992, the same time that the country's name officially was changed from the Mongolian People's Republic to Mongolia and the Communist gold star was removed from the national flag. The first elections under the new constitution in June again produced a MPRP victory, and the party's candidate also won the presidency in an election held in 1993.

By the time of the 1996 parliamentary elections, Mongolia's main opposition parties had organized themselves into the Democratic Union. It won the elections decisively, finally ending more than seven decades of MPRP rule. However, the presidential election of 1997 was won by the MPRP candidate, Natsagiin Bagabandi. In July 2000 the MPRP overwhelmingly retook control of parliament, winning almost every seat. At the end of the year, the main parties of the Democratic Union and several other groups reorganized themselves as the Democratic Party. That did not help them in the 2001 presidential election, which was won again by the MPRP candidate, Bagabandi.

The results were dramatically different in the 2004 parliamentary elections. By then most of the parties opposed to the MPRP had reorganized once again, this time into the Motherland-Democracy Coalition. Its main issue was the economy, in particular slow growth and a halt to certain reforms. Despite these problems, the MPRP was expected to win. However, in a very close election that surprised most observers, the MPRP barely edged Motherland-Democracy by two seats, 26 to 34. Four seats went to minor parties, while the remaining two in the 76-seat parliament were officially undecided but claimed by Motherland-Democracy. The two leading parties then formed a governing coalition, with the new prime minister coming from the Motherland-Democracy Coalition.

Overall, a decade after communism, Mongolia seems to have established a reasonably democratic political system. At the same time, with a small population scattered over a huge expanse, it must overcome potential disunity along regional lines. Mongolia has made some progress toward a free-market economy but remains poor and heavily dependent on foreign aid. Living standards, education, and health care all remain at lower levels than they were ten years ago.

The precarious situation the country finds itself in is well illustrated by a museum in a small town about 460 miles (735 kilometers) southwest of Ulan Bator. It houses ancient Buddhist artifacts—including silver statues, jewelry, and books—that were collected in the nineteenth century by a revered Buddhist monk. After his death, one of his followers, having taken an oath to protect the collection, established a museum to house them and became its curator. That job passed to his descendants: The proper heir in each generation was identified with a special birthmark on his back. In 1937, fearing Mongolia's Communist regime would destroy the collection, the great-great-grandson of the original curator, a man named Tudev, began putting the treasures in his care in crates and burying them. He had buried only about 10 percent before government soldiers destroyed the museum and its contents. What he saved remained underground for two generations. Not until 1990, with communism in Mongolia dead and itself all but buried, did Tudev's grandson and the current curator, whose name is Arltangerel, dig up some of the hidden treasure and establish a new museum. He did not dig up all the crates because he lacked the space for their contents. Nor, with the small amount of government funding he received, is Arltangerel able to properly protect the artifacts he has on display. He and his friends act as guards for the collection. The forty-one-year-old Arltangerel does have a designated successor, his eleven-year-old son, who, like his father, carries the distinguishing birthmark. But the curator is worried. As he told an American reporter in the summer of 2002, "I am the only person who knows the location of the crates, so they are safe. Our museum is not safe."[1] Mongolia, like Arltangerel, who struggles so hard to protect his people's heritage, is a country with many challenges ahead.

MAPS AND FLAGS OF EAST ASIA

R U S S

KAZAKHSTAN

MONG

Hovsgol
Nur

Uvs
Nur

ALTAI MOUNTAINS

GOBI

UZBEKISTAN

40

38

TURKMENISTAN

KYRGYZTAN

TIEN SHAN MOUNTAINS

XINJIANG

TAJIKISTAN

Tarim

Lop Nor

TAKLIMAKAN DESERT

AFGHANISTAN

KUNLUN MOUNTAINS

C H

PLATEAU OF TIBET

PAKISTAN

TIBET

Mekong

Indus

H I M A L A Y A S

Brahmaputra

Lhasa

NEPAL

INDIA

BHUTAN

BANGLADESH

MYANMAR

20

Scale 1:48,000,000

0   800 kilometers

0   800 miles

60   80   100

I A

120   140

MONGOLIA

• Ulan Bator

OLIA

MONGOLIAN PLATEAU

DESERT

MANCHURIAN PLAIN

Tumen

• *Mt.Paektu*

NORTH KOREA

Yalu

TAEBAEK RANGE

NORTH CHINA PLAIN

• **Beijing**

Pyongyang

Seoul

SOUTH KOREA

YELLOW SEA

Korea Strait

Tsushima Strait

Hiroshima

Nagasaki

Ishikari

HOKKAIDO

• Sapporo

Seikan Tunnel

JAPAN

JAPANESE ALPS

HONSHU

Tokyo

Yokahama• • *Mt. Fuji*

Lake Biwa

Kyoto•

• Osaka

Inland Sea

SHIKOKU

KYUSHU

SEA OF JAPAN

I N A

SICHUAN PLAIN

Yangtze

• **Shanghai**

EAST CHINA SEA

Ryukyu Islands *Okinawa*

Pearl

Matsu

TAIWAN STRAIT

Kinmen

The Pescadores

• Taipei

▲ *Jade Mtn.*

TAIWAN

P A C I F I C   O C E A N

VIETNAM

Quiongzhou Strait

BASHI CHANNEL

• **Hong Kong**

MACAU

LAOS

SOUTH CHINA SEA

Hainan Isl.

PHILIPPINE SEA

60

80

100

• Astana

K A Z A K H S T A N

M O N G

UZBEKISTAN

40

38

TURKMENISTAN

Bishkek •
Tashkent •   **KYRGYZTAN**

X I N J I A N G

• Dushanbe
TAJIKISTAN

Tarim

AFGHANISTAN

Kabul •

C   H

Islamabad •

P A K I S T A N

T I B E T

Mekong

Indus

Delhi •

Brahmaputra

• Lhasa

NEPAL

• Kathmandu

Thimpu •
BHUTAN

I N D I A

BANGLADESH

Dhaka •

20

MYANMAR

Scale 1:48,000,000

0 _____ 800 kilometers

0 _____ 800 miles

PEOPLE'S REPUBLIC OF CHINA

Five has always been considered a lucky number in China: There are ancient references to the Five Elements, Five Rulers, etc. There are also five traditional ethnic groups in the country—the Han (or Chinese), the Manchu, the Mongols, the Tibetans, and the Hui (or Muslims) of Sinkiang. When the People's Republic of China was established on October 1, 1949, the small stars on its flag were said to stand for its four social classes, and the large star represents the Chinese Communist Party. Red is the traditional color of the Han and the Communists.

NORTH KOREA

The Russians occupied the northern part of Korea after World War II. The Communist government created in that territory proclaimed the Democratic People's Republic of Korea on September 9, 1948, under a flag that had been adopted on July 10. (Previously, North Korea used the same flag as South Korea.) The commitment of the country to communism was symbolized by the red star and the red stripe of the new flag. The white stripes were meant to stand for dignity, strength, and purity. the blue stripes stood for the nation's commitment to peace.

SOUTH KOREA

The first national flag of Korea was adopted on August 18, 1882, utilizing ancient symbols of the nation. White stands for peace and the traditional clothing worn by Koreans. The central t'aeguk, or yin-yang, emblem is an old Chinese symbol representing such opposites as light and dark, good and evil, old and new, and male and female. The black bars, some broken and some unbroken, stand for the four seasons, the four cardinal directions, as well as the sun, moon, earth, and heaven. The flag was adopted by the Republic of Korea in 1950 and confirmed in October 1997.

JAPAN

Flags with a sun symbol have been used in Japan dating from at least the twelfth century. No national flag was introduced, however, until August 5, 1854, when the country began commercial contacts with other nations and needed an ensign for its ships. In 1870 the same Sun Disk Flag was approved for use on land. The red sun refers to the nickname for Japan—Land of the Rising Sun—and to the mythical origin of the first emperor as son of the sun goddess Amaterasu. The national flag was confirmed on August 13, 1999.

MONGOLIA

The national flag of Mongolia was red with gold symbols when China recognized the independence of the country in 1945. It also included a stripe of light blue in the center because historically that color represented the Mongolian people. The symbols on the flag have both ancient and modern meanings. Originally the design, known as the soyonbo, expressed Buddhist religious values. The star of communism appeared over the soyonbo until the one-party government ended in 1992. Possible new designs were considered for the Mongolian flag, but on January 12, 1992, it was decided to retain the 1945 flag except for the Communist star.

REPUBLIC OF CHINA

The Kuomintang (Nationalist party), a revolutionary organization, adopted its blue flag with a white twelve-rayed sun in 1895. In 1928 that flag was used as the canton (a rectangular space in the upper left-hand corner of the flag) for the new national flag of the Republic of China; the field was red. The three colors stand for the "Principles of the People"—nationalism, democracy, and socialism. After their defeat in a long Chinese civil war, Guomindang forces retreated to the island of Taiwan in 1949. This flag still flies over that island today.

C H R O N O L O G Y

2200–1700 B.C.
- Mythical Xia dynasty in China.

1766–1100 B.C.
- Shang dynasty in China.

1100–256 B.C.
- Zhou dynasty in China.

722–481 B.C.
- China's Spring and Autumn period.

551–479 B.C.
- Lifetime of Confucius.

403–221 B.C.
- China's period of Warring States.

221–206 B.C.
- Qin dynasty unifies China.
- "Burning of the Books" by Qin Shihuangdi in China.
- China's Great Wall built by connecting walls already in existence.

206 B.C.–A.D. 220
- Han dynasty in China.

108 B.C.
- Korean kingdom of Chosøn conquered by China's Han dynasty.

A.D. 2
- First census in China.

589–618
- Sui dynasty in China.

607
- First Japanese mission to the court of the emperor of China.

618–907
- Tang dynasty in China.

676
- Silla kingdom drives out Chinese forces and unites Korea for the first time.

712
- Appearance of *Record of Ancient Matters* (*Kojiki*), Japan's oldest written record. *Chronicles of Japan* (*Nihoh Shoki*) appears in 720.

960–1279
- Song dynasty in China.

1008
- *The Tale of Genji* appears in Japan.

1162–1227
- Lifetime of Ghenghiz Khan; beginning of Mongol conquests.

1192
- Yoritomo granted title of shogun by Japan's emperor, beginning 676 years of shogun military rule.

1274
- Japanese samurai, with the help of a storm, beat off Mongol invasion.

1272–1292
- Marco Polo in China at court of Kublai Khan.

1279
- Mongols conquer China and establish Yuan dynasty.

1281
- Japanese again defeat Mongol invasion, this time with the help of the huge storm known as the kamikaze, or divine wind.

1368
- Mongols driven from China. Ming dynasty established.

1392
- Yi dynasty founded in Korea; it lasts until 1910.

1514
- Portuguese, the first Europeans to reach China by sea, land in Guangzhou (Canton).

1542
- Portuguese land on Kyushu in Japan.

1592–1598
- Korea invaded by Japan; Admiral Yi Sun-shin invents the ironclad turtle ships whose victories help drive the Japanese from Korea in 1598.

1603
- Tokugawa shogunate established in Japan. Within a few decades, Japan begins policy of isolation from the outside world.

1637
- British land in Guangzhou.

THE HANDBOOK OF EAST ASIA

1644
China

- Manchus conquer China and establish Qing dynasty.

1662–1683
China

- Ming loyalist Koxinga controls Taiwan, using it as a base of resistance against Manchu-controlled mainland.

1839–1842
China

- First Opium War ends with Treaty of Nanjing in 1842.

1850–1864
China

- Taiping Rebellion
- 1852: Yellow River dikes collapse and river cuts a new route to the sea.
- 1856–1860: Second Opium War ends with Treaty of Tianjin in 1860.

1853
Japan

- Centuries-long isolation ends when American fleet under Commodore Perry enters Tokyo Bay.

1868
Japan

- Meiji Restoration.

1873
Japan

- Baseball introduced by an American teacher.

1894–1895
China/Japan

- Japan defeats China in the Sino-Japanese War and annexes Taiwan (then called Formosa).
- Formosan Democratic Republic, the first republic in Asian history, independent from May to October 1905 before being crushed by Japanese military force. Taiwan then ruled as a colony for the next fifty years.

1900
China

- Boxer Rebellion against foreigners in China.

1904–1905
Japan

- Japanese defeat Russia in the Russo-Japanese War and consolidate influence in southern Manchuria and in Korea.

1910
Japan/Korea

- Japan annexes Korea.

1911
China
- Revolution ends monarchy after more than 2,000 years.

Mongolia
- Declares independence from China.

1912
China
- Guomindang (GMD), or Nationalist Party, founded.
- Chinese republic established.

1919
China
- Street protests begin May Fourth Movement.

1921
China
- Chinese Communist Party (CCP) founded in Beijing.

Mongolia
- Communists take control of the country.

1923
Japan
- Great Kanto Earthquake hits Tokyo and Yokohama, killing more than 140,000 people.

1924
Mongolia
- Communists declare Mongolian People's Republic.

1926
Japan
- Hirohito becomes emperor.

1926–1927
China
- Northern Expedition—GMD military campaign to unify China includes attack on CCP.

1931
China
- Worst 20th century Yangtze River flood in terms of lives lost; 145,000 people die and 28 million are affected.
- Yellow River flood kills almost 4 million people.

China/Japan
- Japanese seize Manchuria, rename it Manchukuo.

1934–1935
China
- CCP Long March led by Mao Zedong to escape renewed GMD attack.

1937
China/Japan
- Japanese begin full-scale invasion of China; CCP and GMD form temporary alliance against Japanese.
- Rape of Nanjing by Japanese army.

1938
China
- Government destroys Yellow River dikes to slow Japanese advance; 900,000 are killed in resulting floods.

1941

Japan

- Japan bombs Pearl Harbor on December 7; United States enters World War II.

1945

China

- Japanese occupation of Taiwan ends; island returned to Chinese sovereignty.

Japan

- Hiroshima and Nagasaki attacked with atomic bombs; Japan surrenders, ending World War II.
- U.S. begins occupation of Japan, which lasts until 1952.

Korea

- Japanese colonial control ends. Peninsula is divided, supposedly temporarily, at the 38th parallel, with Japanese forces surrendering to United States troops in the south and Soviet troops in the north.

1946–1949

China

- GMD/CCP civil war.

1947

China

- February 28th incident—protest on Taiwan against GMD corruption—suppressed with great loss of life.

Japan

- New democratic constitution written by the United States takes effect.

1948

Korean Peninsula

- North and South Korean regimes established.
- Kim Il Sung becomes leader of North Korea.

1949–PRESENT*

(*For the post-1949 period, the Republic of China will be referred to as Taiwan.)

1949

China

- Founding of the People's Republic of China announced in Beijing by Mao Zedong.

Taiwan

- Guomindang under Chiang Kai-shek flees to the island and governs it as the Republic of China, claiming to be the legitimate government of all of China.

1950-1953

North and South Korea

- Korean War; United States and China also involved.

1951
Japan
- United States and many other World War II Allies sign peace treaty with Japan.

1952
Japan
- U.S. occupation ends. Japan and United States sign mutual security treaty.
Mongolia
- Khorloogiyn Choibalsan dies.

1953
China
- First Five-Year Plan begins.

1954
Japan
- Self-Defense Force is established.

1955
Japan
- Liberal Democratic Party (LDP) formed.

1958–1960
China
- Great Leap Forward, including establishment of people's communes.
- Mao Zedong replaced as president of China by Liu Shaoqi.

1959
- Tibetan revolt against China is crushed; Dalai Lama flees to India.

1960
South Korea
- Syngman Rhee forced from office by demonstrations after fraudulent election.

1961
South Korea
- Park Chung Hee comes to power in a military coup.

1964
Japan
- Tokyo hosts Summer Olympics.

1966–1969
China
- Cultural Revolution launched by Mao.
- Liu Shaoqi dies in prison.

1971
China
- Lin Biao tries and fails to overthrow Mao; Lin dies in plane crash in Mongolia.
China/Taiwan
- PRC is admitted to the United Nations in place of the ROC, which is expelled.

1972
Japan
- United States ends occupation of Okinawa.
- Sapporo hosts Winter Olympics.

1972–1976
South Korea
- Economy grows at rate of 11 percent per year.

1975
Taiwan
- Chiang Kai-shek dies.

1976
China
- Mao Zedong dies in September; Jiang Qing arrested in October.

1978
China
- Deng Xiaoping clearly solidifies power, announces China will "seek truth from facts" and slowly begins economic and technological reforms called Four Modernizations.

Taiwan
- Chiang Ching-kuo becomes president of the ROC.

1979
China
- Wei Jingshen calls for "Fifth Modernization" of democracy and is sent to prison.

China/Taiwan
- United States establishes diplomatic relations with the PRC, having withdrawn diplomatic recognition from the ROC on December 15, 1978. However, the United States continues to support the ROC under the Taiwan Relations Act of 1979.

South Korea
- Park Chung Hee assassinated, and military in effect takes control.

1983
China
- Deng launches "Anti-Spiritual Pollution" campaign to combat Western democratic ideas.
China
- First "Strike Hard" anticrime campaign begins; claims an estimated 30,000 lives before ending in 1986.

1986
Taiwan
- Democratic Progressive Party (DPP) is allowed to organize.

1987
Taiwan
- President Chiang Ching-kuo lifts martial law, in effect since 1949.

South Korea
- Demonstrations force regime to make democratic reforms.

1988
Taiwan
- Chiang Ching-kuo dies and is succeeded by Lee Teng-hui, the first Taiwanese to become president of the ROC.

South Korea
- Seoul hosts Summer Olympics.

1989
China
- Tiananmen Square pro-democracy demonstration; CCP regime ends the demonstration by killing thousands of students and workers. Beijing is under martial law until January 1990.

Japan
- Hirohito dies; Akihito becomes emperor.
- Stock market scandal leads to resignation of three ministers.

1990
Japan
- Recession begins; stock market shrinks by half over next three years.

Mongolia
- Free elections won by ex-Communist Mongolian People's Revolutionary Party (MPRP).

1991
South and North Korea
- Both countries join the United Nations.

1992
Mongolia
- New post-Communist constitution adopted.
- Democratic Union wins elections, ending seven decades of MPRP rule.

1992–1997
China
- Economic reforms under Deng Xiaoping lead to growth in economy from about $369 billion to $697 billion, while population increases by less than 3 percent. Surge in foreign investment in new Special Economic Zones.

1993
China
- Jiang Zemin becomes president of PRC.
- Second "Strike Hard" campaign begins.

South Korea
- Kim Young Sam takes office, becoming first president since 1960 who is not a military man.

1994
North Korea
- Kim Il Sung dies; succeeded by his son, Kim Jong Il.
- Tension with the United States over North Korea's nuclear program leads to the Agreed Framework in October.

1995
Japan
- Kobe earthquake kills more than 6,000 people.
- Aum Shinrikyo terrorist group releases nerve gas in the Tokyo subway, killing twelve and injuring thousands.

North Korea

- Food shortages lead to mass famine that continues for several years.

1996
Taiwan

- Voters receive the right to vote directly for president. Lee Teng-hui is reelected, the first Chinese leader in history to be elected by the people he is governing.

1997
China

- Deng Xiaoping dies.
- "Deng Xiaoping Theory" written into new PRC constitution, joining "Mao Zedong Thought."
- Hong Kong reverts to Chinese sovereignty.

Mongolia

- MPRP candidate, Natsagiin Bagabandi elected president.

1998
Japan

- Nagano hosts Winter Olympics.

South Korea

- Long-time opposition leader Kim Dae Jung takes office as president.

1999
China

- 10,000 Falun Gong members demonstrate in Beijing, demanding official recognition as a religious group; many are arrested.
- Macau reverts to Chinese sovereignty.

North Korea

- Pyongyang tests its new Taeopodong-1 missile, with a range of 900 to 1,200 miles (1,500 to 2,000 kilometers).

Mongolia

- Beginning of severe winter that kills millions of livestock. Animals continue to die until 2001.

2000
China

- Russian president Vladimir Putin visits Beijing, signaling an improvement in Russo-Chinese relations.

Taiwan

- DPP leader Chen Shui-bian elected president; first peaceful transition of power from one party to another in any Chinese state.

Mongolia

- MPRP wins parliamentary elections.

2001
China

- PRC jet fighter collides with U.S. spy plane over international waters off southern China, leading to several months of tension between the two countries.

- Third "Strike Hard" campaign begins, with about 3,000 people executed between April and September; campaign is scheduled to last until 2003.
- PRC signs treaty of friendship and cooperation with Russia during Jiang Zemin's visit to Moscow.
- PRC admitted to the World Trade Organization.

Taiwan

- ROC admitted to the World Trade Organization.

Japan

- Prime Minister Koizumi visits Shinto shrine where World War II war criminals are among the 2.5 million war dead honored.
- Drifter kills eight children in elementary school.

North Korea

- *Newsweek* magazine calls North Korea the worst country in the world.

Mongolia

- Bagabandi reelected president.

2002
China

- Hu Jintao succeeds Jiang Zemin as CCP general secretary.

Japan

- Aide to Prime Minister Koizumi says Japan has the right to have nuclear weapons.

- Reformist politician Yasuo Tanaka elected governor of Nagano Prefecture.
- North Korean spy boat raised.
- Five Japanese kidnapped by North Korea in the late 1970s return home for a visit.

Japan/South Korea

- Tokyo and Seoul cohost the World Cup soccer tournament, amid squabbling with each other. South Korea reaches the semifinals before being defeated.

North Korea

- United States declares North Korea in violation of the 1994 Agreed Framework.
- Pyongyang admits restarting its nuclear weapons program.

2003
China

- Hu Jintao succeeds Jiang Zemin as PRC president.

Japan

- Launches two spy satellites to monitor North Korea.
- New laws give government much greater power in military emergencies.

South Korea

- Roh Soo Hyun inaugurated as president.

North Korea

- Announces it is withdrawing from armistice talks meetings with the United States.
- Announces it has reprocessed 8000 plutonium fuel rods and has a "nuclear deterrant."

2004

Taiwan

- Chen Shui-bian reelected president in very close election.
- Chen's DPP and the Taiwan Solidarity Union fail to win majority in parliamentary elections.

South Korea

- Roh Moo Hyun is impeached by parliament.
- Roh's newly formed Uri Party wins parliamentary elections.
- Roh's impeachment over-turned by South Korea's supreme court.

North Korea

- Six-nation talks on Pyongyang's nuclear program collapse.

Mongolia

- MPRP loses almost half of its parliamentary seats to newly formed Motherland-Democracy Coalition. The two parties join in a governing coalition.

ENCYCLOPEDIA

AKIHITO (1933–)

Emperor of Japan. Born in 1933, Akihito ascended to Japan's Chrysanthemum Throne (the chrysanthemum is Japan's national flower) at his father Hirohito's death in 1989. Like his father, Akihito is an expert amateur marine biologist. Unlike his father, Akihito traveled widely before becoming emperor, visiting Great Britain, the United States, Canada, South America, and many Asian countries. He broke with tradition in 1959 when he married a commoner and then again in the years that followed when he and the empress (only by marriage, she cannot be Japan's ruler) raised their three children at home. Their first son, Crown Prince Naruhito, was born in 1960. The royal couple has tried to be more accessible to the public than their predecessors. They took a subway ride for the first time in 1986 and over the years visited forty-five of Japan's forty-seven prefectures. The emperor even occasionally held press conferences. However, a press conference in June 2002 showed that much had not changed. True, the empress broke tradition by speaking frequently, about half as much as the emperor. But all questions were submitted weeks in advance, and those that were answered rarely touched on important issues. Reporters were given seven pages of instructions about how to behave in the emperor's presence. All wore black suits, as did their cameramen. While some Japanese clearly wanted the royal couple to be closer to the public, for some conservatives even a carefully scripted press conference was going too far. One well-known author, apparently not accepting the 1946 royal edict denying that the emperor is divine, complained sarcastically that "holy people, sacred people, are not to be seen in public, not to be talked about." He added, "For example, no Japanese government would print the emperor's face on a postage stamp."[1]

ANIME

Japan's long tradition of adult comic books—today comic books account for 60 percent of all printed publications in Japan—gave birth to a new tradition in animation in the form of animated films. In Japan people of all ages watch animated movies. They are produced for television, as original videos, and, most notably, as full-length feature films. These lavish and often sophisticated films are referred to as *anime*, a Japanese word derived from French. Their subject matter ranges from science fiction and fantasy to action adventure, romance, and historical drama. Remarkably realistic and detailed visually, these animated films are often graphic in terms of both violence and their sexual content. The master of Japanese animation is

Haya Miyazaki, head of Japan's famous Studio Ghibli since 1984. His films have drawn record audiences for years: In 1998 one of his films shattered the box office records set by the American movie *E.T.* In 2001, Miyazaki's *Sen to Chihiro* (*Spirited Away*), a fantasy about a ten-year-old girl trapped in a bathhouse with gods and spirits, was the number one film in Japan. It sold 21 million tickets, the equivalent of 17 percent of Japan's population. One fifteen-year-old fan explained part of the reason for its success by suggesting that the film "is so Japanese. The music, the culture, the background are closer to the Japanese people. My grandparents love Miyazaki's anime."[2]

The Japanese are not alone in their enthusiasm for anime and Miyazaki's work. In 1998 the Walt Disney studios signed an agreement with the director to release subtitled and dubbed versions of his films. Their decision is easy to understand. Jeffrey Katzenberg, the cofounder of DreamWorks, observed in 2002 while on a visit to Tokyo that "Japanese animation is the envy of the world."[3]

BASEBALL (BASUBORU)

Baseball is extremely popular in East Asia. It has been played in Japan ever since an American teacher introduced the sport to the country in the early 1870s. Today, baseball is as popular in Japan as it is in the United States, and the level of play is very high. The Japanese love their baseball, or *basuboru*, as they call it. Baseball is the number one sport in Japan in terms of both active participants and spectators. There are two professional leagues, whose pennant races are followed obsessively by millions. Each year the leagues draw a total of 15 million fans to their ballparks and entertain tens of millions more on television. The league champions meet to decide the national champion in a seven-game Japan Series. Each professional team is allowed to have two foreign players, and hundreds of Americans have played in Japan since professional baseball began there in the 1930s. The big change in recent years is that Japanese players are beginning to play in the American major leagues. The first successful players were pitchers, but now some position players are beginning to make their marks

as well. The most successful Japanese player in the American major leagues is outfielder Ichiro Suzuki, better known in both Japan and the United States as "Ichiro." Before coming to the United States, Ichiro was a seven-time batting champion in Japan. Playing for the Seattle Mariners in 2001, Ichiro was the American League's batting champion, rookie of the year, and most valuable player. Ichiro, whose

name appropriately means "fast man"—he also led the league in stolen bases—is a genuine superstar, a brilliant defensive as well as offensive player. His second major-league season in 2002 was almost as strong as his first. In 2004, his fourth season, Ichiro set a major league record for hits in a single season, breaking a mark that stood for 84 years. His huge success, and the success of other players like Hideo Nomo and Kazuhiro Sasaki, is a mixed blessing for Japanese baseball, however, as many Japanese fans are worried that many of their best players will start playing in the United States. And that in fact is what is happening. In 2003, Hideki Matsui, Japan's leading home run hitter, joined the New York Yankees and soon established himself as a major league star.

Baseball also is a popular sport in South Korea, where Americans introduced the sport around 1906. South Korea's professional league began play in 1982 and since has expanded from six to eight teams. A handful of South Korean players, all pitchers, have made it to the American major leagues and done quite well. Amazingly, baseball also is played in North Korea. The game was denounced as "a sport of American imperialism" and banned by the Communist regime in the 1940s but was allowed again in the 1990s. Baseball has a very large following in Taiwan, where it was introduced by the Japanese when they annexed the island in 1895. Little League teams from Taiwan won the Little League World Series seventeen times between 1969 and 1997. However, Taiwan withdrew from organized Little League Baseball in 1997, when it was accused of sending teams to compete in the World Series with players taken from a larger talent pool than elsewhere and training out of season. Taiwan has two professional leagues. The first began play in 1990 but was hurt badly by a gambling/game-fixing scandal late in the decade. A rival league was formed, and the leagues now compete for fans rather than cooperate. Both are struggling to survive because of the lingering effects of the scandal. In an apparent effort to help out, Taiwan's president Chen Shui-bian declared 2001 to be Taiwan's year of baseball. Baseball is even played in the People's Republic of China, but only on an amateur basis.

The capital of the People's Republic of China, like the country itself, is a giant. The Beijing municipality, which surrounds the traditional city core, has an area of about 6,564 square miles (16,800 square kilometers), about the size of Belgium. Its population of about 12.5 million makes it China's second-largest city after Shanghai. Beijing is the hub of China's political, cultural, financial, and educational life. It is also surrounded by a huge industrial area developed under the Communist regime.

There have been settlements in the Beijing region for at least three thousand years, but the city's history dates from the thirteenth century, when the Mongol conquerors of China built their capital there between 1260 and 1290. China's capital was shifted to Nanjing for thirty-five years after the establishment of the Ming dynasty. Then the imperial court was moved back and the city was given its current name, Beijing, which means "northern capital." Much of the city was rebuilt according to a plan that followed the Chinese principle of *feng shui*, or "wind and water," which seeks harmony between man and nature. At the center of the city was the emperor's enormous new

palace. It took a workforce of 100,000 artisans and a million forced laborers seventeen years to build, covers an area of 170 acres (70 hectares), and contains more than 8,700 rooms. Between 8,000 and 10,000 people lived there. The palace, known as the Forbidden City, was home to China's emperors until the 1911 Revolution ended the dynastic system. Today it is a gigantic museum. After losing its status as China's capital—and its name, which was changed to Beiping, or "northern peace"—in 1928, Beijing again became China's capital (and regained its name) with the founding of the PRC in 1949. It was in Beijing that Mao Zedong announced the establishment of the PRC to a crowd of a half million people crowded into Tiananmen Square, just outside the Forbidden City. Forty years later, that square, quadrupled in size in the 1950s under Mao, was the scene of the massive pro-democracy rally that the Communist regime crushed at the cost of thousands of lives.

Beijing's growth during the first four decades of Communist rule added vast blocks of dreary apartment complexes and industrial developments to the city's landscape. The Communists also demolished old city walls and gates to create wide avenues. At the same time, many fine examples of architecture from imperial China's last two dynasties survived. Some of them are surrounded by beautiful parks that provide a peaceful escape from Beijing's crowded and hectic streets.

Since the economic reforms of the 1980s and 1990s modern high-rise buildings, shopping malls, and freeways have been added to the mix. As these projects go up, much of old Beijing is coming down. In particular, old neighborhoods made up of the thousands of alleyways known as *hutongs* that run between tightly packed courtyard houses are disappearing. What is not disappearing, but becoming more prevalent, is air pollution. Sandstorms blowing in from the Gobi Desert to the west combined with the fumes, smoke, and industrial emissions of the city itself have given Beijing some of the worst air quality in the world.

CHEN SHUI-BIAN (1950-)

President of the Republic of China (Taiwan), 2000– .When Chen Shui-bian was born to a family of poor farmers in late 1950, the year of the tiger, he was so weak that his parents did not register his birth with the authorities. In early 1951, the year of the rabbit, when young Chen had overcome the odds and survived, as would become his habit, his parents finally registered their son. He turned out to be true to the year of his real birth, much more a tiger than a rabbit.

Chen's family borrowed money to put him through school. He responded by finishing at the top of his class at every level through high school. He then earned the highest grade on the exams for admission to the law department at the National Taiwan University and again ranked first when he took the national bar examination. He became a successful lawyer specializing in maritime law. In 1980 he was asked to help defend a pro-democracy activist who had been arrested. After the trial—his client was convicted but saved from the death penalty—Chen entered politics. He was elected to the Taipei city council, quickly gaining a reputation as an outspoken opponent of the authoritarian GMD regime. In 1985, at a political rally, his wife was run down by a truck and paralyzed from the waist down. Most observers believe that the incident was not an accident. In 1986, Chen was arrested and sentenced to eight months in jail. Despite the hardship he and his family faced, he did not despair, perhaps inspired by his wife who, in her wheelchair, successfully ran for a seat in the Taiwan legislature. After his release from prison, Chen became his wife's legislative assistant, continued to practice law, and joined the opposition Democratic Progressive Party (DPP). He quickly emerged as a DPP leader, especially in framing its official policy as it moved toward open advocacy of Taiwan's independence from China.

Chen was elected to the Taiwan legislature in 1989 and reelected in 1992. In 1994 he was elected mayor of Taipei. He was extremely successful, presiding over the building of a desperately needed subway system, slum clearance, the building of small parks throughout the city, and many other improvements. He also attacked corruption in city government. Despite his record, Chen lost his bid for reelection in 1998. He responded by running for president in 2000, becoming the first opposition candidate to win that office. His vice presidential running mate was a woman, Lu Shiu-lien. Their inauguration was yet another historic landmark: the first peaceful transfer of power from one party to another in any Chinese state. Chen was reelected to a second term in 2004.

DALAI LAMA (1935-)

The current Dalai Lama, Tenzin Gyatso, is the fourteenth in a chain reaching back to the fourteenth century. The term is a title, not a name, and means "ocean-wide," suggesting enormous wisdom. The Dalai Lamas have been the spiritual and temporal rulers of Tibet since the seventeenth century. According to tradition, each Dalai Lama is the reincarnation of his predecessor, and all in turn of the Bodhisattva, or Buddha of Compassion, an ancient deity who is also the patron deity of Tibet. Tenzin Gyatso was recognized as the reincarnation of his predecessor, the thirteenth Dalai Lama, at the age of two and enthroned as the fourteenth Dalai in 1940, just before his fifth birthday. His education began at the age of six and lasted until the age of twenty-five.

The Dalai Lama fled Tibet with tens of thousands of his followers in the wake of the unsuccessful Tibetan rebellion against Chinese rule in 1959. He then became Tibet's leading international spokesperson and advocate while also speaking out on other human rights issues. In that effort he met with many religious leaders of other faiths, including Pope Paul VI, Pope John Paul II (five times), the archbishop of Canterbury, numerous other Protestant leaders, and leaders of the Jewish faith. Over the years he won enormous respect worldwide, despite constant propaganda attacks against him by the PRC. In 1989 he was awarded the Nobel Peace Prize. In accepting the award, the Dalai Lama stressed his concern for all oppressed people and solidarity with all those who work for freedom. He also repeated his conviction that the struggle for the liberation of Tibet must remain nonviolent.

The Dalai Lama continues to be one of the world's most respected religious and moral leaders. He speaks English very well, and has spoken at American college campuses and appeared on American television. He continues to live the life of a Buddhist monk, with prayer and meditation a central part of this daily routine. When asked about his sources of inspiration, he often cites the following verse from the Buddhist saint Shantideva:

> For as long as space endures
> And for as long as living beings remain
> Until then I too abide
> To dispel the misery of the world.

HIROSHIMA

Hiroshima is both a city and a symbol. As a city it is a prosperous industrial and commercial center of more than one million people on southern Honshu. As a symbol it stands for the indescribable horrors of nuclear war.

During World War II, in addition to its role as a communications and transportation center, Hiroshima was home to the Second General Army Headquarters, which was responsible for the defense of southern Japan. In August 1945 about 350,000 people were in Hiroshima, about 43,000 of them Japanese soldiers. Except for Kyoto—which American leaders decided not to bomb because of its historical importance to Japan—Hiroshima was the largest Japanese city that had not yet been attacked by American B-29 bombers. Just after 8:15 in the

morning on August 6, 1945, an American B-29 dropped an atomic bomb on Hiroshima. The explosion killed at least 80,000 people and destroyed most of the city. On August 9, another atomic bomb was dropped on the city of Nagasaki on Kyushu, killing at least 35,000 people and destroying a large part of that city. Nobody knows the exact number who died in the two bombings: The best guesses range from more than 100,000 to 200,000 people.

Why did the United States use atomic weapons against Japan at the end of World War II? The answer to this question is relatively straightforward: to end the war as quickly as possible and avoid an invasion of Japan, which would have cost the United States enormous casualties. Although Japan was a defeated and battered country by the summer of 1945, its leaders rejected the idea of surrender as dishonorable. They believed they could wage a final battle on their shores that would cause so many American casualties that the United States would negotiate an end to the war on more favorable terms. America's leaders, with good reason, were convinced that no surrender was in sight. They dreaded the prospect, after the extraordinarily fierce and bloody battles for the islands of Iwo Jima and Okinawa, of having to attack the Japanese home islands. Such a battle was certain to be the most costly in American lives of the entire war. The atomic bomb made it possible to force a Japanese surrender without invading the home islands. The actual decision to use the bomb grew directly out of wartime policy: Ever since the United States had started working on the bomb, the assumption was it would be used as soon as it was ready. In August 1945, nothing had happened to cause American leaders to challenge that assumption.

Nor did Japan surrender immediately after the bombing of Hiroshima. The military officers who controlled the government still wanted to continue the fight. After Nagasaki, Emperor Hirohito broke with tradition and personally intervened to get Japan's Supreme War Leadership Council to agree to surrender.

Although the Japanese were shocked by the atomic bomb, in particular that the United States had developed one so soon, they understood that such a weapon could be built some day. Like Germany and the United States, Japan attempted to develop an atomic bomb during World War II. (Fear that Germany would build a bomb was the main reason the United States began its program.) Japan's program had the full support of Prime Minister Tojo, who believed his country's fate could be decided by atomic weapons. The program was under the direction of the distinguished physicist Yishio Nishina but suffered from the start from an inadequate supply of uranium ore. It therefore made slow progress. American bombing raids during late 1944 and early 1945 destroyed key facilities and brought the Japanese atomic program to a virtual halt.

Today, the city of Hiroshima has several memorials and a museum dedicated to the memory of the atomic bombing, most notably the Atomic Dome, which marks ground zero, the Peace Memorial Park, and the Peace Memorial Museum. While deeply moving and unnerving, some of these memorials also are examples of Japan's selective memory of the war that has so angered her neighbors and victims. The Peace Memorial Museum, for example, chronicles the terrible suffering the bomb caused on August 6, 1945, but obscures the fundamental reason the bomb was dropped. It pays no attention to what Japan did throughout East Asia and in the Pacific in the years prior to the bombing of Hiroshima, when it waged a war of aggression that took the lives of millions of people.

A similar lapse in memory involves non-Japanese who died at Hiroshima. Tens of thousands of Korean forced laborers who had been taken from their homes and put to work in Japan to help the war effort were in Hiroshima on August 6, 1945. Thousands died, no one knows how many, but perhaps as many as one in ten of the overall total. However, while the Peace Memorial Park dates from the early 1950s and the Peace Memorial Museum opened in 1955, no monument to the Koreans who died at Hiroshima was erected until 1970. Nor was it built by the Japanese, whose government had brought the Koreans to Hiroshima in the first place. Rather, the monument was built by the Korean Residents Association in Japan. Even then, the Korean monument was not allowed in the Peace Memorial Park until 1999, when it was finally moved to a site inside the park. A month later, twenty-nine years after it was first dedicated, the memorial received its first official visit from a Japanese prime minister, Keizo Obuchi. The Korean monument reminds visitors that none of the Japanese memorials mention the Koreans who died at Hiroshima.

HONG KONG

The British colonized the area in southern China that became Hong Kong in three stages. They took the island of Hong Kong after the First Opium War in 1842, a small area on the mainland called the Kowloon Peninsula after the Second Opium War in 1860, and a much larger area on the mainland called the New Territories in 1898. These areas constituted the British colony of Hong Kong until it was returned to Chinese sovereignty in 1997. Between the 1840s and 1997, Hong Kong became a thriving commercial and light-industrial center and, with its excellent natural harbor, one of the world's busiest ports. Hong Kong also became incredibly crowded. By the time of its return to Chinese sovereignty, more than 6.6 million people lived within its small area of 423 square miles (1,098 square kilometers). It was in addition an exciting and vibrant city whose shopping and entertainment opportunities lured tourists from all over the world.

One facet of Hong Kong's vibrancy was its film industry, which grew into the world's third largest, trailing only Hollywood and Bombay in the number of films produced each year. Its first star to make an impact beyond East Asia, and probably still its best known, was Bruce Lee. Lee made only a few movies before his untimely death in 1973 at age thirty-two, but his kung fu film *Return of the Dragon* (1972) has been elevated to the status of a cult classic. By the 1990s, Hong Kong directors

and actors had achieved international renown on a more serious level, often working abroad. Perhaps most notable was director John Woo, who became well established in Hollywood, where he directed *Windtalkers*, one of the blockbuster films of 2002.

Hong Kong is one of the PRC's two Special Administrative Regions (SARs). (The other is Macau.) According to the agreement under which Britain returned Hong Kong to China, the PRC is pledged to follow a "one country, two systems" policy for fifty years, meaning that Hong Kong's capitalist system will be left intact and not subsumed into the PRC's socialist economic system. The PRC also promised that Hong Kong would enjoy a high degree of political autonomy. Since the transfer, the PRC has not interfered in Hong Kong's economic life, but limits on political expression clearly have been set in various ways, some subtle and some less so. One of those limits has been in place from the start. Only twenty-four of the sixty members of Hong Kong's legislative council are elected by the people. Six are chosen by Beijing and thirty are chosen by business and other groups that almost always follow orders from Beijing. Pressure from the government, pro-Beijing politicians, and businessmen with ties to Beijing clearly have undermined editorial independence in the local news media. As a result, local journalists now avoid trouble by engaging in self-censorship and not reporting on certain subjects. More overtly, Hong Kong's chief executive, Tung Chee-hwa, ran unopposed for a second term after being endorsed by PRC president Jiang Zemin. As one pro-democracy leader observed, "This isn't an election, it's a farce."[4] Now that it is ruled by the People's Republic of China, Hong Kong seems unlikely to decline completely as an economic center, but it is equally unlikely to maintain its current status. For example, Shanghai already is challenging its status as the financial center of China. It also seems inevitable that Hong Kong will not retain the overall dynamism and vibrance it enjoyed when it was a colony of Great Britain.

HÖVSGÖL NUUR

Mongolia's largest freshwater lake, reaching a depth of 860 feet (260 meters), Hövsgöl Nuur is Mongolia's largest source of freshwater. It is also the fourteenth-largest freshwater source in the world, with more than 1 percent of the world's total supply. Forty-six rivers feed the Hövsgöl Nuur, but only one, the Egiin Gol, leaves it. Because of the lake's remoteness in a region of

mountain forests, its waters probably are the most pristine and unspoiled in the world. The Mongols have a simple word for the Hövsgöl Nuur that reflects their feeling and respect for the lake: They call it "mother."

HU JINTAO (1942–)

General secretary of the Chinese Communist Party, 2002– , and president of the People's Republic of China, 2003– . Hu first made his mark and impressed Deng Xiaoping in 1989 by violently crushing unrest in Tibet in 1989 and keeping the region under a tight lid during the Tiananmen Square crisis. In 1992, Deng appointed Hu to the seven-member Politburo Standing Committee, the CCP's highest policy-making body. He is considered a completely conventional Communist and has been a loyal supporter of Jiang. He took control gradually: He assumed the position of CCP general secretary in the fall of 2002 and became president of the PRC in March 2003, in both instances succeeding Jiang Zemin. In 2004 he succeeded Jiang as chairman of the powerful Central Military Commission

Hu Jintao comes from one of China's poorest provinces and is educated as an engineer. He belongs to the "fourth generation" of CCP leaders: Jiang belongs to the third, Deng belonged to the second, and Mao and his closest colleagues belonged to the first. His formative experiences are from the era of the Cultural Revolution, so stability is certain to be a central concern. Little is known about his ideas or his thinking about foreign policy. His credentials as a reformer are suspect. According to one pro-reform party intellectual, Hu is "certainly smart and adept at protecting himself, but we have no idea where he stands on crucial issues."[5] Hu made his first visit to the United States in April 2002.

JIANG ZEMIN (1926–)

General secretary of the Chinese Communist Party, 1989–2002, and president of China, 1993–2003. Educated as an engineer, Jiang joined the CCP in 1946 and survived the various eras of turmoil under Mao Zedong in the 1950s and 1960s without serious injury to his career or person. He began to rise in the party hierarchy in the 1980s with the help of leading reformers close to Deng Xiaoping. Jiang became mayor of Shanghai in 1985 and joined the Politburo in 1987. Part of his success was his ability to shift between supporting modernizing reforms and successfully suppressing dissent without using excessive violence. During the Tiananmen Square crisis of 1989, Jiang sided with the hardliners regarding what to do in Beijing, but was able to keep things under control in Shanghai without using force. Jiang's standing as a economic reformer who could be tough on prodemocracy dissenters led Deng to choose him as his successor. He became president of the CCP in 1993 and successfully consolidated his power after Deng's death in 1997. Jiang gradually left political life between 2002 and 2004, yielding his political positions to Hu Jintao.

KIM DAE JUNG (1925–)

President of South Korea, 1997–2003. Like his country, Kim Dae Jung is a survivor. He was born into a farming family on an island off Korea's southwest coast and graduated from a commercial high school. During the Korean War he worked for a firm shipping supplies, landing in a North Korean prison from which he escaped. After the war he ran a small newspaper before entering politics. Elected on his third try to the national assembly, Kim quickly established himself as a pro-democracy leader during the dictatorial rule of Park Chung Hee. He shocked both Park and Korea as a whole by winning more than 43 percent of the vote when he ran unsuccessfully against Park in the 1971 presidential election. Kim's bold opposition to Park's increasingly dictatorial rule nearly cost him his life. In 1973 he was seized by Park's agents while in Japan and released only after a strong protest from the United States. He was then put under house arrest. In 1976 he was given a five-year sentence and, when released in 1978, again placed under house arrest. In 1980, this time for opposing military rule, Kim was arrested and sentenced to death, a sentence later commuted to life in prison. Two years later he was allowed to go to the United States.

Kim's supporters feared for his life when he returned to Korea in 1985. Again he was put under house arrest. In 1987 he was cleared of all charges against him. He ran unsuccessfully for president in 1987 and 1992, before winning the office in the 1997 election. One of his most important initiatives was the "sunshine" policy of promoting ties with North Korea. Kim's lifetime of standing firm for democracy and peace was recognized in 2000 when he was awarded the Nobel Peace Prize.

Kim's presidency was been without personal hardship. In 2001 members of his wife's family were involved in a scandal, and in 2002 two of his sons were jailed for accepting bribes.

KIM IL SUNG (1912–1994)

Dictator of North Korea, 1948–1994. Kim Il Sung's original name was Kim Sung Chu, but he took the name of a famous early twentieth-century Korean guerrilla fighter while himself fighting against the Japanese occupation of Korea during the 1930s. Kim Il Sung, trained in Moscow, became the leader of Korea's Communists in 1945 and North Korea's leader in 1948. He launched the Korean War in an attempt to conquer all of Korea in June 1950 and had to be saved from total defeat by Chinese intervention. He ruled as an absolute dictator until his death in 1994 and was succeeded by his son, Kim Jong Il.

KIM JONG IL (1942–)

Leader of North Korea since 1994 and son of Kim Il Sung. Little is known of Kim Jong Il and most of what is officially said about him cannot be trusted. His official biography says he was born in an anti-Japanese guerrilla camp deep in the woods of North Korea in 1942, but he was most likely born in Siberia, in the Soviet Union, in 1941. Kim may have changed the date of his birth because 1942, as an even year, is considered a better

birth year and also more closely matches the birth date of his father, Kim Il Sung. Among the younger Kim's ideas that impressed Kim Il Sung was that North Korea should copy Mao Zedong's destructive Cultural Revolution. Kim Jong Il's training for North Korea's top job seems to have included preparing state-sponsored terrorism against South Korea, the worst incident being the bombing of a Korean Airlines jet in 1987 that killed all 115 people aboard. Kim Jong Il did not take the title of president of North Korea having had his late father designated the country's "eternal president" in 1998. Kim Jong Il was rarely photographed until his historic 2000 meeting with South Korean president Kim Dae Jung.

KIM JONG NAM (1972–)

Heir apparent to the North Korean leadership and son of Kim Jong Il, Kim Jong Nam is the number two leader in North Korea after his father. His status as heir apparent in effect makes North Korea the world's only hereditary Communist dynasty. Kim Jong Nam's major appearance on the world stage was a bizarre incident in 2001, when he entered Japan illegally on a passport from the Dominican Republic, apparently without his father's knowledge. He was traveling with two women in their thirties and a four-year-old boy. After being caught and revealing his true identity, he told officials he wanted to take the boy to Tokyo Disneyland. Kim Jong Nam's visit to Japan, aside from the weird way he entered the country, caused an international incident because North Korea and Japan do not have diplomatic relations, and talks to normalize relations had been stalled for months. It was, in any event, a short and unsuccessful visit. Kim was deported under heavy guard three days after he arrived. He, and the little boy, never got to Disneyland.

KOIZUMI, JUNICHIRO (1942–)

Prime minister of Japan since 2001. Born in 1942, Koizumi comes from a political family: Both his grandfather and father served in parliament. Koizumi earned a university degree in economics before entering politics, eventually winning election to the parliamentary seat his father had once held. Although he could not have advanced very far in Japanese politics by straying too far from convention, Koizumi is not cut from the same colorless cloth as most Japanese politicians. He has at times been willing to support unpopular causes. During 1996 and 1997, for example, in his capacity as minister of health and welfare he defied the ministry of finance and its concerns about tax revenue to put some teeth in Japan's program to curb tobacco sales. He also broke certain common political conventions, among them the custom of ministers accepting political contributions from companies in industries their ministries supervised. As one adviser remembered, "He [Koizumi] would decline all donations from related industries, even flowers."[6]

Charismatic, handsome, and plainspoken, Koizumi is divorced, which is unusual for Japanese politicians. Before becoming prime minister, he openly frequented Tokyo's hostess bars—but only until 8:30 in the evening, after which he went home and listened to opera, at least according to close associates. Immediately after taking office, Koizumi did not follow the usual rules in choosing the cabinet. He selected people who were close to him rather than those suggested by party bosses. A month later, he rejected the advice of bureaucrats by ordering the government to obey a court order and pay compensation to leprosy patients for discrimination they had suffered at the hands of the state. He also apologized to those patients.

Koizumi has not shunned controversy as prime minister. Known for his nationalist leanings, Koizumi angered China's neighbors in August 2001 when he visited a Shinto shrine that honored Japanese World War II dead, including convicted war criminals. Meanwhile, he strengthened his standing among Japanese conservatives by supporting an expanded role for Japan's military. After the terrorist attack on the World Trade Center in New York City on September 11, 2001, Koizumi sent Japanese warships overseas for the first time since 1945 in support of American military action in Afghanistan. He also proposed increasing the powers of Japan's armed forces in an emergency. More controversially, Koizumi gave tacit support to officials who suggested that, given the dangers it faced from its neighbors, Japan should consider ending its post-World War II ban against acquiring nuclear weapons.

All of these factors cast Junichiro Koizumi in a mold different from that of the other prime ministers who have governed Japan in the post-World War II period.

KOREAN WAR

The Korean War began in June 1950 when North Korean forces crossed the 38th parallel hoping to overrun South Korea and unify the entire peninsula under Communist rule. The United States, backed by a U.N. resolution condemning the

North Korean aggression, sent troops to defend South Korea. U.S. troops and smaller contingents from fifteen other U.N. members officially fought under U.N. command. There was no declaration of war; the conflict officially was called a police action. The commander of U.N. forces in Korea was General Douglas MacArthur, one of the heroes of the American victory over Japan in World War II.

The Korean War went through three phases. Between June and September the North Koreans held the advantage. Seoul fell in a matter of days, and soon U.N. forces were confined to a small area around the port of Pusan on Korea's southeast tip. MacArthur then undertook a daring and dangerous landing at the port of Inchon near Seoul behind North Korean lines. The North Korean army panicked and fled north. Within weeks the U.N. forces were at the 38th parallel. The decision was then made to push northward and destroy the North Korean regime, despite warnings from the People's Republic of China that it would enter the war if American forces approached the Chinese border at the Yalu River. As American Marines neared the Yalu in late November, they were attacked by hundreds of thousands of Chinese troops that had infiltrated into Korea. The U.N. forces were driven back south of the 38th parallel, Seoul falling for the second time. At this point a bitter dispute between MacArthur and President Harry Truman about how to conduct the war under these new conditions led to Truman's decision to fire MacArthur for insubordination. It took months of heavy fighting for U.N. forces to reach the 38th parallel and retake Seoul. The front stabilized there as negotiations for a cease-fire lasted until July 1953.

The armistice signed in July 1953 ended the Korean War but did not bring peace, as no formal treaty has ever been signed. The United States provided most of the air and naval forces on the U.N. side and about one third of the ground forces. South Korea provided about 60 percent of the U.N. ground forces. The fifteen other member nations provided the rest; some also contributed to the air and naval forces. More than 54,000 Americans died in the war, about 33,000 in combat and the rest from other causes, and more than 100,000 were wounded. South Korean losses were 59,000 killed and 291,000 wounded. The Chinese and North Koreans have never divulged their military casualties; the best guess is that together they suffered a half million dead and a million wounded. Among the dead was the son of Mao Zedong. Civilian casualties also are unknown, but it is certain that the dead and wounded ran into the millions. The Korean War left most of the peninsula in ruins, including both Seoul and Pyongyang.

LAOGAI OF THE PRC AND THE NORTH KOREAN LABOR CAMPS

The laogai, China's system of forced labor camps, is the largest of its kind in the world. Because the PRC refuses to provide information about these camps, no one knows for certain how many there are and how many prisoners they hold. According to Harry Wu, executive director of the Laogai Research Foundation and a prisoner in the camps for nineteen years, there are at least 1,100 camps that currently hold about 6.8 million prisoners. The laogai was set up in the early days of the Communist regime with the help of experts from the Soviet Union. Wu estimates that since then about 50 million people have passed through the system.

Laogai means "reform through labor." To the PRC leadership, reform means giving up any thought of real political reform in China. As Wu puts it, "The laogai is not simply a prison system; it is a political tool for maintaining the Communist Party's totalitarian rule."[7] Wu also points out that the laogai is a moneymaker. One third of the PRC's tea, 60 percent of its vulcanizing chemicals, a significant part of its cotton crop, and a large variety of other products are produced in the laogai, many of which are exported and find their way to unsuspecting Western consumers and companies. Laogai sales certainly run into the billions of dollars. Conditions in the camps are brutal. A twelve-hour workday, often under extremely hazardous conditions, is typical. It usually is followed by two-hour study periods in which prisoners must listen to government propaganda. Some prisoners labor as much as eighteen hours per day. The camps are dreadfully overcrowded (two prisoners typically share a bed), food quality is poor, and medical care is inadequate. The laogai is also a source of tens of thousands of human organs that are taken from executed prisoners and then transplanted in Chinese hospitals in patients able to pay for them.

Smaller in size but if anything more brutal is the North Korean labor camp system. It holds an estimated 200,000 prisoners. Since 1972 an estimated 400,000 people have died in these camps. It is easy to understand why. Workdays can start as early as 5:30 in the morning and continue until 11 at night. The camps are horribly overcrowded and working conditions often life-threatening. Many North Korean refugees who illegally cross the border into China and are then deported back to North Korea end up in the labor camps. If they are pregnant women, they have their pregnancies ended with abortion injections. Babies that are born are killed; sometimes the mothers are forced to do the killing themselves. While North Korean secrecy prevents exact numbers from being known, an organization called Human Rights Without Frontiers estimated that in 2001 several hundred babies were killed in the camps.

In the twentieth century, forced labor was one of the worst features associated with Communist rule. Although most Communist regimes collapsed in the last decade of that century, forced labor survives in East Asia's two Communist states.

MACAU

The oldest European settlement in East Asia, Macau began as a Portuguese colony in the mid-sixteenth century. It is about 40 miles (60 kilometers) west of Hong Kong. Its 9.18 square miles (23.8 square kilometers) consists of a peninsula and two small islands. Macau was returned to Chinese sovereignty in 1999 with the same fifty-year "one country, two systems" policy that governed the return of Hong Kong and, like Hong Kong, is now a Special Administrative Region. About 414,000 people

live in Macau. The city has long had a seedy reputation because of its huge criminal-infested gambling industry, which has survived Macau's transfer from Portuguese to Chinese control. As one Chinese businessman commented as he was leaving a casino in late 2001, "I would never bring my children here."[8] Some Macau businessmen have plans to clean up the city's image and make it a tourist center, but that plan will have to succeed against formidable odds.

MARTIAL ARTS

East Asia is the birthplace of a variety of forms of self-defense and combat with ancient roots that are usually referred to as the martial arts. They are also a form of therapeutic exercise, and overall the majority of people who practice the martial arts do so as exercise. Tai chi, a system of slow graceful movements, is the most popular form of exercise in China and the most practiced martial art in the world. Most if not all martial arts seem to have originated in China among Buddhist monks, but as they spread to Japan and Korea they evolved into distinctive new forms that have since become associated with those countries. Whatever their individual form, all the East Asian martial arts have a spiritual basis that stress the idea of allowing *qi*, or cosmic energy, to flow thorough one's body. All stress discipline and self-control, patience and humility, and—when it comes to combat—deflecting an opponent's strength and using it to one's own advantage.

Some of the best-known martial arts in the West originated in Japan or Korea. Judo in its original form called jujutsu (or jujitsu) developed in Japan during the Edo period (1603–1868). In the 1880s it was modified by eliminating dangerous holds so it could be practiced as a competitive sport. Karate, which means "empty hand" in Japanese, began in the early seventeenth century on Okinawa. It was developed by native Okinawans as a means of defense against the Japanese, who had just conquered the island. Kendo, "the way of the

sword," is based on sword-fighting techniques of the samurai warriors. Ninjutsu, whose practitioners as seen in action movies are known in the West as ninja, involves both armed and unarmed combat. Among the specialties the ninja mastered was assassination, which they carried out by a variety of means. The best-known Korean martial art is taekwondo, a form of kicking and punching that came to Korea from China. Today there are more than 1,100 schools teaching taekwondo in South Korea.

ONJUMG-RI

Imagine taking a cruise ship to a resort and, after you land at a dock, traveling to your destination along a specially built road on which soldiers stand at every crossing. Local villagers use a parallel road visible in the distance. Arriving at the resort, which is in a picturesque mountain region, you find it is ringed by a 7-foot (2-meter) fence topped with both barbed and electric wire. When you visit a nearby national forest, you use special bathrooms for foreign tourists. Natives are directed to out-houses to keep them separate from the foreigners.

That is the situation at Onjumg-ri, a mountain resort in North Korea's Kumgang Mountains just north of the 38th parallel. North Korea needs tourist money to prop up its economy, which is why in 1998 it permitted a South Korean company to open the resort and bring in tourists via ship from South Korea. At the same time, the North Korean regime forbids all contact between the local residents and the tourists, as any "capitalist" influence is seen as a threat to the regime. "I have worked here for three months and I have never met anyone in the village," the resort manager told a Western journalist.[9] Even the garbage on the cruise ships is considered a potential security risk. Each ship must take it along on its return journey.

OSHIMA: THE ISLAND OF THE OLD

On Oshima, a fish-shaped island in the Inland Sea, the gray future of an aging Japan has arrived with a vengeance. People in their eighties outnumber teenagers by more than three to one; the figure for people in their seventies is seven to one. Schools are abandoned, as are homes. Young people who have left the island to find employment have not been replaced with new children. Meanwhile, their parents and grandparents have aged. Some still work. A taxi driver is 83, a paper "girl" 84, a barber—still able to wield a straight razor—is also 84, and a policeman a youthful 60. He belongs to the minority: Half of the population of Oshima is over 65. The woman who gets up at 4:30 every morning to deliver meals-on-wheels to one hundred housebound people is 84. She took care of her mother until her death at the age of 104.

On Okikamuro, a smaller island off Oshima's southern tip, the population is even older. There the population has dropped from 500 to 230 over the past 20 years. Half the homes on the tiny island are abandoned.

Oshima and Okikamuro are examples of what ultimately happens to a society where the birthrate plummets far below replacement level while those already living live longer. It is a prospect that deeply worries many Japanese leaders. One solution is large-scale immigration, but that is something the Japanese have decisively rejected until now. Failing that, Japanese who make up the workforce in the middle of the twenty-first century will have to carry an enormous tax burden to care for their elders. Meanwhile, Japan's population will continue to fall unless the birthrate rises dramatically.

PYONGYANG

North Korea's political capital and industrial center is also Korea's oldest city. It served as the capital of several Korean kingdoms, beginning with Chosøn more than two thousand years ago. It has been destroyed during war many times, including by the Japanese in 1592, by the Manchus early in the seventeenth century, during the Sino-Japanese War of 1894–1895, and during the Korean War of 1950–1953. The city stands on a bluff overlooking the Taedong River and is North Korea's showpiece. It is filled with monuments and landmarks honoring the Great Leader Kim Il Sung, including Kim Il Sung Square, Kim Il Sung Stadium, Kim Il Sung University, and the Kim Il

Sung Higher Party School. There are many open green spaces and hardly any traffic. Although enforcement has been relaxed in recent years, the North Korean government has tried to improve the look of its main city by keeping people who don't meet certain standards of attractiveness off the streets. Included in this list are the very old, people with disabilities, and pregnant women. Pyongyang is the most desirable place in North Korea, and only those with the right backgrounds and total loyalty to the regime are permitted to live there.

ROH MOO HYUN (1946–)

President of Korea since 2003. Roh Moo Hyun was born into a poor family and never attended college. Instead, he studied for South Korea's extremely difficult bar exam on his own and in 1975 passed it on his first try. Roh was active in South Korea's pro-democracy movement during the 1970s as a human rights lawyer. He entered politics in 1988 as a member of the opposition United Democratic Party. During the 1990s, he suffered a series of election defeats before finally winning a seat in parliament in 1998. His political views place him on the left of South Korea's political spectrum. He has urged economic reforms that will benefit the less privileged groups in South Korea and has strongly supported Kim Dae Jung's sunshine policy regarding North Korea. Roh also has been critical of the United States, which has 37,000 troops in South Korea to protect it from the heavily armed North Koreans, for "bossing around" his country while taking too hard a line in dealing with Pyongyang. At the same time, on his first day in office he said he would work hard to maintain South Korea's alliance with Washington. Roh backed up his promise later in 2003 by sending almost 700 troops to Iraq to help the United States effort there. Despite opposition at home, Roh's government deployed 3,000 more troops to Iraq in 2004.

SAMURAI

The samurai emerged as a warrior class in feudal Japan during the twelfth century. Their code of conduct drew from Shinto, Buddhist, and Confucian ideas. That code came to be called the *bushido*, or way of the warrior. It demanded absolute loyalty to one's lord (or *daimyo*), indifference to pain or death, total self-control, rejection of any kind of deceit or subterfuge, and benevolence to the oppressed. A samurai had to defend his honor at all costs, which included never surrendering to an enemy; he was expected to die fighting. To save his honor, a samurai was expected to commit suicide by disembowelment, a ritual known as *seppuku*, or hara-kiri. During the Meiji era many former samurai played important roles in Japan's modernization as government officials, soldiers, and businessmen. The samurai code was intensely patriotic, and it made its presence felt during World War II, when hundreds of thousands of Japanese soldiers fought to the last man in hopeless battles rather than surrender. It also was felt in Japan's cruel treatment of prisoners of war, including many Americans, who died at an appalling rate while in Japanese hands.

SEOUL

Seoul, which means "capital," was founded as the capital of Korea's Yi dynasty in 1392 and has retained that status for more than six hundred years, although since 1948 it has been the capital of only half the Korean Peninsula. The capital of South Korea, Seoul is also home to more than a fifth of its population. Seoul literally rose from the ashes after the Korean War to become a thriving modern metropolis. It is home to eighteen universities, fifteen colleges, South Korea's major industrial companies, the country's government, and many cultural and artistic institutions. It was in Seoul in 1919 that Korean leaders defied the Japanese occupiers and declared Korea's independence, an act that was met with massive repression. The Koreans have a saying: "If you have a horse, send it to Cheju Island; if you have a son, send him to Seoul." The point is that the horse will thrive on the lush grasses of subtropical Cheju Island, and one's son will be able to build his future amid the opportunities available in Seoul.

SHANGHAI

Shanghai is China's largest city, most important seaport, and leading industrial city. The city core of about 145 square miles (375 square kilometers) is home to about 8 million people,

while the Shanghai municipality covers an area of about 2,400 square miles (6,318 square kilometers) and has a rapidly growing population that has reached about 14 million. Shanghai was a small town until China was forced to open it to foreign trade in 1842 by the terms of the Treaty of Nanjing. Shanghai then grew rapidly. It became China's major port and commercial center as well as a city known for its opium dens, gambling houses, brothels, and gangs that engaged in almost every form of vice and exploitation. A large part of the city known as the International Settlement was under the control of foreign powers and guarded by their troops. That area today is Shanghai's main commercial section. The Communist revolution ended all that activity, both the commercial and the criminal, turning Shanghai into a dull but law-abiding city.

When Deng Xiaoping began his economic reforms, he designated Shanghai as the city that would lead the effort as it became China's banking and financial center. The building and development boom brought fancy office buildings, luxury high-rise residences, expensive hotels and department stores, gleaming banks, and new highways, bridges, and other massive construction projects. Shanghai has become a showcase for China's economic growth, but also a showcase for its new runaway inequalities—its crowded streets filled with the stylish rich who live in the new high-rise buildings and homeless beggars who barely survive—that so violate the basic promise of Mao Zedong's Communist revolution.

The first regular traffic between East Asia and Europe was along the Silk Road, which led from China across Central Asia and the Middle East to the shores of the Mediterranean Sea. The route crossed mountains and deserts via a series of oases. Rarely did a single individual travel the entire route; instead, goods were passed from caravan to caravan until they reached their destinations. The trade in silk from China to the Roman Empire began in the first century A.D. While silk was the most important product the Chinese had to sell, they also exported other goods to the West. Because there were few Western goods the Chinese wanted other than colored glassware, over the centuries huge amounts of silver flowed from the West to the Middle Kingdom. The Silk Road also was the information highway of its time, with ideas and technical knowledge flowing in both directions. The

Silk Road went through various periods of decline and recovery, depending on whether China and other powers along the route were able to maintain safety for the caravans. The discovery of a sea route from Europe to East Asia marked the end of the long and colorful history of the Silk Road.

SUMO

Sumo, the Japanese form of wrestling, is generally considered the country's national sport. The sport is wrapped in an elaborate aura of Shinto religious ceremony, feudal tradition, and theatrical formality. The bouts themselves usually are very short, on average lasting about six seconds. Two huge men dressed in traditional loincloths try to push each other out of a small circle or force a part of the body other than the feet to touch the ground. As soon as one of those things happens, usually within a matter of seconds, the bout is over. The preliminaries, which include throwing salt to purify the ring, usually last longer than the matches themselves. Sumo's Shinto roots are ancient, but the sport itself was formalized in the seventeenth century. Sumo wrestlers are huge, especially by Japanese standards, frequently weighing more than 300 or even 400 pounds (136 to 182 kilograms). About six hundred are active at any one time, with the top fifty in effect constituting the elite group that compete in major tournaments and receive salaries. At the very top is the rank of grand champion, or *yokozuna*, which is rarely held by more than four men at any one time.

TAIPEI

The capital of the Republic of China, Taipei is also the economic and cultural center of Taiwan. The city dates from the eighteenth century and the arrival of immigrants from Fujian province on the mainland. It began to grow when it was made a provincial capital in 1885 and developed even more under the Japanese occupation (1895–1945). The Guomindang (GMD) made it their headquarters when they fled from the mainland to Taiwan in 1949. Modern Taipei is the result of rapid growth and development that began in the 1970s and turned the city into a crowded, noisy, bustling metropolis that is home to more than 10 percent of Taiwan's people. One of the city's most important recent additions is its subway system, which can carry people underneath the traffic-choked streets to most parts of the city.

Just north of the city is the National Palace Museum, home of the largest collection of Chinese artifacts in the world. The collection dates from an emperor of the Song dynasty and was the private preserve of China's emperors until the Revolution of 1911. It then became the contents of a museum inside Beijing's Forbidden City. The collection was packed into 7,000 crates and moved several times during the 1930s and 1940s to save it from the Japanese. Facing defeat at the hands of the Communists, the GMD moved the entire collection to Taiwan. The museum that houses the collection in Taipei today was opened in 1965. It is one of the few things that passed through China's twentieth century wars unscathed: During all the moves by foot, rail, oxcart, truck, raft, and whatever else was available over three decades, not a single piece in the collection was lost or broken.

TAKHI

Unlike domesticated horses that may have returned to the wild in places like the western United States, the takhi are wild animals like zebras: They cannot be tamed. Takhi have heavier skulls and jaws, thicker necks, and shorter legs than other horses as well as zebralike erect manes and zebra stripes on their legs.

They are light tan with white on their bellies in the winter; their color darkens to blend with the steppe background in the spring as the snow melts. The takhi went extinct in the wild in the late 1960s. All of the animals alive today are descended from a dozen that were caught and sent to zoos about a hundred years ago. About thirty horses were reintroduced to the wild in Mongolia in the 1990s; they now number about two hundred. (The rest of the takhi live in captivity.) The special respect the Mongols have for the takhi is reflected in their name: the word *takhi* means "spirit" or "spiritual" in Mongolian.

THREE GORGES DAM

The dam being built about midway along the course of the Yangtze River will be the largest in the world. It will stand 600 feet (180 meters) high and 1.4 miles (2.25 kilometers) long. The water behind it will form a reservoir 400 miles (640 kilometers) long, the largest in the world, with an area as large as the city of Los Angeles. The dam will fulfill the old dream of controlling the waters of the Yangtze to prevent the floods that have brought so much hardship to the people of China. It will produce electric power equal to one fifth of China's current

capacity and promote industrial development of an economically backward inland region. Shipping on upper reaches of the river also will be improved. The project is expected to cost about $20 billion by the time it is completed in 2009.

Although the giant dam has the strong support of the Chinese government, not everyone is so enthusiastic. It will flood one of the most scenic places in China, the Yangtze River's famous Three Gorges. At least two million people will lose their homes, valuable farmland will be lost, and important archaeological sites will disappear forever. The environmental damage from changing the flow of the river probably will be extensive. Just the construction work alone is likely to pollute the river in the area of the dam. Perhaps worst of all is the danger that the dam, which will be in an earthquake zone, might collapse. The human toll of such an event along the crowded Yangtze would be astronomical. Many experts have pointed out it would have been economically more efficient, environmentally less damaging, and safer to build smaller dams on several of the Yangtze's tributaries, but that advice was rejected by China's leadership.

TIBET

Tibet, called Xizang in Chinese, emerged as a united kingdom in the seventh century. It was a militarily powerful state able to wage war on several of its neighbors, including China. The seventh century was also when Buddhism began to spread in Tibet, although it took a century to became fully established as the dominant religion there. Tibet's political unity collapsed in the middle of the ninth century, marking the end of the era when its armies would threaten its neighbors. Despite the end of its military power, Tibet managed to remain independent of China for most of its history. Ironically, it was only non-Chinese dynasties—the Mongol Yuan dynasty in the thirteenth century and the Manchu Qing dynasty in the seventeenth century—that were able to incorporate Tibet into the Chinese Empire. Qing rule, however, was tenuous, especially as the dynasty weakened during the nineteenth century.

In 1912 the Dalai Lama, the Buddhist religious leader who since the seventeenth century also had been the ruler of Tibet, declared Tibet's independence from China. That independence was not recognized by China or the international community. However, weakened first by civil strife and then by the Japanese invasion, China for several decades after 1912 was in no position to impose its will on Tibet.

That changed when the Communists took power in 1949. In 1950 the PRC invaded and took control of the plateau in what they called the "liberation" of Tibet. Most Tibetans saw it as foreign aggression. The next year China signed an agreement promising Tibet autonomy and noninterference in its society, a promise it soon violated. Tibetan resistance to Chinese rule simmered and finally flared into open revolt in 1959, which the Chinese brutally suppressed. The Dalai Lama fled Tibet with about 60,000 followers for exile in India, where he remains to this day as the head of what he calls a government in exile.

There are several points that seem reasonable to make about Tibet. The Chinese claim on Tibet is not strong, either from a historical and cultural point of view. At the same time, it is important to remember that Tibet was not what Americans would consider a free society during centuries of rule by the Dalai Lamas. It was a theocracy controlled by Buddhist monks in which ordinary people enjoyed few freedoms. Yet Lamaism, the Tibetan form of Buddhism, is at the core of Tibetan national identity and has long commanded the loyalty of almost all Tibetans. Furthermore, the history of PRC rule over Tibet is one of consistent and often brutal human rights abuses. From the 1950s through the 1990s, unknown numbers of Tibetans, but at a minimum tens of thousands, have been arrested and sent to labor camps for resisting Chinese rule. Many have died in those camps.

In 1965, Tibet officially became the Tibet Autonomous Region (TAR). The TAR was smaller than the Tibet that existed before 1949, as large chunks of its eastern sections were taken away and attached to Chinese provinces. Tibet's shrunken borders left about half of all ethnic Tibetans outside the TAR. Then came the dreadful Cultural Revolution. Tibet, with its deeply religious population, suffered terribly during that three-year rampage in which traditional beliefs and practices were attacked throughout China. Red Guards destroyed more than four thousand monasteries as the Chinese government tried to wipe out all religious observance. The end of the Cultural Revolution brought some relief, and in the late 1970s, Beijing began easing some of its controls on Tibet. Resistance, while usually at a low ebb, nonetheless was constant. In 1989 a new set of disturbances led Beijing to impose martial law until 1990. In the decade that followed the economic reforms of Deng Xiaoping improved living conditions for many Tibetans, but the region remained one of the poorest in China. Tibetans also were disturbed by Chinese immigration, fearing that eventually they would become a minority in their own land.

Some Tibetans, especially the better-educated young people, support modernization under Beijing's rule. Tibet now has a growing middle class. Lhasa, its capital, was once known strictly the center of Tibetan Buddhism, the home of the Dalai Lama, a city of temples and shrines, and the destination of uncounted pilgrimages by generations of the faithful. Today Internet cafes, karaoke bars, cabarets, and discos where young people enjoy themselves have been added to the mix. For Beijing, modernization clearly is a vehicle to break the hold of traditional beliefs on the people and reconcile them to Chinese rule. Yet for most Tibetans the Chinese always have been and remain foreign conquerors and occupiers who are trying to destroy their way of life.

TOKYO

Tokyo is the capital and most important city in Japan, the core city in the world's largest megalopolis, and the most important corporate and communications center in East Asia. Its economic power makes it one of the most important cities in the entire world. Tokyo proper alone covers an area of 240 square miles (620 square kilometers). There is virtually nothing a city should have, or shouldn't, that Tokyo lacks. It is Japan's administrative, economic, financial, cultural, and educational center, the home to more than a hundred colleges and universities. Its nightlife and shopping areas are among the most lively in the world. It is one of the world's most modern cities, in part because of rebuilding after the earthquake of 1923 and the American bombing of the city during World War II. Tokyo has the use of a large natural harbor in the city of Yokohama about 20 miles (32 kilometers) to the south and a modern man-made harbor at the mouth of the Sumida River, which cuts through the city before emptying into Tokyo Bay.

Tokyo began as the village of Edo in the twelfth century when a local lord built a fort where the Sumida River reaches the sea. The name Edo means "gate of the river." Edo remained a sleepy backwater until it was made the capital of the Tokogawa shogunate in 1603, after which it grew into a major city. With the Meiji Restoration in 1868, Edo became Tokyo, meaning "eastern capital," and retained its status as the capital of Japan. In the twentieth century the city went through two catastrophes: the earthquake of 1923 that killed 140,000 people and the American bombing of the city that left half of it in ruins during 1944–1945. Unquestionably one of the world's great cities, Tokyo and its ultramodern bridges, buildings, and other structures are living on borrowed time. Every seventy years the Tokyo region is hit by a major earthquake; it is now almost a decade overdue.

TUNG CHEE-HWA (1928–)

Chief executive of the Hong Kong Special Administrative Region. A shipping magnate with close ties to Beijing, Tung became Hong Kong's first chief executive after the city's return to Chinese sovereignty in 1997. Upon winning PRC president Jiang Zemin's endorsement, he ran unopposed for a second term and, not surprisingly, won. His position reveals the political reality and emptiness of the PRC's "one country, two systems" policy. Taiwanese president Chen Shui-bian has called Tung a "puppet of Beijing," and most of the people of Hong Kong seem to agree. As one pro-democracy advocate told a Western journalist, "If the outcome [of the election] is predetermined, how can you expect the public to be engaged. People are demoralized."[10]

ULAN BATOR

Ulan Bator is the political capital of Mongolia and also its cultural, economic, and transportation center. Almost a third of the country's population live there. The city was founded in 1649 as a monastery town and at the start of the nineteenth century had more than one hundred monasteries and temples. As much as half the population at that time was made up of monks and nuns. Almost all of those religious buildings were destroyed during the 1930s, although some survived and are either museums or once again occupied by monks. Beginning in the 1930s, and in the decades that followed, dreary Soviet-style apartment blocks took over much of the city. The city received its current name, which means "Red Hero," in 1924. Mongolia's only university, founded in 1942, is in Ulan Bator, as is a library with many old Mongolian, Tibetan, and Chinese manuscripts. A new addition is the Museum for Politically

Repressed People, which is run by the daughter of a Mongolian Communist leader who resisted Stalin's orders and was shot in 1937. An event called the Naadam festival is held each year in Ulan Bator. Its roots date from the days of the conquering Mongol armies, and its main events are horse racing, archery, and wrestling. During the Communist era the event was called People's Revolutionary Day, but now its original name, which simply means "holiday" or "festival," is again in use.

WEAPONS OF MASS DESTRUCTION

PEOPLE'S REPUBLIC OF CHINA

The PRC has the world's fourth—possibly the third—largest arsenal of nuclear weapons, well behind the United States and Russia and probably just a bit behind France. It tested its first atomic bomb in 1964 and its first thermonuclear, or hydrogen, bomb in 1967. It also has a large ballistic missile force to deliver those weapons, including about twenty to twenty-five long-range DF-5 missiles capable of reaching the United States. However, the DF-5 missiles are liquid powered, which means they take a long time to prepare for launching and are therefore vulnerable. By 2001, China had tested a solid-fueled, three-stage DF-31 missile for the first time. It has a range of almost 5,000 miles (8,000 kilometers). As of 2002, China had one nuclear submarine capable of launching nuclear missiles, but it apparently was not operational. China has been making a major effort to modernize its nuclear weapons, which is one reason its spying on the United States has caused so much concern. China also has exported nuclear technology, especially to Pakistan, despite signing the Nuclear Non-Proliferation

Treaty (NPT) of 1968 in 1992. In 1996 it signed the Comprehensive Test Ban Treaty (CTBT), which bans all nuclear weapons tests, both in the atmosphere and underground.

The PRC also has biological and chemical weapons, although the details of its arsenal remain secret.

NORTH KOREA

In his 2002 State of the Union Address, just four months after the September 11, 2001, terrorist attack that destroyed the World Trade Center in New York City, President George W. Bush listed three countries as forming an "axis of evil" that threatened the United States by their support of terrorism and attempts to develop weapons of mass destruction. Two were Muslim states in the Middle East: Iran and Iraq. The third was a Communist state in East Asia: North Korea.

North Korea began a nuclear research program in the mid-1960s with the help of a nuclear reactor from the Soviet Union at a town called Yongbyon, about 50 miles (80 kilometers) north of Pyongyang. In 1985, it signed the 1968 Nuclear Non-Proliferation Treaty but did not permit the International Atomic Energy Commission (IAEA) to make inspections. In fact, by the 1980s, North Korea was expanding its nuclear facilities. It modernized its Soviet reactor, began building a second reactor, and built a plutonium reprocessing plant. The reprocessing plant was of particular concern, as it gave North Korea the capacity to produce materials that could be used to make a nuclear bomb. Activity related in one way or to North Korea's overall nuclear program—including mining, research, fuel fabrication, power generation, and waste storage—was being conducted at more than a dozen sites scattered throughout the country. In 1992, North Korea finally allowed the IAEA to inspect its facilities. The agency's findings were ominous, suggesting that North Korea might have reprocessed enough plutonium for one or two nuclear weapons. In 1994, American fears that the North Koreans were about to produce weapons-grade plutonium led to a crisis between the two nations. It was resolved in October of that year by the Agreed Framework, under which North Korea agreed not to build nuclear weapons in exchange for an international aid package. In 2002 the United States declared that North Korea was not in compliance with that agreement. In the fall, Washington announced the North Koreans had admitted violating the 1994 agreement by restarting their nuclear weapons program. The new project was based on producing a bomb made from enriched uranium, an effort aided by technology obtained from Pakistan. In December 2002, Pyongyang announced it was reactivating its five-megawatt reactor at Yongbyon and removed all international surveillance equipment from a storage facility where spent nuclear fuel rods were stored. In January 2003, it withdrew from the Nuclear Nonproliferation Treaty. The next month the United States announced that North Korea indeed had reactivated the Yongbyon reactor. Later that year, North Korea announced it had reprocessed enough plutonium fuel rods to make six atomic bombs. In mid-2004, talks to resolve the continuing crisis between North Korea and the United States failed.

Pyongyang also developed biological weapons, despite having signed the Biological Weapons Convention (BWC) in 1987 banning such activity. By 2000, North Korea had probably developed anthrax bacteria, botulinum toxin, and plague bacteria and was producing chemical weapons at a dozen weapons facilities. It had thousands of artillery shells capable of delivering those chemical weapons and placed within range of the DMZ, where American troops are stationed, and Seoul.

On top of all of that, the North Koreans from the 1970s worked to develop ballistic missiles to deliver their weapons of mass destruction. They began with Soviet-supplied Scud missiles with a range of 180 miles (300 kilometers), which they copied and built at home. Many of those missiles were sold to Iran, which used them in its war against Iraq. By the late 1980s, North Korea was building Scud missiles with a range of 300 miles (500 kilometers). In the early 1990s the North Koreans tested a new missile, the Nodong, with an estimated range of 600 to 800 miles (1,000 to 1,300 kilometers), and in 1998 they tested the multiple-stage Taeopodong-1. Its range was 900 to 1,200 miles (1,500 to 2,000 kilometers). The next step, already under development, is the Taeopodong-2, which might have intercontinental range and be able to reach the United States.

By 2000, North Korea had deployed about six hundred missiles, including one hundred Nodongs. It also had turned the spread of WMD into its most profitable business. North Korea had sold missiles, missile components, or technology to Iran, Libya, and Syria—all on the U.S. list of nations that support international terrorism—as well as to Egypt and Pakistan. Reliable intelligence reports also have revealed North Korean involvement in Iran's nuclear program, a Libyan/Egyptian nuclear center, and in Syrian biological and chemical weapons laboratories. All of this enormous expenditure on mass destruction was done as the North Korean economy unraveled and, by the late 1990s, as mass famine stalked the land.

JAPAN

Japan has not developed nuclear weapons. However, that might change. A number of important politicians have argued that Japan cannot continue to remain without a nuclear deterrent in the face of Chinese and North Korean nuclear arsenals. Japan is considered a "virtual nuclear power." It has developed missiles that can launch satellites which can easily be converted to carry nuclear warheads. It also has a highly advanced nuclear power industry that has given it a large supply of weapons-grade uranium. Prime Minister Koizumi has not publicly supported Japan's development of nuclear weapons, but, perhaps more significantly, he has not repudiated several people who have. One Japanese response to Chinese and North Korean nuclear weapons programs has been to accelerate its spy satellite program.

WEB-CAPABLE PHONES

The "thumb generation" has arrived in Japan: millions of young people who communicate with thumb-operated Web-capable phones. Japan leads the United States in the mass use of cell phones equipped for e-mail. There are 50 million in Japan today, up from 10 million two years ago, or four for every ten

Japanese. With these phones it is possible to send and receive messages in university lectures, crowded commuter trains, and other places where talking on cell phones often is not permitted. One result is that young Japanese thumbs are becoming bigger and more muscular, hence the new term *oya yubi sedai,* or "thumb generation." As young thumbs get faster, television stations are holding thumbing speed contests. Although Japan's thumb generation is in love with their new phones, there is at least one downside to them: Doctors are beginning to see cases of thumb stress.

WORLD CUP OF SOCCER, 2002

International sporting events are supposed to bring nations together for friendly competition that promotes goodwill, but that is not necessarily what happens when Japan and South Korea are involved. The animosity left over from the past often runs too deep. This certainly was the case in the 2002 World Cup. Japan and South Korea competed intensely for the right to host the competition. Finally the international body that controls the tournament imposed a compromise, making the two East Asian nations cohosts for the 2002 event. That did not stop the South Korean–Japanese competition. When Japan built or renovated ten stadiums, South Korea outdid its cohost by building ten brand new stadiums, none of which it needed. The two East Asian neighbors argued about whether the event should be called Japan-Korea or Korea-Japan and who would get which matches such as the opening match and the final. (The event was called Korea-Japan and Japan got the final match.) The bitterness ran very deep, especially in South Korea. As one Korean working at the event commented, "Many people would rather have no World Cup than to share one with Japan."[11]

Both nations hired foreign coaches and spent huge amounts of money to get their teams ready for the tournament, each determined to do better than the other. The South Korea coach came from Holland, and he began by bringing a strong dose of European democratic culture to South Korea's Confucian and hierarchical soccer world. He refused to select his players according to family lineage, age and experience, or academic background. Instead, he introduced what for South Korean soccer was a revolutionary idea: The best players, those who performed, whatever their age or background, would play. As one approving fan commented, "He taught us that someone's background did not matter. Someone is just someone. [He] chose players who could play, not for any other reason."[12] And South Korea's Dutch coach got results. A country that had never won a game in five previous World Cup appearances reached the semifinals of the tournament, a great achievement. Even better, it occurred on the same day that Japan was eliminated. In the end, in this competition with Japan, the Koreans, who have usually suffered at the hands of their more powerful neighbor, came out on top. To many of them that seemed more important than hosting, or winning, the World Cup.

XINJIANG

The Xinjiang Autonomous Region in northwestern China is the largest region in the country, comprising one sixth of its total area. It also has valuable mineral resources, the most important being oil. In 1949, when the Communists came to power, 85 percent of the population was made up of Turkic-speaking Muslim Uighurs, who arrived in the region about a thousand years ago. Since then a steady influx of Han Chinese has turned the Uighurs into a minority of about 47 percent in their own land. Urumqi, the region's capital city, is now 80 percent Han Chinese. For many Uighurs, who have consistently opposed Chinese rule since the eighteenth century, their only hope to preserve their identity in their homeland, which they call East Turkestan, is to become independent of China. For the Chinese government, Uighur separatism is a potential domino that could cause others to fall, and is thus a threat to the unity of China. The result is a tense and dangerous situation the Beijing regime has kept under control only through harsh and sustained repression.

The Chinese Empire only rarely controlled this part of inner Asia, through which the Silk Road once passed. The Han dynasty controlled the region between the first century B.C. and the second century A.D., and the Tang dynasty held it loosely for a while until driven out in the eighth century. Not until the Manchus conquered the region in the mid-eighteenth century did it again come under the control of the Middle Kingdom. The Manchus called the region the New Territory, or Xinjiang in Chinese. Manchu control, never very strong, was punctuated by several Muslim rebellions. After the fall of the dynastic system in 1911, warlords controlled the region for a while. After 1928 the Nationalist regime could do little more than claim sovereignty over the region. Xinjiang was the scene of several more anti-Chinese rebellions in the 1930s and 1940s and, in 1944, the proclamation of a short-lived Republic of East Turkestan.

After 1949 the new Communist regime successfully asserted its control over the region. It made Xinjiang an autonomous region in 1955, a gesture that had little meaning since Xinjiang, like the rest of China, was tightly under the control of the government in Beijing. Unrest and Muslim separatist activity in the region began to increase in the 1990s. This occurred in part because of hopes inspired by the disintegration of the Soviet Union in 1991, which resulted in independence for five Muslim states in Central Asia. Chinese repression has surged as well, becoming a cause of more resistance even as some Muslim separatists were executed or sentenced to long prison terms. Xinjiang became the only region of the country where political dissenters were regularly executed. Between early 1997 and early 1999, at least 190 people were executed for political or separatist activities. The Uighurs responded with violence of their own, including a number of terrorist attacks. Both the repression and the separatist resistance spilled over into the new century. So did Chinese immigration into the region, further tilting the demographic balance against the Uighurs. Although the Beijing government clearly had a diffi-cult situation on its hands, the balance of power in Xinjiang, combined with the government's readiness to use force, increasingly favored the Chinese.

ZORIG, SANJAASURENGIYN (1962–1998)

In October 1998, Mongolia was shocked when Zorig was stabbed to death by masked assailants. Mild-mannered and highly principled, Zorig played a leading role in Mon-golia's pro-democracy movement in 1989–1990. He was considered a potential candidate for prime minis-ter at the time of his murder. Tens of thousands of mourners marched in the funeral procession of the man widely considered the father of Mongolian democracy. In 1999 a statute of him was unveiled opposite Ulan Bator's central post office. His murderers have never been brought to justice.

NOTES

Chapter One
(no notes)

Chapter Two

1. Quoted in Arthur Cotterell, *China: A Cultural History* (New York: New American Library, 1988), p. 71.
2. Quoted in Hilda Hookham, *A Short History of China* (New York: New American Library, 1972), p. 51.
3. Quoted in Keith Buchanan, Charles P. FitzGerald, and Colin A. Ronan, *China* (New York: Crown Publishers, 1980), p. 59.
4. John King Fairbank, *The United States and China*, 4th ed., enlarged (Cambridge, MA: Harvard University Press, 1983), p. 171.
5. Quoted in Orville Shell and Joseph Esherick, *Modern China* (New York: Random House, 1972), p. 21.
6. Quoted in Edward L. Shaughnessy, general ed., *China: Empire and Civilization* (New York: Oxford University Press, 2000), p. 231.
7. *Selected Works of Mao Zedong*, Vol. 5 (Beijing: Foreign Languages Press, 1977), pp. 16–17.
8. Quoted in June Grasso, Jay Corrin, and Michael Kort, *Modernization and Revolution in China* (Armonk, NY: M.E. Sharpe, 1991), p. 164.
9. Stuart Schram, ed., *Chairman Mao Talks to the People: Talks and Letters, 1858–1971* (New York: Pantheon Books, 1974), pp. 92–93.
10. Quoted in Roderick MacFarquhar, *The Origins of the Cultural Revolution, Vol. 2: The Great Leap Forward, 1958–1962* (New York: Columbia University Press, 1983), p. 200.
11. Quoted in Roxane Witke, *Comrade Chiang Ching* (Boston: Little, Brown & Co., 1972), p. 325.
12. Orville Shell, *To Get Rich Is Glorious*, revised and updated ed., (New York: New American Library, 1986), p. 54.
13. Quoted in Shell, p. 96.
14. Patrick Henry, the American revolutionary, delivered his famous "give me liberty or give me death" speech during a debate in the Virginia Assembly in 1775. Lord Acton, the British historian, wrote "Absolute power corrupts absolutely" in a letter to a colleague in 1887. Martin Luther King gave his "I have a dream" speech at civil rights rally in Washington, D.C., in 1963.
15. *Selected Works of Deng Xiaoping* (Beijing: Foreign Languages Press, 1994), pp. 360–361.
16. *The New York Times*, December 8, 2001.
17. *The New York Times*, July 16, 2001.

18. *The New York Times*, December 26, 2001.
19. *The New York Times*, December 30, 2001.
20. *The New York Times*, November 2, 2001.
21. Willy Lam, "Hu Jintau's Move to Consolidate Power," *China Brief: A Journal of News and Analysis*, September 30, 2004, 4.

Chapter Three
1. *The New York Times*, April 24, 2001.

Chapter Four
1. *The New York Times*, November 27, 2001.
2. Quoted in W. Scott Morton, *Japan: Its History and Culture.* (New York: McGraw Hill, 1994), p. 20.
3. *The New York Times*, July 1, 2001.
4. *The New York Times*, April 1, 2002.
5. *The New York Times*, June 7, 2001.
6. *The New York Times*, October 16, 2001.
7. *The New York Times*, October 16, 2001.
8. *The New York Times*, April 22, 2001.
9. *The New York Times*, May 9, 2002.
10. *The New York Times Magazine*, July 1, 2001.
11. *The New York Times*, January 15, 2001.
12. *The New York Times Magazine*, July 1, 2001.
13. *The New York Times*, March 29, 2002.

Chapter Five
1. Quoted in Andrew C. Nahm, *Introduction to Korean History and Culture* (Elizabeth, NJ, and Seoul, Korea: Hollym International Corporation, 1993), p. 2.
2. Quoted in *The Boston Globe*, March 21, 2002.
3. Christopher Hitchens, "The Worst of the Worst," *Newsweek*, July 9, 2001.
4. Quoted in *The New York Times*, February 19, 2002.

Chapter Six
1. Quoted in *The New York Times*, August 12, 2002.

Encyclopedia
1. Quoted in *The New York Times*, June 21, 2002.
2. Quoted in *The New York Times*, January 3, 2002.
3. Quoted in *The New York Times*, January 2, 2002.
4. Quoted in *The New York Times*, March 1, 2002.
5. Quoted in *The New York Times*, April 27, 2002.
6. *The New York Times*, June 26, 2001.
7. Harry Wu, "Labor Camps Reinforce China's Totalitarian Rule," 1999 <http://www.cnn.com/SPECIALS/1999/china.50/red.giant/prisons/wu.essay/ (June 14, 2002).
8. *The New York Times*, December 20, 2001.
9. *The New York Times*, January 20, 2002.
10. Quoted in *The New York Times*, March 1, 2002.
11. Quoted in the *New York Daily News*, June 19, 2002.
12. Quoted in *The New York Times*, June 21, 2002.

INDEX

Page numbers in *italics* refer to illustrations.

267